1,001
THINGS
EVERYONE
SHOULD KNOW
ABOUT
AMERICAN
HISTORY

**Signers of the Declaration
of Independence.**
CULVER PICTURES, INC.

1,001
THINGS
EVERYONE
SHOULD KNOW
ABOUT
AMERICAN
HISTORY

JOHN A. GARRATY

DOUBLEDAY

New York London Toronto Sydney Auckland

Published by Doubleday, a division of
Bantam Doubleday Dell Publishing Group, Inc.
666 Fifth Avenue, New York, New York 10103

DOUBLEDAY and the portrayal of an anchor with a dolphin are
trademarks of Doubleday, a division of Bantam Doubleday Dell
Publishing Group, Inc.

Library of Congress Cataloging-in-Publication Data
Garraty, John Arthur, 1920—
    1,001 things everyone should know about American history
/ John A. Garraty.
        p.   cm.
    1. United States—History—Miscellanea.   I. Title.   II.
Title: One thousand one things everyone should know about
American history. III. Title: One thousand and one things
everyone should know about American history.
E178.6.G25 1989   88-14446
973—dc19   CIP

BOOK DESIGN BY MARYSARAH QUINN

PHOTO RESEARCH BY SABRA MOORE
AND JULIE TESSER

ISBN: 0-385-24432-0
Copyright © 1989 by John A. Garraty
All Rights Reserved
Printed in the United States of America
April 1989

FIRST EDITION

TABLE OF CONTENTS

INTRODUCTION

When readers complained that Charles A. Beard's *An Economic Interpretation of the Constitution of the United States* (1913) presented a distorted view of the character and motives of the Founding Fathers, Beard liked to deflect their attacks by pointing out that he had called the book "*An* Interpretation of the Constitution," not *the* interpretation. To those who may disagree with my choice of items in this book, I offer the same defense: My "1,001 Things that Everyone Should Know About American History" are certainly not *the* 1,001 things, or even my opinion of what the 1,001 most important things about American history are. Indeed, I have steered away from things that I was pretty sure everyone does know about the subject almost as carefully as I have avoided topics that no one but a professional historian is likely to be familiar with. Instead, I have concentrated on subjects that people who are interested in American history will recognize, things they "know about" but may not remember exactly. There is nothing in the following pages that might not be included in a college American history textbook or that a good high school teacher might not draw upon to illustrate a lecture or to stimulate class discussion.

My selection is just that—a selection, not a definitive collection of essential information. Mostly I have depended on what has come to mind (on what *I* know about American history, which is obviously only a fraction of what "should" be known about the subject). I have spent a good deal of time checking facts and quotations in order to make sure that I have recalled them correctly, but I have not "researched" any of the topics on my list in the sense of making sure that I have not left out some vital item. In other words, I have deliberately tried to preserve a random quality in the work, the rationale being that any of my 1,001 items could be deleted in favor of something else—that the number of interesting things about American history is practically limitless. I have tried

Major General William Henry Harrison.
CINCINNATI HISTORICAL SOCIETY.

Walter Johnson.
CULVER PICTURES, INC.

to describe my selections in a precise and interesting way, when appropriate adding details or pointing out connections that readers may not be expected to have known. At the same time, I hope and expect that readers of my "things" will frequently be led by them to recall other "things that everyone should know."

As its deliberately random character suggests, my book is designed to entertain more than to instruct. It has a logical structure, as the Table of Contents will reveal, but it can be opened at random and read at any length without confusion. Yet the sections have patterns of their own; the items are arranged in chronological order, causes come before effects, and so on. And though this is not a "serious" book in any conventional sense, I believe readers will find that a good deal of the material I have chosen is inspiring. I confess that I have included some items only because they are amusing, or in order to stick pins in inflated reputations. But many of the people I have called attention to really were heroes, and a large percentage of the quotations, documents, speeches, and private letters that I have chosen should make any American proud of the country and its past. There is a good deal of material by and about Thomas Jefferson here, by no means all of it complimentary, but among it is my favorite Jefferson quotation, a line from a letter he wrote shortly before his death: "The mass of mankind has not been born with saddles on their back, nor a favored few booted and spurred, ready to ride them legitimately, by the grace of God." (See number 283, following.)

This book has grown out of an article I published in the December 1986 issue of *American Heritage.* The idea was suggested to me by the editor of *American Heritage,* my friend Byron Dobell. Some years earlier, when he was editor of *Esquire,* Dobell had commissioned a piece called "100 Things That Every College Graduate Should Know." This was a real grab bag of information, and it produced a mailbag of reader responses. Dobell convinced me that an article on what people should know about American history would produce a similar response and, as he usually is, he was right. (My main creative contribution was to include 101 things rather than 100.)

Like its predecessor in *Esquire,* the article inspired a large response from readers, many of them, I must confess, pointing out careless errors I had made in describing some of the items. Newspapers picked up the article, and I found myself being interviewed on radio talk shows all over the country. Dobell authorized a second "101 Things" article, and on my own I then decided to undertake this book. I wish here to thank Byron most warmly for choosing me to bring his idea to fruition. I am also indebted to Patrick Williams of Columbia University for his assistance in locating, gathering, and checking material, and to Marshall DeBruhl and Herman Gollob, my past and present editors at Doubleday, for their advice and support.

John A. Garraty
Sag Harbor, N.Y.

Joseph Smith.
LIBRARY OF CONGRESS.

Two perspectives on slavery.
CULVER PICTURES, INC.

Brinkmanship, cartoonist Herblock's 1956 view. HERBERT BLOCK, *HERBLOCK'S SPECIAL FOR TODAY,* 1958.

ALSO BY JOHN A. GARRATY

Silas Wright

Henry Cabot Lodge: A Biography

Woodrow Wilson: A Great Life in Brief

The Nature of Biography

From Main Street to the Left Bank:
Students and Scholars Abroad

Right Hand Man: The Life of George W. Perkins

A Guide to Study Abroad

The American Nation:
A History of the United States

The New Commonwealth

Interpreting American History:
Conversations with Historians

Unemployment in History

American History

The Great Depression

PART I
Politics

COLONIAL AMERICA
Good Phrases for Big Issues

Karl Bodmer's print of Plains
Indian artifacts, 1830s.
LIBRARY OF CONGRESS.

1 The Columbian Exchange. This phrase, the title of a book by the historian Alfred W. Crosby, Jr., describes the interaction of the Old World and the New. Crosby was concerned with the way microbes, plants, and animals moved from one hemisphere to the other and how these "exchanges" affected life. In a larger sense there was also a cultural exchange, and it was not entirely in one direction. The Indians were profoundly affected by European tools, weapons, and ideas, but the Europeans were influenced too—in the way they dressed; how they fought; and, in many instances, how they thought.

2 Headright. To encourage settlement, colonial governments issued rights to take specified amounts of unoccupied land, usually fifty or one hundred acres, for each person arriving in their territories. The headright went to whoever paid the passage of the newcomers, not necessarily to the immigrants themselves.

3 Quitrent. Holders of headrights generally had to pay a small annual fee to the issuing authority. A quitrent was a tax rather than a rent, since the person paying it had legal title to the land; unlike modern property taxes, however, the amount was fixed and unrelated to the value of the land.

4 Indentured Servant. Since many Europeans who wished to come to the colonies could not afford passage money, they indentured themselves to ships' captains or established colonists, agreeing to work for a set term—usually between five and seven years—in exchange for their passage. They were subject to strict control by their masters, but when their terms were completed the masters were obliged to provide them with some farm tools, seed, and other essentials so they could strike out on their own. The headright associated with each indentured servant went to the master, who was the person responsible for bringing the servant to the colony.

5 Triangular Trade. This was the system developed in the northern colonies in order to acquire English manufactured goods despite the fact that they could not raise the crops (such as sugar and tobacco) for which there was a large demand in England. By trading grain, fish, and other things that could be produced in these colonies to southern European countries and in the Caribbean sugar islands, northern merchants obtained wine, fruit, and the semitropical goods the English wanted. These they exchanged in the mother country for the manufactured goods that were in demand back home. This indirect trade was not necessarily three-sided. It took many forms, the most notorious involving the purchase of molasses in the Caribbean, the distilling of the molasses into rum in New England, the exchange of the rum for slaves in West Africa, and the sale of the slaves to the Caribbean sugar planters.

6 Salutary Neglect. The British policy of allowing the American colonies a great deal of freedom in economic matters, especially those related to trade, de-

despite the restrictions imposed by the Navigation Acts. The policy was devised by Sir Robert Walpole, who was Prime Minister from 1721 to 1742. He believed that since the colonies were growing and England was enjoying prosperous times, it was best to let well enough alone.

Sir Robert Walpole. COURTESY OF CULVER PICTURES, INC.

7 Virtual Representation. The British argument that the Americans were represented in Parliament despite the fact that they did not elect any of the members of that body. This made sense to the British because although members of the House of Commons were elected by the voters of particular districts, they often did not reside in those districts. It was assumed that each member represented the entire empire.

Virtual representation did not make sense to colonists, however, because in America, representation was *direct*. It was assumed that delegates to the local assemblies represented only the people of the districts that elected them.

Town meeting in America, 1760. LIBRARY OF CONGRESS

THE PROVIDENTIAL DETECTION

Anti-Jefferson cartoon, 1800. THE AMERICAN ANTIQUARIAN SOCIETY.

8 The Revolution of 1800. The election of Thomas Jefferson as President in 1800 seemed an event of revolutionary significance to many people, not the least of whom was Jefferson himself. The election marked the first true change of party control of the government, for the Jeffersonians gained an overwhelming victory in the congressional elections as well. But no revolution took place; the basic structure of the government was not altered, and while the Jeffersonians took power and proceeded to change the policy of the government, they did so peacefully.

Nicknames

Portrait on oak panel thought to be Miles Standish. *MEMORIAL HISTORY OF BOSTON 1880,* JUSTIN WINSOR, COURTESY OF THE NEW YORK PUBLIC LIBRARY.

9 Captain Shrimp. The name was given to Myles Standish by Thomas Morton of Merrymount. The reference, of course, was to Standish's diminutive size.

10 **Light-Horse Harry.** Henry Lee, Revolutionary War cavalry officer, friend of George Washington (it was this Lee who described Washington as "first in war, first in peace, and first in the hearts of his countrymen"), and the father of Robert E. Lee.

11 **Champagne Charlie.** Charles Townshend, British Chancellor of the Exchequer, who pushed the Townshend Acts (taxing tea, glass, paint, paper, and other products imported into the colonies) through Parliament in 1767.

12 **Gentleman Johnny.** General John Burgoyne, the dashing British commander who lost the crucial Battle of Saratoga in 1777. Along with six thousand Redcoats, supporting Indian and Loyalist forces, and a hundred-odd cannon, Burgoyne had marched from Canada through the northern wilderness with no less than thirty carts loaded with his and his mistress's personal possessions.

1789–1860

Good Phrases for Big Issues

13 **American System.** A scheme designed by Henry Clay in the 1820s. Clay sought to form a coalition of eastern and western interests in Congress. In return for western support of protective tariffs that would benefit eastern manufacturers, the Easterners would vote for bills providing federal expenditures on roads and canals. These would reduce the cost of transporting manufactured goods to the West and make it possible for western farmers to sell their produce to the industrial workers in the East.

14 **Gerrymander.** The technique of redrawing the boundaries of election districts so as to maximize the number of seats controlled by the dominant party. The term came into use in 1812 after Governor Elbridge Gerry of Massachusetts redrew boundaries in such a way that one district in Essex County had a particularly contorted

THE GERRY-MANDER.

Woodcut in the *Boston Gazette*, March 26, 1812.
LIBRARY OF CONGRESS.

shape. When a critic, seeing a map of the county, said that the district looked like a salamander, another cried out, "Gerrymander," and the name stuck.

15 **Impressment.** Under British law, any subject of the crown could be drafted into the Royal Navy in an emergency. In wartime, captains sometimes stopped even neutral ships on the high seas and carried off any British-born sailors aboard. Thousands of men were impressed in this manner during the Napoleonic Wars. Since many American sailors were of British origin, and since the British

Scarf commemorating battleships in the War of 1812.
OLDS COLLECTION, PEABODY MUSEUM COLLECTION.

operated on the principle "once an Englishman, always an Englishman," the impressment of such sailors from American vessels caused bitter resentment in the United States. The anger was even greater in the many cases when Americans who were *not* British-born were impressed. Though by no means the only one, impressment was an important cause of the War of 1812.

16 **The Spoils System.** This was the political practice of treating government jobs as "the spoils of war." After each election, the winning party discharged many perfectly competent clerks, postmasters, and other members of the bureaucracy and replaced them with "loyal" members of their own party. The system of rewarding one's supporters existed from the beginning of the Republic, but it was "perfected" in the 1820s and 1830s by the politicos of the Albany Regency (see numbers 38, 285) and by other partisans of Andrew Jackson.

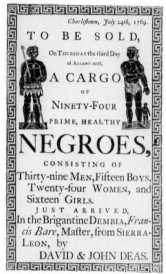

Charlestown, July 24th, 1769.

TO BE SOLD,

On THURSDAY the third Day of AUGUST next,

A CARGO

OF

NINETY-FOUR

PRIME, HEALTHY

NEGROES,

CONSISTING OF

Thirty-nine MEN, Fifteen BOYS, Twenty-four WOMEN, and Sixteen GIRLS.

JUST ARRIVED,

In the Brigantine DEMBIA, *Francis Bare*, Master, from SIERRA-LEON, by

DAVID & JOHN DEAS.

Advertisement for African slaves, 1769. THE AMERICAN ANTIQUARIAN SOCIETY.

17 **The Peculiar Institution.** A southern euphemism for slavery. The term was not intended to be pejorative; by "peculiar," Southerners meant particular or unique, not odd or queer.

18 **Rotation in Office.** This was the belief, developed during the presidency of Andrew Jackson (1829–37), that government employees ought to be "rotated" to make room for others. "No man has any more intrinsic right to official station than another," Jackson said. The system was an intrinsic part of the spoils system (see number 16), but in theory was to be applied without regard for party allegiance.

Puck's view of the Spoils System under Benjamin Harrison, 1889. *PUCK, JULY 24, 1889.*

19 **Nullification.** A constitutional argument developed by John C. Calhoun of South Carolina in *Exposition and Protest,* 1828. Calhoun claimed that since the separate states existed before the United States and had created the new government by drafting the Constitution, a state could decide for itself what the Constitution meant and "nullify," within its boundaries, any law of Congress it deemed unconstitutional. South Carolina put the theory into practice by declaring the Tariff Act of 1832 "unauthorized by the Constitution," but after President Jackson warned that he would hang Calhoun "as high as Haman" and treat any attempt to prevent the enforcement of the law as treason, Congress passed a new "compromise" tariff and South Carolina repealed its Ordinance of Nullification (see number 177).

20 **Manifest Destiny.** This term, coined by John L. O'Sullivan in 1845 in his *United States Magazine and Democratic Review,* reflected the expansionist spirit of the era. It was, wrote O'Sullivan, "our *manifest* [read, 'obvious'] *destiny* to overspread the continent." Belief in Manifest Destiny was characteristic of

21 **Young America.** This term came into use in the 1840s to describe an attitude of mind that involved not only national expansion but a mindless confidence in the worldwide triumph of republicanism and democracy. To a considerable degree, not always understood by people with these ideas, Young America was a way of distracting people from the ominous threat to peace and order posed by the growing concern about the future of slavery.

Nicknames

22 His Rotundity. John Adams, so called because of his portly shape and possibly because of his belief that a President should be treated with the dignity and punctilio commonly supplied to monarchs.

23 Magnus Apollo. DeWitt Clinton, longtime mayor of New York, governor of New York,

Governor DeWitt Clinton opening the locks of the Erie Canal.
PAINTING BY ABRAHAM C. D. TUTHILL, SHELBURNE MUSEUM.

United States senator, and unsuccessful Federalist candidate for President in 1812, because of his large size and impressive appearance. Despite the many offices he held, Clinton's most important achievement was his planning and carrying to completion in 1825 of the

24 Big Ditch, the 363-mile-long Erie Canal, between the Hudson River and the Great Lakes, which sped the development of the West and made New York City, in Clinton's words, "the emporium of commerce, the seat of manufactures, [and] the focus of great moneyed operations."

25 Czar Nicholas. Nicholas Biddle, president of the Second Bank of the United States in the 1820s and 1830s, because of the large influence he exerted on other, smaller banks, and to some extent on contemporary political affairs. Critics called the Bank

26 The Monster because its large size gave it great influence over the economy. But many businessmen, especially those interested in raising capital, opposed the Bank because it restrained state-chartered banks that tended to overextend themselves.

Andrew Jackson slays the bank hydra. CULVER PICTURES, INC.

27 Prince Hal. Henry Clay, whose admirers saw a resemblance between Clay's dashing, somewhat unconventional political style and the personality of the hero of Shakespeare's *Henry V*. Clay was also known as

Currier & Ives print of Henry Clay. COURTESY OF THE NEW YORK PUBLIC LIBRARY.

28 Harry of the West, and while a youth as

29 The Mill Boy of The Slashes, because the part of Hanover County, Virginia, where he grew up was called "The Slashes." Later in life he was called

30 **The Great Pacificator** and **The Great Compromiser,** because of his skill at working out inter-sectional political deals (see number 178).

31 **Sharp Knife.** The name given to General Andrew Jackson by his Creek Indian foes after the Battle of Horseshoe Bend in Alabama in 1814.

Daniel Webster.
CULVER PICTURES, INC.

32 **Black Dan.** A name given to Daniel Web-ster because of his swarthy complexion and dark eyes. Webster's admirers also called him

33 **Godlike Daniel** be-cause of his imposing

appearance and magisterial style.

34 **The Cato of the Sen-ate.** Silas Wright of New York, a prominent Democratic politician in the 1830s and 1840s. The Cato he was likened to was Mar-cus Porcius Cato (the Elder), the ancient Roman states-man known for his simple manners and high moral standards.

1848 engraving of Martin Van Buren. COURTESY OF THE NEW-YORK HISTORICAL SOCIETY.

35 **The Little Magi-cian.** Martin Van Buren of New York, also known as

36 **The Red Fox** and

37 **The American Tal-leyrand,** because he was a crafty and inventive political manager. His New York political machine was known as

38 **The Albany Regency,** because, during the 1820s and 1830s, it ran things while Van Buren spent most of his time away in Washington as sena-tor, Secretary of State, Vice President, and finally as President.

39 **His Accidency.** John Tyler, so called after he succeeded to the presi-dency upon the death of Wil-liam Henry Harrison in 1841. Since this was the first time that a President had died in office, there was some question as to the ex-tent of Tyler's authority.

John Tyler. THE CHICAGO HISTORICAL SOCIETY.

40 **Prince John.** John Van Buren, son of Martin, given the name by political opponents while he was attaché at the American legation in London during his father's service as minis-ter there in the early 1830s. He was also, for obvious rea-sons, known as

41 Young Fox. He was active in New York Democratic politics for decades, first as leader of the radical Barnburner faction (see number 50), and later as a member of the faction opposed to the Civil War.

42 Bully. Congressman Preston S. Brooks of South Carolina, who was given the name by northern critics after he attacked Senator Charles Sumner of Massachusetts with a gutta-percha cane to avenge insulting remarks Sumner had made about proslavery Senator Andrew P. Butler, who was Brooks's uncle. Southerners took a different view of Brooks. After he was censured for his actions by the House of Representatives, he resigned, returned to South Carolina (where he was presented with a number of souvenir canes to replace the one he had broken while beating Sumner), and easily won re-election.

43 The Pathfinder. John C. Frémont, so called because of his long career as an explorer and surveyor, and his excellent published reports of his explorations, written with the help of his wife, Jessie, daughter of Senator Thomas Hart Benton (see number 620).

A John Frémont campaign ribbon. PRIVATE COLLECTION.

Senator Stephen A. Douglas. FREDERICK HILL MESERVE COLLECTION.

44 The Little Giant. Senator Stephen A. Douglas of Illinois, also known as

45 The Steam Engine in Britches because of his short stature (he had a massive head and trunk perched on stubby, almost dwarfish legs), his colorful personality, and his self-confident political style.

46 The Forty Thieves. The New York City Board of Aldermen in the 1850s.

Party and Factional Nicknames

47 Quids. Short for "Tertium Quids," or "third thing." This was a term loosely applied to those supporters of Jefferson who became disaffected with him and his policies as President, and who tended to vote with the Federalists. On the national level, the most important—and certainly the most vituperative—was John Randolph of Roanoke, Virginia (see number 277).

John Randolph of Roanoke. CULVER PICTURES, INC.

48 Bucktails. A Jeffersonian faction of the early nineteenth century in New York State, opponents of the faction headed by DeWitt Clinton, known unimaginatively as the Clintonians.

49 War Hawks. A group of congressmen (Henry Clay prominent among them) who, for complicated reasons, favored going to war with Great Britain in 1811–12.

50 Barnburners and Hunkers. Radical and conservative factions of the New York Democratic Party in the 1840s. The Barnburners were opposed to slavery and were said by their opponents to be "willing to burn down the barn to get rid of the rats." The source of "Hunker" is more obscure; perhaps, being conservative, they were thought to be "hunkering down" before the winds of change.

51 Know-Nothings. The members of the American Party, originally a secret society (the Order of the Star-Spangled Banner) that flourished in the 1850s. The party was militantly patriotic, anti-Catholic, and anti-immigrant. When queried about the organization, its adherents were schooled to reply: "I don't know." The party was strong in the Midwest in the 1850s, electing more than forty congressmen in 1854.

Know-Nothings song sheet. CULVER PICTURES, INC.

1837 cartoon satirizing Whig Party member Martin Van Buren. CULVER PICTURES, INC.

52 Conscience Whigs and Silver Grays. Northern members of the Whig Party, mostly New Englanders, who strongly opposed slavery in the 1840s and 1850s were called Conscience Whigs; northern members of the party who were willing to cooperate with the southern or "Cotton" Whigs were known as Silver Grays.

53 Doughfaces. Northerners who supported southern policies on slavery and territorial government before the Civil War. Some-

times described as "northern men with southern principles."

Slogans

Commentary on the Embargo Act of 1807. CULVER PICTURES, INC.

54 O Grab Me. From the word "embargo" spelled backward. The term was concocted by opponents of the Embargo Act of 1807, which sought to deal with the impressment of American seamen—and other violations of the rights of neutrals during the Napoleonic Wars—by forbidding all exports. Eventually even supporters of the embargo began to use the term.

55 Corrupt Bargain. A charge made by supporters of Andrew Jackson before and during the 1828 presidential campaign. In 1824 none of the four candidates won a majority in the electoral college, but Jackson had the largest total, 99. John Quincy Adams had 84, William H. Crawford 41, and Henry Clay 37. The election was therefore thrown into the House of Representatives, where Clay used his influence to swing the election to Adams. When Adams then appointed Clay as his Secretary of State, the Jacksonians charged that a deal had been made.

56 **Tippecanoe and Tyler Too.** A slogan used by the Whigs in 1840 when William Henry Harrison, the hero of the Battle of Tippecanoe, was their presidential candidate and John Tyler his running mate. The battle fought in 1811 in Indiana resulted in the breakup of the Indian confederacy organized by Tecumseh, a Shawnee chief, and his brother Tenskwatawa, who was known as "the Prophet." (See numbers 538, 539.)

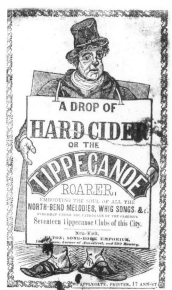

Harrison 1840 campaign songbook. THE CINCINNATI HISTORICAL SOCIETY.

57 **54-40 or Fight.** A Democratic rallying cry in the 1840s, referring to the dispute over whether the United States or Great Britain owned the Pacific Northwest. The region had been under joint control since 1828. American expansionists demanded that the United States take over the entire region, which extended to 54°40′ North latitude. However, in 1846, President James K. Polk agreed to a compromise with the British, dividing the region at the 49th parallel.

58 **Bleeding Kansas.** The name applied by abolitionists and other opponents of slavery to the chaotic situation that developed in Kansas Territory in the mid-1850s. With the territory open to slavery as a result of the Kansas-Nebraska Act, pro- and antislavery supporters rushed to the state to try to capture the government. Fighting broke out between proslavery "Border Ruffians" from Missouri and antislavery settlers, some armed with "Beecher's Bi-

Border ruffians invading Kansas. CULVER PICTURES, INC.

bles"—rifles named after the Reverend Henry Ward Beecher, an abolitionist. John Brown's raid at Pottawatomie is the best known of the numerous atrocities of the period.

59 **Free Soil, Free Speech, Frémont.** Slogan of the new Republican Party in 1856. It referred to the Republicans' demand that slavery be banned in the western territories and that efforts to suppress abolitionist literature in the South be ended. It was adapted from the 1848 slogan of the Free Soil Party, which was "Free Soil, Free Speech, Free Labor, Free Men." John C. Frémont was the Republican candidate.

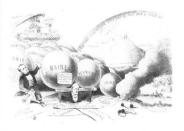

"The Balls Are Rolling, Clear the Track," John C. Frémont campaign, 1856. COURTESY OF THE HARVARD COLLEGE LIBRARY

60 **Cotton Is King.** Argument of southern disunionists in the late 1850s, who claimed that the North would not resist secession because its economy and that of Great Britain and other European powers were so dependent on southern cotton.

THE CIVIL WAR
Nicknames

Abraham Lincoln songbook.
THE MUSEUM OF AMERICAN POLITICAL LIFE, UNIVERSITY OF HARTFORD

61 Honest Abe. People actually called Lincoln this long before he became famous. During the latter stages of the Civil War, he was also referred to as

62 Father Abraham.

63 Unconditional Surrender. Ulysses S. Grant, a play on his initials made after he informed a Confederate general seeking an armistice: "No terms except an unconditional and immediate surrender can be accepted." The nickname would probably not have come into use had Grant not, upon entering West Point, changed the names his parents gave him ("Hiram Ulysses" to "Ulysses Hiram") in order to avoid the initials "H.U.G." He was registered at the Point, however, as "Ulysses Simpson," Simpson being his mother's maiden name, and he let that stand.

64 Stonewall. Confederate General Thomas J. Jackson, who got the name during the Battle of Bull Run when another officer, observing the tough defense put up by Jackson's troops, said: "There is Jackson standing like a stone wall."

General Thomas J. Jackson. BRADY COLLECTION, THE LIBRARY OF CONGRESS.

65 Little Phil. General Philip H. Sheridan was given this name by admiring cavalrymen because he was a very small man. President Lincoln said of him: "This Sheridan is a little Irishman, but he is a big fighter."

66 Beast. Benjamin Franklin Butler (see numbers 75, 657), the name given him during the Civil War by outraged citizens of Union-occupied New Orleans. To stop local women from insulting Union soldiers, General Butler issued an order that such persons should be treated "as a woman of the town plying her avocation."

67 Fighting Joe. Union General Joseph Hooker, who got the name in 1862. The nickname was not given him because of his aggressive tactics, though he was anything but a cautious or timorous commander. During General George B. McClellan's 1862 campaign against Richmond, a last-minute Associated Press dispatch reached the *New York Courier and Enquirer* just as the paper was going to press. It began: "Fighting—Joe Hooker . . . ," meaning that what followed was to be added to earlier accounts of the action involving Hooker's corps. The compositor, however, set it up as a heading, "Fighting Joe Hooker," and after publication the name caught on (see also 854, 889). In 1863, after Lincoln —somewhat against his better judgment—had put Hooker in command of the Army of the Potomac,

Hooker suffered a disastrous defeat at the Battle of Chancellorsville. To his credit, Hooker disliked his nickname, saying, "It sounds to me like Fighting Fool."

68 Slow Trot. Union General George H. Thomas, so called because of his careful, seemingly unimaginative way of organizing for battle. He was actually a brilliant tactician and an excellent battlefield commander, as is demonstrated by his better-known nickname

69 Rock of Chickamauga, given him after his troops withstood a furious Confederate assault on their positions in that battle.

70 Young Napoleon. General George B. McClellan, so called because he somewhat resembled *the*

General George B. McClellan.
CULVER PICTURES, INC.

Napoleon in physical appearance, grandiose style, and his inflated sense of his own importance.

71 Napoleon in Gray. Confederate General Pierre G. T. Beauregard, who was both of French descent and an excellent tactician (see number 874).

Civil War cartoon.
CULVER PICTURES, INC.

72 Copperheads. Northern Democrats who opposed Lincoln's vigorous prosecution of the Civil War and favored a negotiated settlement that would permit the retention of slavery. The leading Copperhead, Ohio Congressman Clement L. Vallandigham, was imprisoned by the military, but released and banished to the Confederacy by President Lincoln.

Slogans

73 Vote Yourself a Farm. This refers to the Republican Party's promise in the 1860 campaign to give land in the

West to anyone who would settle on it. Unlike so many campaign promises (especially those involving gifts of any kind), this one was kept by passage of the Homestead Act of 1862.

"Old Abe's Last Joke," *New-York Illustrated News,* June 2, 1864.
CULVER PICTURES, INC.

74 Don't Swap Horses in the Middle of the Stream. Republicans offered this advice to voters in 1864, when Lincoln was running for a second term.

1865–1900

Good Phrases for Big Issues

75 Waving the Bloody Shirt. This post–Civil War Republican tactic involved reminding northern voters that the South was made up mostly of Democrats and that many northern members of that party had been, at best, lukewarm about resisting secession. The term came into use after Congressman Benjamin F. Butler (see number 66) displayed before his colleagues the bloodstained shirt of a Northerner who had been flogged in Mississippi. The "bloody shirt" was used by Republicans for decades as a way of diverting attention from politically embarrassing contemporary issues.

A *Puck* cover of the Bloody Shirt, May 16, 1888. *PUCK,* MAY 16, 1888.

76 Robber Barons. This name was applied to the ultra-rich industrialists of the late nineteenth century, such as railroad magnates Cornelius Vanderbilt and Jay Gould and oil tycoon

Robber barons, as seen by *Puck,* March 10, 1897.
CULVER PICTURES, INC.

John D. Rockefeller (see number 461). It originated in the 1860s, but became a symbol of corporate power and the evils of unrestrained economic freedom only with the publication of Matthew Josephson's bestseller *The Robber Barons* in 1934.

77 The Large Policy. The program of late nineteenth-century expansionists. Influenced by the closing of the frontier, the successes achieved by European imperialists, the importance of developing markets for American manufactures, the strategic concepts of Captain Alfred Thayer Mahan (see number 798), and racist arguments about the white man's burden, the expansionists urged the building of a modern navy, the construction of a canal across Central America, and the acquisition of the Hawaiian Islands and other "strategic" spots in the Caribbean and Pacific regions.

78 The Open Door. The name given to the policy developed by Secretary of State John Hay in his "Open Door Notes." Concerned by the way Great Britain, France, and Germany were establishing spheres of influence in the crumbling Chinese Empire, Hay in 1899 asked the pow-

ers to agree to respect the trading rights of all nations in their spheres. Their response was noncommittal at best. Shortly thereafter the nationalist-inspired Boxer Rebellion broke out in China, and in July 1900 Hay dispatched a second round of Open Door Notes, stating that the United States believed in "the territorial and administrative entity" of China and in "the principle of equal and impartial trade with all parts of the Chinese Empire." The Open Door policy worked well enough so long as no power was willing to use force to obtain and maintain special advantages.

Nicknames

James C. Blaine meets Columbia, July 17, 1884. COURTESY OF THE NEW-YORK HISTORICAL SOCIETY.

79 The Plumed Knight. James G. Blaine, so called by his many Republican admirers and by numbers of Irish-Americans who normally voted Democratic. Most Democrats called him other things (see number 558). This name was bestowed upon Blaine by Robert Ingersoll, a spellbinding orator of the era, in a speech placing his name into nomination for President at the 1876 Republican Convention. That nomination, however, went to

80 His Fraudulency, Rutherford B. Hayes, who won the presidency in the famous disputed election of 1876 (see number 180).

Rutherford B. Hayes and Lucy Hayes, 1852.
HAYES MEMORIAL LIBRARY.

81 Lemonade Lucy. A name that was given to Hayes's wife because she would allow no liquor in the White House.

82 The Ohio Icicle. Senator John Sherman, sponsor of the Sherman Antitrust Act of 1890, was so dubbed because of his stiff, colorless personality. Sherman is thought to have invented the political term "to mend some fences."

83 Silver Dick. Congressman Richard P. Bland of Missouri, so called during his long career in the House (1873–99) because of his persistent advocacy of the free coinage of silver.

84 Czar. The name given to Congressman Thomas B. Reed of Maine, because of the way he controlled the business of the House during his two terms as speaker, 1889–91 and 1895–99. Among other witticisms, Reed has been credited with the line "A statesman is a politician who is dead."

Congressman Thomas B. Reed of Maine, 1899. *EXPANSION: BAIT'S BEST CARTOONS FROM THE MINNEAPOLIS JOURNAL,* 1899, COURTESY OF THE NEW YORK PUBLIC LIBRARY.

85 Pitchfork Ben. Benjamin Tillman, governor of South Carolina (1890–94), U.S. senator (1895–1918), so called because when campaigning for the Senate in 1894 he promised that if elected he would stick a pitchfork in President Grover Cleveland's ribs.

86 The Dude President. Chester A. Arthur, so called because he was a particularly flashy dresser.

87 Sockless Jerry. Jeremiah Simpson, rough-hewn Populist congressman from Kansas in the 1890s, who got his name after he claimed scornfully in the 1890 campaign that his Republican opponent, James R. Hallowell, wore silk socks.

Jeremiah Simpson.
THE KANSAS STATE HISTORICAL SOCIETY, TOPEKA

88 The Sage of Nininger. Ignatius Donnelly, reformer, perennial third-party candidate for office, novelist, Populist orator and idea man, named after the Minnesota town he had founded.

89 The Peerless Leader. The perennial (three-time) Democratic presidential candidate William Jennings Bryan of Nebraska, also known as

90 The Great Commoner because of his stress on being a product of and a representative of "the people." When the free silver issue surfaced in the 1890s, Bryan, who was then in the House of Representatives, announced, "The people of Nebraska are for free silver. Therefore I am for free silver. I'll look up the reasons later." Early in his career Bryan was known as

91 The Boy Orator of the Platte because of his remarkable oratorical talents (see number 412).

William Jennings Bryan. *THE VERDICT SUPPLEMENT,* NO. 11.

92 Queen Lil. The name given by American expansionists to Queen Liliuokalani, last ruler of the Hawaiian Islands and ardent exponent of "Hawaii for the Hawaiians" at the time of the American-sponsored revolution in the islands in 1893.

93 The Rough Rider. Theodore Roosevelt was so named after the regiment of that name, composed of a motley mixture of cowboys, adventurers, and odd characters, raised and led by Roosevelt to fight in the Spanish-American War. (He was also known as "T.R." and as "Teddy," which latter name he disliked intensely.)

"Teddy to the Rescue of Republicanism!" *The Verdict,* **October 10, 1899.** THE NEW YORK STATE HISTORICAL ASSOCIATION, COOPERSTOWN.

Party and Factional Nicknames

94 Carpetbaggers. The Northerners who moved to the states of the former Confederacy after the Civil War and became active in politics as civil servants and elected officials. They were uniformly members of the Republican Party. The term, applied by unfriendly Southerners, was a reference to the luggage made of carpeting material in which they presumably transported all their worldly belongings.

Journalist Carl Schurz, as seen by *Harper's* **cartoonist Thomas Nast, November 9, 1872.** CULVER PICTURES, INC.

95 Scalawags. Southern whites who cooperated with the occupying forces after the Civil War and were presumed to be in favor of treating the former slaves as equals. Most white Southerners considered scalawags even more reprehensible than carpetbaggers.

96 Redeemers. Conservative whites who won control of the southern states after the withdrawal of federal troops in the 1870s. They claimed to be moderates who would advance the interests of the region by cooperating with northern industrialists and developers, but they stood uncompromisingly for white supremacy.

97 Bourbons. Conservative northern and eastern Democrats of the period who favored "retiring" the "greenbacks" (paper money unbacked by specie) and returning to the gold standard. In the 1890s most of them bitterly opposed all efforts to increase the coinage of silver. In the South, Redeemers were also called Bourbons.

"The Financial Balance and How to Keep It," *The Daily Graphic,* January 11, 1878. COURTESY OF THE NEW-YORK HISTORICAL SOCIETY.

98 Stalwarts and Half-Breeds. Post–Civil War Republican factions, both mainly interested in office as a source of patronage, the Stalwarts blatantly so. The Half-Breeds behaved more circumspectly in hopes of obtaining the cooperation of the

99 Mugwumps. Eastern Republicans in the 1870s and 1880s, not active politicians, who opposed all the more sordid aspects of the political management of

the era and favored civil service reform. They were strongly opposed to James G. Blaine; this was still another of the reasons (see numbers 558, 559) why Blaine was not elected President in 1884.

Politicians on guard against Mugwumps, *Puck,* June 23, 1886. *PUCK,* JUNE 23, 1886.

Slogans

100 Seward's Folly. The response of critics to Secretary of State William H. Seward's purchase of Alaska from Russia in 1867. The argument was that the price ($7.2 million for what appeared to be a frozen wilderness) was far too high.

"The Official Seal," *Harper's Weekly* view of the Alaskan purchase, April 27, 1867. *HARPER'S WEEKLY,* APRIL 27, 1867.

101 A Public Office Is a Public Trust. This Democratic campaign slogan of 1884 was designed to remind voters, not very subtly, that the Republican candidate ("Blaine, Blaine, James G. Blaine, the continental liar from the State of Maine") was believed to have sold favors to a railroad while serving as Speaker of the House of Representatives in the 1870s (see number 558).

Grover Cleveland's 1884 campaign slogan. CULVER PICTURES, INC.

102 Twisting the British Lion's Tail. A nineteenth-century political technique (one of which Blaine was a master) involving criticism of Great Britain in general and British policies in particular in order to win the support of Irish-Americans, who resented British control of Ireland.

103 Remember the Maine. Rallying cry of those eager to go to war with Spain in order to free Cuba after the USS *Maine* was blown up in Havana Harbor in February 1898.

Sinking of the *Maine*, February 15, 1898.
CHICAGO HISTORICAL SOCIETY.

1901–40

Good Phrases for Big Issues

104 **Muckraking**. The name given to the investigative journalism that flourished in the early twentieth century. Muckrakers such as Lincoln Steffens and Ida M. Tarbell exposed the graft, corruption, and other sleazy aspects of the Progressive Era. Theodore Roosevelt compared the more sensationalistic of these journalists to John Bunyan's "Man with the Muck-Rake" in *Pilgrim's Progress,* who was so concerned with the filth he was raking up that he missed a "celestial crown" when it was offered him.

105 **The Roosevelt Corollary**. President Theodore Roosevelt's modification of the Monroe Doctrine. Since the Doc-

trine committed the United States to keeping European nations from using force in the Western Hemisphere when their "rights" were threatened, the United States must intervene in their stead to prevent "chronic wrongdoing" by Latin-American governments.

106 **Dollar Diplomacy**. William Howard Taft's less bellicose way of dealing with the same problem. Taft reasoned that the United States' development of strong economic interests in the Caribbean region would serve as a stabilizing influence, making military intervention unnecessary.

Taft campaign postcard, 1908.
THE MUSEUM OF AMERICAN POLITICAL LIFE, UNIVERSITY OF HARTFORD

107 **Missionary Diplomacy**. Woodrow Wilson's approach to

Latin-American problems. Wilson thought Dollar Diplomacy ignoble; he proposed to deal with other nations "upon terms of equality and honor." But he was also determined, as he put it to a British diplomat, "to teach the South American republics to elect good men!" In the end he intervened more frequently and more forcefully in the region than either Roosevelt or Taft.

Woodrow Wilson lectures Mexico, *Punch*, August 27, 1913.
PUNCH, AUGUST 27, 1913.

108 **The Noble Experiment**. The prohibition of the manufacture, distribution, and sale of alcoholic beverages after the passage of the Eighteenth Amendment was described by President Hoover as an "experiment noble in purpose."

109 **The Stimson Doctrine**. This was the policy announced in 1932 by

President Hoover's Secretary of State, Henry L. Stimson, after the Japanese invasion of Manchuria: the United States would not recognize the seizure of territory when it violated existing treaty rights. When Stimson proposed expanding his doctrine to include economic sanctions against Japan, President Hoover rejected the idea on the ground that it would be "like sticking pins in a tiger."

110 **Hoovervilles.** During the Great Depression of the 1930s, shantytowns inhabited by unemployed people sprang up on wasteland in and around the nation's cities. Critics dubbed these settlements "Hoovervilles," in part because President Hoover had been most reluctant to provide direct federal aid to the jobless.

Hooverville, 1930s.
LIBRARY OF CONGRESS.

111 **Hundred Days.** The period from March 9 to June 16, 1933, the length of the first session of the first New Deal Congress, during which a flood of legislation aimed at fighting the Depression was enacted.

"The Galloping Snail," drawing by Bert Thomas, March 20, 1933. *THE DETROIT NEWS,* COURTESY OF THE FRANKLIN DELANO ROOSEVELT LIBRARY

Nicknames

William Howard Taft. *LOS ANGELES TIMES,* SEPTEMBER 28, 1909.

112 **Big Bill.** William Howard Taft, because of his girth—he weighed over three hundred pounds. Quite different, though also a very large man, was

113 **Big Bill.** William Dudley Haywood, the radical leader of the Western Federation of Miners, who in 1905 was a founder of the

114 **Wobblies.** The Industrial Workers of the World, an organization noted for violent strikes and an anticapitalist philosophy.

Industrial Workers of the World sticker, 1910s. THE NATIONAL ARCHIVES.

115 **Honey Fitz.** John Fitzgerald, Boston political boss, best known for being the namesake of his grandson, President John Fitzgerald Kennedy. Fitzgerald got the name because of his skill at singing "Sweet Adeline." He was also known as

116 **Fitzblarney** for more easily understandable reasons.

117 **Uncle Joe.** Joseph G. Cannon, Republican congressman from Illinois, sometimes known as "Hayseed" and "Foul-mouthed Joe," autocratic speaker of the House of Representatives, 1903–11.

118 The Scholar in Politics. Senator Henry Cabot Lodge of Massachusetts, because he had a Harvard Ph.D.—earned in 1876 under Henry Adams (see number 438)—and was the author of biographies of Washington, Hamilton, and Webster, and of many other books and essays. The fact that Woodrow Wilson was also a Ph.D. (Johns Hopkins, 1886), and was also known as a scholar in politics, was thought by some to explain Lodge's intense dislike of the President.

Henry Cabot Lodge.
LIBRARY OF CONGRESS.

119 Peck's Bad Boy. Title given to President Woodrow Wilson by unscrupulous political opponents because of his supposed illicit relationship with a divorcée, Mrs. Mary Allen Peck.

120 The Duchess was Florence Kling Harding, wife of President Warren G. Harding.

Florence Kling Harding.
LIBRARY OF CONGRESS.

121 The Lone Eagle. The name given to Charles A. Lindbergh, Jr., after his solo flight from New York to Paris in 1927. But much earlier, in the 1890s,

122 The Lone Eagle was the brilliant Wall Street speculator Bernard Baruch, so called because his success was achieved despite his apparent lack of interest in rumors, inside information, and the opinions of other Wall Street types, such as his contemporary

123 Bet-You-a-Million Gates. John Warne Gates, a steel manufacturer known for his "fatal passion for speculation" and his daring, often somewhat shady combinations and takeovers.

124 Black Jack. General John J. Pershing, the name given him by West Point cadets because of the strict discipline he maintained while assigned there in the late 1890s. Pershing had previously commanded the Tenth Cavalry, an all-black unit, and was devoted to that regiment. This roused the scorn of the cadets.

General John J. Pershing.
U.S. ARMY PHOTOGRAPH.

125 The Radio Priest. Father Charles E. Coughlin, whose controversial broadcasts on political and economic topics attracted an audience of millions in the 1930s. Coughlin first supported and then bitterly attacked Franklin D. Roosevelt and the New Deal. When his talks became increasingly more anti-Semitic and pro-Fascist, he was ordered by his bishop to cease broadcasting.

Father Charles E. Coughlin.
BROWN BROTHERS.

126 Hell 'n' Maria. Charles G. Dawes, chairman of the board of directors of General Electric, so called because that was a favorite expletive of his.

127 The Unholy Thing with a Holy Name. This was what the Irreconcilables (see number 133) called the League of Nations.

128 Silent Cal. Calvin Coolidge, who had little to say and said it economically, as for example,

"The business of the United States is business," and (when asked if he intended to seek re-election in 1928) "I do not choose to run." Then there is the no doubt apocryphal tale about the interviewer who said, "Mr. President, I made a bet that I could get more than two words out of you"—to which Coolidge replied, "You lose."

Calvin Coolidge celebrates the Fourth of July, 1927, Rapid City, S.D. WIDE WORLD PHOTOS.

129 The Happy Warrior. Governor Alfred E. Smith of New York, who was given this name by Franklin D. Roosevelt in the course of a speech nominating him for President at the 1924 Democratic National Convention.

130 The Kingfish. Senator Huey P. Long (see number 473), because of his total dominance of his native state of Louisiana.

131 Cactus Jack. Vice President John Nance Garner, who got the name during his thirty-year career as a Texas congressman.

John Nance Garner, 1939.
LIBRARY OF CONGRESS.

Party and Factional Nicknames

132 Bull Moosers. Members of the Progressive Party formed by

Progressive Party campaign button, 1912.
THEODORE ROOSEVELT ASSOCIATION.

Theodore Roosevelt when he ran for President in 1912. The name originated when Roosevelt said upon being nominated, "I feel like a bull moose."

133 **The Irreconcilables.** Senators, most but not all Republicans, who were adamantly opposed to the League of Nations and who, therefore, voted against ratification of the Versailles Treaty after World War I. Not to be confused with the "reservationists," who were willing to vote for the treaty if various changes were made.

Slogans

134 **Perdicaris Alive or Raisuli Dead.** This phrase (actually a telegram sent by Secretary of State John Hay to the Sultan of Morocco) was used by the Republicans to help re-elect Theodore Roosevelt in 1904. Ion Perdicaris had been abducted in Morocco by a bandit named Ahmed ibn-Muhammed Raisuli. Perdicaris, who was Greek by birth and whose American citizenship was actually open to question, was released, though not because of Hay's telegram. How times have changed!

135 **He Kept Us Out of War.** This phrase was used by the Democrats in the 1916 presidential election. It was adopted after Martin Henry Glynn, a former governor of New York, defended Woodrow Wilson's neutrality policy at the Democratic Convention. Glynn drew thunderous applause by repeatedly pointing out that, in various crises in the past, the United States had avoided getting involved in foreign conflicts. This showed that American neutrality in the European war was very popular.

Woodrow Wilson campaign truck, 1916. UPI/BETTMANN NEWSPHOTOS.

136 **Keep Cool with Coolidge.** Republican advice during the 1924 presidential campaign, probably an attempt to make a virtue of Calvin Coolidge's colorless personality and taciturn style (see number 128).

A Coolidge campaign sticker, 1924. THE MUSEUM OF AMERICAN POLITICAL LIFE, THE UNIVERSITY OF HARTFORD

137 **A Chicken in Every Pot** (and a car in every garage): A slogan of the Republicans in the 1928 presidential campaign, the reference being to what they called "Coolidge prosperity."

138 **Who but Hoover?** Slogan of black Republicans in the 1932 presidential election. While most blacks were not very happy with Hoover, the prospect of voting for Roosevelt, who had not shown much interest in the problems of blacks and who seemed sure to be dependent on southern Democrats, was even less attractive. Four years later, influenced by New Deal reforms, blacks voted overwhelmingly for Roosevelt.

NRA songsheet, 1930s. COURTESY OF THE NEW-YORK HISTORICAL SOCIETY.

139 **We Do Our Part.** The motto of NRA, the New Deal's National Recovery Administration, used in conjunction with the famous Blue Eagle emblem to identify the products of companies that had adopted NRA codes of fair business practice.

140 Every Man a King. The slogan of the Share Our Wealth movement of Louisiana Senator Huey Long (see number 130). The movement was a product of the Great Depression. Long proposed to confiscate all personal fortunes of more than $5 million and all incomes of over $1 million, and to use the money to give every American family a house, a car, and an annual income of $2,000 or more.

Huey P. Long's Share Our Wealth Society button. SPECIAL COLLECTIONS, HILL MEMORIAL LIBRARY, LOUISIANA STATE UNIVERSITY.

141 Let's Get Another Deck. This was a Republican response in 1936 to Franklin Roosevelt's New Deal. When that failed, the Republicans tried

142 Two Good Terms Deserve a Rest in 1940, with equal lack of success.

SINCE 1940
Good Phrases for Big Issues

143 Truman Doctrine. President Harry S Truman's response to a British Government message that it was no longer financially capable of supporting anti-Communist forces in Greece. In March 1947 Truman asked Congress for $400 million "to support free people who are resisting attempted subjugation by armed minorities or by outside pressures." This was an early sign of the

144 Cold War. The name given the tension and mutual suspicion that marked relations between the Soviet Union and the United States after World War II. From the American perspective, the Russians seemed bent on spreading their system throughout the world; the Russian perspective is less clear because the Soviet archives are closed. The Cold War subsided somewhat after the defusing of the Cuban Missile Crisis in 1962.

New York models picket Russian furs, 1952.
UPI/BETTMANN NEWSPHOTOS.

145 Détente. A diplomatic term taken from a French word meaning a lowering of pressure, in particular the reduction of tensions between nations. It has been used most recently to describe the improvement of relations between the United States and the Soviet Union.

Political embrace, Nixon and Brezhnev.© FUNY, *THE NEW YORK TIMES.*

146 Silent Majority. A term given currency by President Richard M. Nixon during the Vietnam War. In a speech in November 1969, Nixon suggested that despite the criticisms of his policy by liberal opponents of the war, a "silent majority" of the American people approved of what he was doing.

Nicknames

147 **Tail Gunner Joe.** Senator Joseph R. McCarthy of Wisconsin, who claimed falsely to have been a tail gunner on American bombers during World War II.

Joseph McCarthy, 1946.
UPI/BETTMANN NEWSPHOTOS.

148 **Engine Charlie.** Charles E. Wilson, President Eisenhower's Secretary of Defense, so called when he was head of General Motors in order to distinguish him from

149 **Electric Charlie,** the Charles Wilson who was head of the General Electric Company.

150 **Dugout Doug.** The name given General Douglas MacArthur by GIs pinned down by the Japanese on the Bataan peninsula in the Philippines in the early days of World War II, because MacArthur

spent most of his time in the relative safety of Corregidor Island (see number 930). The men realized that they were slated for (at best) captivity, while MacArthur would, albeit for sound military reasons, be evacuated before the inevitable surrender. They composed a song to the tune of "The Battle Hymn of the Republic," one verse of which ran:

Dugout Doug's not timid, he's just cautious, not afraid,
He's protecting carefully the stars that Franklin made,
Four-star generals are rare as good food on Bataan
And his troops go starving on . . .

General Douglas MacArthur.
THE NATIONAL ARCHIVES.

151 **Uncle Joe.** Joseph Stalin, who was so called by President Franklin Roosevelt at the Yalta Conference in 1945.

Joseph Stalin, 1953.
WIDE WORLD PHOTOS.

152 **The Bridegroom on the Wedding Cake.** Thomas E. Dewey, because of his small stature and rather formal, dapper appearance. The name was given him during the 1944 presidential campaign, apparently by Alice Roosevelt Longworth (Theodore Roosevelt's daughter), though she denied having originated it (see number 448).

153 **Lord Root of the Matter.** Harry Hopkins, a friend and adviser to President Franklin Roosevelt. The name was given him by Winston Churchill, who was impressed by Hopkins's ability to analyze complex situations and, by logical arguments, convince others that these analyses were correct.

154 **The Wizard of Ooze.** Illinois Senator Everett M. Dirksen, so called because of his florid, overly formal, but generally good-humored oratorical style.

155 **Landslide.** Lyndon B. Johnson, who got the name because of the paper-thin margin by which he was elected to the Senate in 1948.

156 **Tricky Dick.** Richard M. Nixon, because of his shifty, calculating political style. The phrase long antedated the Watergate scandal.

Richard Nixon in close-up.
LIBRARY OF CONGRESS.

James Earl Carter.
JIMMY CARTER LIBRARY

157 **Jimmy.** James Earl Carter, so known at least as far back as his campaign for governor of Geor-

gia in 1966. Worth mentioning only because after he became nationally prominent the continued use of the nickname by Carter himself started a nickname epidemic among politicians that still rages. See, for example, Bob Dole, Tip O'Neill . . .

158 **The Steel Magnolia.** Rosalynn Carter, wife of Jimmy, who was given the name because beneath her low-keyed, earnest, "southern belle" exterior, she seemed a person with a strong will and firmly held opinions.

159 **Panama Howie.** Name given to Senator Howard Baker of Tennessee by conservative Republicans. They strongly resented his support of the treaty providing for the turning over of the Panama Canal Zone to the Republic of Panama.

160 **The Teflon President.** Description applied to Ronald Reagan, because his mistakes never seemed to "stick" to him or reduce his popularity with the voters.

Party and Factional Nicknames

161 **Dixiecrats.** Name applied to conserva-

tive "states' rights" Democrats who opposed the reelection of President Harry S Truman in 1948. They supported J. Strom Thurmond, who received 39 electoral votes, but their defection and that of left-leaning Democrats who supported Henry A. Wallace did not prevent Truman from winning the election.

162 **Boll Weevils.** The term applied during Ronald Reagan's first term to Democratic congressmen from southern states who supported the President's policies of cutting social programs and spending more money on defense. The term has a long history in the South as a mild pejorative for renegade Democratic politicians.

163 **Hawks and Doves.** During the Vietnam War, those who fa-

A hawkish LBJ. DRAWING BY PAUL BACON, COURTESY OF *THE NEW YORK TIMES BOOK REVIEW*, 1967

vored pursuing the war vigorously were known as Hawks. Those who sought to end the fighting were Doves. The names were applied to people of one or the other persuasion generally; these were not political factions in the narrow sense of the term.

Slogans

164 **Had Enough?** A question that was asked by the Republicans in the 1946 congressional elections. The argument was that after so many years of "Democratic rule," it was "time for a change."

165 **Massive Retaliation.** Secretary of State John Foster Dulles's substitute for the Democrats' containment policy. Any Soviet or Red Chinese aggression could be nipped in the bud by threatening to respond to such with nuclear weapons. This "atomic diplomacy" was also said to provide the cheapest possible defense—"more bang for the buck."

166 **A Choice, Not an Echo.** The rallying cry after World War II of conservative Republicans who resented what they saw as their party's tendency to run candidates willing to accept many New Deal re-

forms. When, in 1964, the conservatives succeeded in nominating Barry Goldwater for President, they proclaimed,

167 **In Your Heart You Know He's Right.** This promoted the Democrats to retort,

168 **In Your Guts You Know He's Nuts.** Despite having poked fun at the Democratic presidential candidate Adlai Stevenson's intellectuality in the 1952 and 1956 campaigns by referring to him and his supporters as

169 **Eggheads,** in 1964 Republicans tried to use

1952 campaign, Adlai Stevenson.
CARTOON BY JOSEPH PARRISH,
COURTESY OF THE CHICAGO
HISTORICAL SOCIETY

170 **Au H$_2$O,** the chemical symbols for gold and water, as a slogan. It went over with the voters no better than the rest of their campaign.

171 **All the Way with LBJ.** Democratic suggestion that Lyndon B. Johnson should be elected in his own right in 1964.

Johnson sweeps the states, 1964.
SARK

172 **Nixon's the One.** A Republican slogan in the 1968 presidential campaign, sometimes used by the Democrats on posters bearing a photograph of a very pregnant black woman.

173 **It's Morning in America Again.** This phrase was used by the Republicans in the 1984 election. It referred to the apparent change in mood in the country from pessimism and cynicism to optimism and good feeling.

COMPROMISES

In an intensely competitive political society, where 55 percent is a sweeping victory and 60 percent a landslide, success in politics often depends upon the art of compromising. American history is full of instances of wheeling and dealing, in which one group has agreed to something it dislikes in exchange for something it wants very much—or, to put a better face on the practice, instances in which politicians have taken into account the needs of others as well as themselves and have tried to do what was best for the entire country. Here are some examples:

174 The Great Compromise. This was the agreement reached at the Constitutional Convention between the smaller, less populous states, which wished all states to be represented equally in Congress, and the larger states, which favored representation according to population. The compromise, of course, was to give each state two senators, chosen by its legislature, and to apportion seats in the House of Representatives according to population, electing the members by popular vote.

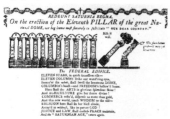

New York approves the Constitution, July 26, 1788.
COURTESY OF THE NEW-YORK HISTORICAL SOCIETY.

175 The Three-Fifths Compromise. This was a deal at the Convention between northern and southern delegates. Northerners wanted to count slaves as property in the apportionment of federal taxes. Southerners wanted to count them as part of the population when determining the size of each state's delegation in the House of Representatives. The compromise was to count each slave as three fifths of a person for both purposes. In practice this favored the South, because no direct taxes were enacted by Congress until after slavery was abolished.

176 The Missouri Compromise (1820) was a compromise involving the admission of Missouri as a slave state. To balance the slave state–free state division in the Senate, Maine—until then a part of Massachusetts—was made a separate state. In addition, Congress barred slavery "forever" from all of the Louisiana Territory north of 36°30′ North latitude, the westward extension of the southern boundary of Missouri. When Missouri submitted a state constitution to Congress in 1821, as required before its formal admission to the Union, another controversy developed over a provision barring free blacks from the state, but this too was compromised. Nevertheless many far-

sighted people recognized that the question of slavery had become a grave threat to sectional harmony. John Quincy Adams called the dispute the "title page to a great tragic volume," and Jefferson said, "We have a wolf by the ears, and we can neither safely hold him, nor safely let him go."

177 The Compromise Tariff (1833). In the late 1820s and early 1830s, northern and western interests had pushed laws through Congress placing high protective duties on imported manufactured goods. Most Southerners disliked these duties because there was little manufacturing in their districts. Passage of the Tariff of 1832 led South Carolina (inspired by its leading statesman, John C. Calhoun) to enact an Ordinance of Nullification (see number 19) that declared the law void in South Carolina and prohibited the collection of tariff duties in the state after February 1, 1833. To prevent the showdown between state and federal authority that would have followed, Henry Clay—whose American System (see number 13) had encouraged the coalition of western and eastern interests that had made passage of the high tariffs possible—engineered the passage of a new tariff that lowered the duties gradually over a period of years. South Carolina then repealed its ordinance before the February 1 deadline.

178 The Compromise of 1850. A complex congressional settlement occasioned by the acquisition of California and the rest of the Southwest after the war with Mexico, which again raised the question of slavery in the territories. After long and at times brilliant debates, Congress passed laws admitting California as a free state and dividing the rest of the Southwest into two territories, which were eventually to be admitted to the Union "with or without slavery," as their residents should decide. In addition, the federal government took over the debts of the state of Texas (which gave up its claim to some western lands). In a further attempt to "settle" the slavery question, Congress abolished the slave

Engraving depicting the Compromise of 1850. Henry Clay is addressing the Senate.
BETTMANN PICTURES, INC.

trade (not slavery itself) in the District of Columbia and passed a Fugitive Slave Act designed to make it easier for slave owners to recover runaways. The ideas behind this compromise were the work of Henry Clay, in old age thought of as "the Great Pacificator" rather than as "Prince Hal," but the legislation was maneuvered through the Senate by Stephen A. Douglas.

179 The Crittenden Compromise, 1860. The proposal advanced by Senator John J. Crittenden of Kentucky, a disciple of Henry Clay (who had died in 1852), to relieve the sectional crisis that resulted from the election of Lincoln as President. Crittenden suggested a constitutional amendment allowing slavery in all territories south of 36°30′ and guaranteeing that no future amendment would seek to tamper with slavery where it already existed. The necessary legislation failed, however, when Lincoln refused to go along with any extension of slavery into new territory.

180 The Compromise of 1877. This deal broke the deadlock created by the disputed results of the 1876 presidential election. In exchange for accept-

ing the Republican version of the results and thus the election of Rutherford B. Hayes, the Democrats were promised that Hayes would remove the last federal troops occupying southern territory and would appoint a Southerner to his Cabinet. The compromise, made in the interest of sectional harmony, marked the end of the Reconstruction Era and of federal efforts to compel white Southerners to treat blacks fairly.

Anti-Reconstruction cartoon. Ulysses S. Grant rides in the carpet bag. CULVER PICTURES, INC.

181 The Atlanta Compromise, 1895. The name given to the policy proposed by Booker T. Washington in his speech at the Atlanta Cotton States and International Exposition (see number 319). Washington urged southern blacks to accept segregation and to concentrate on developing useful skills. Obsequiousness, he intimated, would pay off in the long run. In return Washington urged white Southerners to help black people to get ahead in the world. If they did, he promised, blacks would be "the most patient, faithful, law-abiding, and unresentful people that the world has seen." The policy worked in the sense that it reduced racial tensions and attracted considerable northern philanthropic support for southern blacks, but, as W. E. B. Du Bois and other black radicals pointed out, the psychological cost was high and southern white aid was rarely forthcoming (see number 324).

Booker T. Washington, April 12, 1902. LIBRARY OF CONGRESS.

LANDMARK LAWS

The laws by which Americans are and have been governed are legion. Some are so rarely broken that they could just as well be repealed, while others are so widely ignored that they would best be forgotten. Many were enacted to deal with circumstances that soon changed—because of or in spite of the measures themselves. When pressed, professional historians can explain the tortuous terms of Macon's Bill No. 2, enacted in 1810, but even Representative Nathaniel Macon's biographer in the *Dictionary of American Biography* skims past Macon's Bill No. 1 with the vague description, "a stroke at British shipping." However, many acts of Congress have been truly pathbreaking. Some of the following are as dead today as Nathaniel Macon's second effort, but all of them changed the course of American history in exceptionally significant ways.

182 **Land Ordinance of 1785.** This act of the Continental Congress established the method by which federally owned land was to be divided and sold. New regions were surveyed into square townships, these to be further subdivided into 36 one-square-mile (640-acre) sections and sold at public auction. Proceeds of the sale of section 16 in each township were to be devoted to "the maintenance of public schools." This ordinance, much amended in detail, imposed the checkerboard pattern that still marks most of the land west of the Appalachians.

183 **Northwest Ordinance, 1787.** This measure provided a system of government for western territories. At the very start of the nation's independent existence, it established the principle that as the country grew, new states should be admitted "on an equal footing with the original States in all respects whatsoever." This rejection of the concept of colonial dependency made orderly expansion of the country possible. Slavery was also banned, but since the original ordinance applied only to the region between the Mississippi and Ohio rivers and the Great Lakes, this part of the system was not always included when the ordinance was extended to cover territories farther west.

184 **Homestead Act, 1862.** Although the Ordinance of 1785 and later modifications of it made land available in relatively small units and at prices large numbers of individuals could afford, this Civil War measure was a major advance. It offered 160 acres of "unappropriated public lands" free to those who would agree to use it "for the actual purpose of settlement and cultivation" for five years. Much of the best public land was not opened to homesteaders, but the principle of giving land to anyone who would develop and use it was important. The law is still in effect and is still being used.

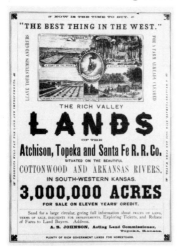

Nineteenth-century railroad poster. THE ATCHISON, TOPEKA & SANTA FE RAILWAY COMPANY

185 Morrill Act, 1862. This law gave each state federally owned land amounting to thirty thousand acres "for each senator and representative in Congress." The sums derived from the sale of the land were to be used to support "colleges for the benefit of agriculture and the mechanic arts . . . without excluding other scientific and classical studies." Over time the "land grant" colleges established under the law have received over thirteen million acres and trained more millions of students.

186 The Pendleton Act, 1883. This law, passed after the assassination of President James A. Garfield, "classified" about 10 percent of all federal jobs and created a Civil Service Commission to administer competitive examinations of applicants for these posts. It also outlawed the solicitation of political contributions from such civil servants. Both the venality and corruption of the patronage system and the growing need for technically trained personnel to run government offices made such a system imperative. Over time the classified service was steadily extended, though of course the giving of jobs as rewards for political services rendered has not totally disappeared.

New commissioners move in to tame unruly railroads. HARPER'S WEEKLY, APRIL 9, 1887.

187 Interstate Commerce Act, 1887. Although directly concerned with eliminating such transportation abuses as the granting of rebates and the use of monopoly power by railroads, the most important part of this act was section 11, which created an Interstate Commerce Commission to regulate railroads and supervise their activi-

ties. The commission was the model for such important federal regulatory bodies as the Federal Trade Commission, the Federal Communications Commission, and the Securities and Exchange Commission.

Woodrow Wilson scrubs up the antitrust laws, 1915. JAY N. "DING" DARLING, DES MOINES REGISTER.

188 Sherman Antitrust Act, 1890. This law made illegal all "combinations in the form of trusts or otherwise" that were "in restraint of trade." It was an attempt to check the growth of large "monopolistic" business enterprises. It took the form it did rather than directly outlawing businesses of a certain size because the right of Congress to do the latter was constitutionally questionable. Congress's right to regulate interstate commerce was clearly established. The law has had a checkered history (currently it is almost a dead letter), but over the years it has been a major force in shaping the thinking of economists, corporate executives, and public officials.

189 Income Tax Act, 1913. A federal income tax had been imposed during the Civil War and again in 1894, but the latter measure was declared unconstitutional by the Supreme Court. After the ratification of the Sixteenth Amendment had authorized such taxes, Congress levied a tax of 1 percent on income above $4,000 and 2 percent on income of more than $20,000. We have never been without one since.

190 Sheppard-Towner Act, 1921. This measure, which provided federal funds for state-administered prenatal and child care programs, was of minor importance in itself—it was continued only until 1929. But it was a landmark nonetheless, the first federally supported health care program in the nation.

191 Immigration Act, 1921. This was not the first law regulating the admission of immigrants but the first to control directly where the immigrants came from. It limited the entry of persons from any nation to 3 percent of the foreign-born people of that nationality resident in the United States in 1910. This "quota system" was made more stringent in 1924 and still more restrictive in 1929. The quota system was abolished in 1965, but even that more liberal law restricted immigration from Western Hemisphere countries to 120,000 persons a year.

192 Agricultural Adjustment Act of 1933. Although not as innovative an idea as its sponsors claimed, this law began the direct subsidy of agriculture that has become standard in the nation. The law was designed to maintain a "balance between the production and consumption of agricultural commodities." To raise deeply depressed farm prices to a level roughly in balance with the prices of manufactured goods, farmers who raised cotton, wheat, and other sta-

Depression-era farmer, 1930 cartoon. © BILLY IRELAND, COLUMBUS (OHIO) DISPATCH.

ple crops were paid to keep a percentage of their land out of production. The law was declared unconstitutional in 1936, but was soon re-enacted in a different form. In still different guises, the policy remains in effect today.

193 Wagner National Labor Relations Act, 1935. This law guaranteed workers "the right of self-organization" and described a list of "unfair labor practices"—among them refusing to bargain with employees collectively rather than individually—that employers were forbidden to use in labor disputes. It created the National Labor Relations Board to supervise union elections and gave it the power to "prevent any person from engaging in any unfair labor practice."

194 Social Security Act, 1935. This omnibus act is best known for its establishment of the old age pension system (the original tax was 1 percent each on workers and employers), but it also created the unemployment insurance system and provided federal grants to the states for dependent children, handicapped people, and the aged poor. The original law did not cover agricultural workers, domestic servants, and other low-paid occupations, and benefits were pitifully small. But both coverage and payments have been steadily expanded, and as President Roosevelt pointed out at the time, it was partially funded by money taken from the paychecks of future recipients so that "no damned politician" was likely to vote to do away with what FDR proudly called "my social security system."

195 **Withholding Tax Act,** 1943. At the time this law, passed during World War II, served the double purpose of bringing in tax money for the war effort more quickly and taking pressure off domestic prices by reducing the take-home pay of wage earners. In the long run it has eased the pain of paying stiff income taxes for honest citizens and substantially increased the task faced by dishonest ones who try to avoid paying their taxes.

196 **Economic Cooperation Act,** 1948. This law put into effect an idea, advanced by Secretary of State George C. Marshall in a famous speech at Harvard in 1947, that was designed to prevent the spread of communism in the nations of Western Europe by providing them with funds to rebuild their war-weakened economies. The economic impact of the measure was enormous, and the policy of giving large sums to foreign countries—as a peaceful way of preventing their falling under the influence of communism in general and the Soviet Union in particular—became firmly established. (See number 638.)

FAMOUS SUPREME COURT CASES

Many of the most important Supreme Court decisions have arisen from relatively minor controversies between individuals or other private interests. Here are some of the most significant.

197 **Marbury v. Madison,** 1803. On his last evening as President, John Adams signed a commission appointing fellow Federalist William Marbury as a justice of the peace for the District of Columbia, but in the confusion of the change of administrations, the commission was not delivered. Jefferson, the new President, ordered it withheld. Hoping to obtain it, Marbury sued the new Secretary of State, James Madison. Speaking through its new chief justice, John Marshall, the Supreme Court ruled that the federal law on which Marbury's suit was based was unconstitutional. This was the first time that a law of Congress was declared unconstitutional by the Court.

198 **Trustees of Dartmouth College v. Woodward,** 1819. In this "Dartmouth College Case," which involved an attempt by New Hampshire to turn Dartmouth into a state college, the Court ruled that the college's charter (granted by King George III before the Revolution) was a contract and therefore could not be altered without the consent of both parties. It was in arguing the college's case that Daniel Webster got off his famous tearjerker: "It is, sir, as I have said, a small college, and yet *there are those that love it.*"

199 **McCulloch v. Maryland,** 1819. John W. McCulloch, cashier of the Baltimore branch of the Bank of the United States, was sued by Maryland because he refused to pay a tax levied on the bank by the state legislature. The case is notable because, in deciding in favor of the bank, Chief Justice John Marshall interpreted the powers of Congress broadly. The Constitution did not specifically grant Congress the right to

create a bank, but a bank was a reasonable way for Congress to exercise powers enumerated in the document. "Let the end be legitimate," Marshall declared, "and all means which are appropriate . . . are constitutional." Since the bank was constitutional and since the Constitution was the supreme law of the land, the state tax on the bank was unconstitutional because "the power to tax involves the power to destroy."

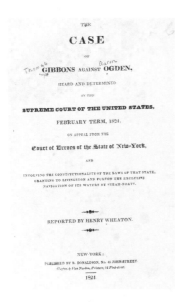

Frontispiece, *Gibbons* v. *Ogden,* 1824. LIBRARY OF CONGRESS.

200 **Gibbons v. Ogden,** 1824–25. Thomas Gibbons and Aaron Ogden were rival ferry boat operators. Ogden had been granted the exclusive right to operate a ferry between New York City and New Jersey by New York State, but

Gibbons set up a competing line. When Ogden sued, the Supreme Court ruled that the New York law was unconstitutional because it interfered with interstate commerce, a prerogative of the federal government. By defining commerce as "intercourse" (not merely the movement of goods), the Court laid the basis for the later federal regulation of radio and television, and of other forms of transportation and communication.

201 **Charles River Bridge v. Warren Bridge,** 1837. This case modified the Dartmouth College case by establishing some limits to the sanctity of contracts. In 1785 the state of Massachusetts had granted a group of businessmen a charter to build a toll bridge across the Charles River between Boston and Charlestown. In 1828, after traffic had increased enormously, the legislature authorized the construction by the state of a competing span, the Warren Bridge. The proprietors of the Charles River Bridge sued, charging violation of contract; but the Court, speaking through Chief Justice Roger B. Taney, declared that the Charles River charter was not exclusive and that "advancing the public prosperity, by providing

safe, convenient, and cheap" transportation was a legitimate public purpose.

202 **Dred Scott v. Sandford,** 1857. Dred Scott, a slave, sued for his freedom on the ground that his master, an army surgeon, had taken him into Wisconsin Territory, whence slavery had been barred by Congress in the Missouri Compromise (see number 176). Since Scott had married while in Wisconsin Territory, freedom for his wife, Harriet, was also at issue. The Court decided against the Scotts, ruling that the Missouri Compromise was unconstitutional because it violated the Fifth Amendment by depriving slave owners of the right to take their property wherever they wanted to. If unchallenged, this line of reasoning would have opened all the West, even Oregon Territory, to slavery.

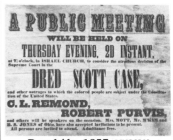

Broadside, 1857. LINCOLN UNIVERSITY, PENNSYLVANIA.

203 **Munn v. Illinois,** 1876. This case involved the refusal of Ira V. Munn, a Chicago grain elevator operator, to obey an 1871 Illinois law regulating the practices of railroads, warehouses, and similar businesses providing services to the public. The Court upheld the Illinois law and seven similar state acts, ruling that "when private property is devoted to a public use, it is subject to public regulation." If people like Ira Munn did not want their activities regulated by the state, "they should not have clothed the public with an interest in their concerns."

204 **Plessy v. Ferguson,** 1896. Homer Adolph Plessy, a light-skinned Louisiana black man, was arrested for sitting in a railroad car reserved by Louisiana law for whites. In a New Orleans state court, his attorneys argued that the law was unconstitutional, but Judge John H. Ferguson ruled against them on the ground that the railroad had provided separate but equally good cars for blacks, as the law required. This line of reasoning was upheld by the U.S. Supreme Court. The case is remembered today mainly for the dissent of Justice John Marshall Harlan. "Our Constitution is color-blind," Harlan wrote. "The arbitrary separation of citizens, on the basis of race . . . is a badge of servitude

wholly inconsistent with civil freedom."

205 **West Coast Hotel Co. v. Parrish,** 1937. Elsie Parrish, a chambermaid employed by the West Coast Hotel Company in the state of Washington, was paid less than the minimum wage that Washington had established for working women and minors. She sued for back pay. Similar state laws had repeatedly been declared unconstitutional, but the Supreme Court upheld this one. The case marked the turning point in the Court's attitude toward social and economic legislation. It remains unclear whether Justice Owen J. Roberts, who switched from con to pro in this 5–4 decision, did so because of President Franklin D. Roosevelt's proposal to "pack" the Court (see number 563).

Mrs. Nettie Hunt shares school desegregation victory with her daughter Nikie, May 17, 1954.
UPI/BETTMANN NEWSPHOTOS.

206 **Brown v. Board of Education of Topeka,** 1954. This is the famous school desegregation

case in which the Court, by a vote of 9 to 0, overturned *Plessy v. Ferguson.* "In the field of public education," Chief Justice Earl Warren stated, "the doctrine of 'separate but equal' has no place."

207 **Baker v. Carr,** 1962. In this case Charles Baker, a citizen of Tennessee, sued Joseph Carr, a state election official. Baker charged that he had been denied the equal protection of the laws guaranteed by the Fourteenth Amendment to the United States Constitution because the state's election districts were of grossly unequal size. (Tennessee had not reapportioned seats in the legislature since the beginning of the century.) The Court agreed; soon other suits were brought in more than thirty states, and the principle of "one person, one vote" in apportioning representation in legislatures became firmly established.

208 **Roe v. Wade,** 1972. Norma McCorvey, a woman prevented from having an abortion by Texas law, sued to have the law overturned. Jay Floyd, attorney for the state of Texas, arguing the issue before the U.S. Supreme Court, claimed among other things that the case should be dismissed as moot, since

the plaintiff had already had her baby. In a controversial decision, the Court ruled in McCorvey's favor, establishing the right of women to have abortions during the early months of pregnancy.

TREATIES

Treaties are legal devices employed by sovereign nations in order to deal with one another. Most either ratify the terms by which wars are brought to an end or (happily) are intended to remove the causes of possible wars before they start. Some of the most important treaties entered into by the United States have been primarily real estate deals. Treaties are negotiated by diplomats, described by people who resent their privileges by such terms as "statesmen sent to lie abroad for their country" and "cookie pushers." This is unfair, but the privileges do exist. As the following examples reveal, an astonishing percentage of the treaties entered into by the United States have been negotiated in Paris, a city noted for its beauty, elegant hotels, fine cuisine, and other attractions too numerous to mention.

209 Treaty of Paris, 1763. This is the multinational pact that ended the Seven Years' War, the American phase of which was called the French and Indian War. The defeated French ceded all of Canada and their claims east of the Mississippi River and south of the Great Lakes to Great Britain, and their claim to New Orleans and the land west of the Mississippi to Spain. The historian Francis Parkman (see number 529) wrote of this treaty: "Half the continent had changed hands at the scratch of a pen."

210 Treaty of Alliance with France, 1778. This treaty was negotiated during the Revolution after the American victory in the Battle of Saratoga. The two countries promised to "aid each other mutually" if France entered the war against Great Britain and declared that the purpose of the pact was "to maintain effectually the liberty, sovereignty, and independence absolute and unlimited of the . . . United States." The French aid, of course, was crucial to the winning of the Revolution.

211 Treaty of Paris, 1783. This treaty ended the American War of Independence. Great Britain recognized the United States as "free, sovereign, and independent." The boundaries of the new nation were set at the Great Lakes, the Mississippi River, and 31° North latitude, the boundary of Florida.

212 Jay Treaty, 1795. In some ways the "final" ending of the Revolution, this treaty, negotiated in London by Chief Justice John Jay, committed the British to removing their troops from forts they had been holding in the Great Lakes region and to compensate American shipowners for vessels and cargoes they had seized in the West Indies. The United States Government agreed to honor prewar debts owed by Americans to British merchants, something many state courts had been refusing to do. The treaty was unpopular in the United States because the British did not agree to respect the rights of neutral vessels on the high seas in time of war.

213 Louisiana Purchase, 1803. This agreement was negotiated in Paris by American diplomats Robert R. Livingston and James Monroe. As "a strong proof of friendship," Napoleon Buonaparte, then First Consul of France, ceded (read: *sold*) to the United States a vast and ill-defined region between the

Mississippi River and the Rocky Mountains for 60 million francs—about $15 million. This territory had been returned to France by Spain in 1800. With good reason the treaty has been called the greatest real estate bargain in history, but at the time the only part of the area important to the United

Monroe and Livingston are shown purchasing Louisiana from Talleyrand.
THE ARCHITECT OF THE CAPITOL

States was New Orleans; control of this city gave farmers in the American West the unrestricted right to float their produce down the Mississippi on rafts and small boats, and to store it until it could be transferred to ocean-going ships. More than a century later—after the assassination of Senator Huey Long in September 1936 (see number 516)— wags gave the name "Second Louisiana Purchase" to the arrangement made between federal officials and members of Long's Louisiana political machine. The government dropped criminal charges against the Louisianans in exchange for their agreement to pay $2 million in back taxes and (more im-

portant) to support Franklin Roosevelt for renomination at the upcoming Democratic presidential convention, something Long had opposed.

214 Treaty of Ghent, 1814. This treaty with Great Britain, negotiated by an American delegation that included Henry Clay, Albert Gallatin, and John Quincy Adams, ended the War of 1812 on the basis of *status quo ante bellum*— that is, without the payment of any indemnity or the transfer of any territory. It was important in that it provided for the future solving of minor commercial and boundary controversies, and is famous because after the signing, but before word reached the United States, the one major American military victory had taken place: the Battle of New Orleans.

Facsimiles of signatures to the Treaty of Ghent, 1814.
CULVER PICTURES, INC.

215 The Rush-Bagot Agreement, 1818. Signed by Secretary of State Richard Rush and "His Britannic Majesty's Envoy Extraordinary," Charles Bagot, this agreement demilitarized the Great Lakes and set the precedent for the weapons-free border between Canada and the United States that now exists. Each side was to have only three small vessels on the Lakes (and one on Lake Champlain), and these "warships" were limited to one 18-pound cannon each.

216 Transcontinental Treaty, 1821. This agreement, negotiated in Washington in 1819 by Secretary of State John Quincy Adams and Luis de Onis, the Spanish minister to the United States, determined the boundary between the United States and Spain's North American possessions. It thereby gave the United States a firm claim to the region between the Rocky Mountains and the Pacific Ocean. As part of the treaty, Spain sold Florida to the United States for $5 million.

217 Webster-Ashburton Treaty, 1842. The vexing problem of determining the border between Maine and Canada was finally settled by this agreement, negotiated by Secretary of State Daniel Webster and Lord Ashburton, British minister to the United States. It gave the United States about two thirds of the territory in dispute. The negotiations are remembered mostly because of the famous "redline map" that Webster showed skeptical commissioners of the state of Maine who were opposed to giving up any of the region. During the peace negotiations at Paris in 1783, Benjamin Franklin had drawn a red line marking the boundary on a map, but there was no copy in the American archives. To persuade the commissioners to go along with a compromise, Webster showed them a map of his devising with a red line that gave most of the disputed area to Canada. In fact, Franklin's line gave most of the land to the United States, though to his credit Webster did not know this.

218 Treaty of Guadalupe Hidalgo, 1848. This treaty—negotiated by State Department clerk Nicholas Trist, President James K. Polk's personal representative— ended the Mexican War. Mexico recognized the Rio Grande as its boundary with Texas and ceded California and nearly all of what is now

the Southwest to the United States for a bit more than $18 million.

219 Treaty of Paris, 1899. This determined the fate of the Philippine Islands after the Spanish-American War. (Spain had agreed in August 1898 to stop fighting, grant Cuba its freedom, and cede Puerto Rico and Guam to the United States.) In Paris, Spain ceded the Philippines to the United States in return for $20 million. The acquisition was opposed by American antiimperialists, and the treaty probably would have been rejected by the Senate if William Jennings Bryan, titular head of the Democratic Party, had not urged Democratic senators to ratify it. He did so, though he was personally opposed to taking the Philippines, in order to make the

The United States acquires the Philippines, *Harper's Weekly*, January 6, 1900. *HARPER'S WEEKLY*, JANUARY 6, 1900.

question an issue in the upcoming presidential election.

220 Versailles Treaty, 1919. Although President Woodrow Wilson participated personally in the enormously complicated negotiations ending World War I, little of this agreement related directly to the United States. Signers, however, thereby became members of the new League of Nations, the constitution of which was an integral part of the treaty. For a mixture of partisan and practical reasons, most of them related to the League, the Senate rejected the entire pact. Separate treaties were then negotiated with Germany and the other enemy nations.

Woodrow Wilson acknowledges the cheers of the Paris crowds, **1919.** U.S. SIGNAL CORPS, THE NATIONAL ARCHIVE.

221 Washington Treaties, 1922. These were three agreements relating to naval disarmament and the Far Eastern relations of the victorious World

War I powers. Besides contracting to reduce the number of battleships in their fleets, they promised to maintain the Open Door in China and otherwise respect one another's interests in the Pacific area. These treaties were relatively toothless, but still less meaningful was the

222 Kellogg-Briand Pact, 1928. This treaty, drafted by French Foreign Minister Aristide Briand and Secretary of State Frank B. Kellogg in Paris and eventually agreed to by sixty-two nations, condemned "recourse to war" without providing any way of punishing nations that took up arms. It has been called "an international kiss."

223 North Atlantic Treaty, 1949. This pact, entered into by the United States and most of the nations of Western Europe, established the North Atlantic Treaty Organization (NATO), a military alliance created to defend Western Europe against possible Soviet aggression.

224 Strategic Arms Limitation Treaty (SALT), 1972. This Soviet-American pact limited the number of antiballistic nuclear weapons each nation could have to two hundred

and stopped their production of nuclear ballistic missiles. A second treaty,

"The Odd Couple," Bill Mauldin, *The Sun Times*, 1973.
© BILL MAULDIN, *THE SUN TIMES* (CHICAGO), 1973.

225 Salt II, 1979, was an agreement calling for a further reduction of nuclear weapons. However, President Carter withdrew it from the Senate (where it would almost certainly have been rejected) after the Russian invasion of Afghanistan in December of that year. In 1988, however, an agreement eliminating intermediate range missiles was successfully negotiated by the two superpowers.

TEMPESTS IN DIPLOMATIC TEAPOTS

226 Destruction of the Caroline, 1837. This incident was an outgrowth of a small and ineffectual Canadian rebellion

against British rule. A group of Canadian "patriots" had seized an island in the Niagara River and were using an American vessel, the *Caroline,* to bring in supplies. To stop this activity, Canadian "loyalists" surprised the *Caroline* at its dock on the New York side of the river and burned it to the water's edge. Despite the demands of local residents that the United States retaliate, President Van Buren issued a proclamation stressing American neutrality in the Canadian conflict, and the British Government denied responsibility for the raid. Nearly three years later, however, the controversy flared up when a Canadian deputy sheriff named Alexander McLeod was arrested in New York and charged with murdering an American who had been killed in the raid. When the British demanded his release without trial, on the ground that he had been acting under orders (an indirect admission of responsibility for the raid), the State Department took the position that the federal government had no jurisdiction in the case. There was much talk of war on both sides of the Atlantic. Fortunately, McLeod was acquitted, the British issued an indirect apology for the attack on the *Caroline,* and, since it was generally agreed that the ship had been used for illegal purposes, the United States did not demand any indemnity.

227 Aroostook War, 1838–39. The peace treaty ending the Revolutionary War had not precisely defined the border between Maine and the Canadian province of New Brunswick, at that time an unpopulated wilderness. Both countries claimed a large region including the valley of the Aroostook River, a land rich in timber. In the late 1830s, Canadian loggers began cutting there. When some Maine residents tried to stop this, the lumberjacks "arrested" a group of them. This led to the calling up of militia by both sides, and Congress authorized the President to summon volunteers to protect American interests in the region. However, a truce was negotiated by General Winfield Scott (see number 629) that left the Aroostook region under American control. The controversy was settled in 1842 by the Webster-Ashburton Treaty (see number 217).

228 Ostend Manifesto, 1854. This document, drafted by the American ministers to Great Britain, France, and Spain, who were meeting at Ostend

in Belgium, was part of an effort of the Administration of President Franklin Pierce to persuade Spain—which was nearly bankrupt—to sell Cuba to the United States. Acting on instructions from Washington, the ministers suggested that if Spain refused to sell the island, "it will then be time to consider the question, does Cuba in the possession of Spain seriously endanger our internal peace?" If so, "we shall be justified in wresting it from Spain, if we possess the power." Whether "wresting" meant annexing Cuba or helping the Cubans to win their independence was unclear from the document, which was supposed to be kept secret. Word of it leaked out, however, and the resulting furor forced the government to release the Manifesto and give up its efforts to obtain Cuba.

229 The Virginius **Affair,** 1873. Another crisis related to Cuba erupted in 1873 when the Spanish gunboat *Tornado* seized the *Virginius*, a vessel flying the American flag and carrying arms to Cuban rebels, and brought it to Santiago. Four of the crew were promptly charged with piracy and executed. This caused concern in Washington, but that was as nothing

compared to the reaction when it was learned that the captain of the *Virginius* and forty-eight more members of the crew, a number of them Americans, had also been executed by a firing squad. This "insult to the American flag" caused great public indignation in the United States. Secretary of State Hamilton Fish (see number 456) instructed the American minister in Madrid to demand the release of the captured ship and its surviving passengers and crew; compensation for those killed; "signal punishment" of the killers; and a salute to the American flag. Failure to accept this ultimatum, Fish went on, would result in the severing of diplomatic relations. The Navy was ordered to concentrate in Florida waters, and coastal defenses were strengthened in anticipation of war. However, investigation soon revealed that the *Virginius* belonged to Cubans and had no right to fly the American flag. The war scare then evaporated.

Captain Frey and the crew of the *Virginius* **prepare for execution, 1873.** CULVER PICTURES, INC.

230 **Chilean Crisis,** 1891. Anti-American feeling in Chile was high in 1891 because the United States had sided with the losing side in a recent successful revolution. One result was that some sailors from the USS *Baltimore,* on shore leave in Valparaiso, were set upon by a mob. Two of the sailors were killed. President Benjamin Harrison thereupon demanded "prompt and full reparation" for what he characterized as an "insult . . . to the uniform of the United States sailors," and when this was not forthcoming, he sent a message to Congress, virtually inviting the legislators to declare war. The Chileans then backed down and met Harrison's terms. The incident had serious repercussions, however, because it cast a pall over American relations with all the Latin-American nations.

231 **The Venezuela Boundary Controversy,** 1895. The boundary between the Republic of Venezuela and British Guiana had never been precisely drawn. Venezuela claimed more territory than it was probably entitled to, but the British also overstated their case and (more important) refused to submit the controversy to arbitration. The question assumed critical dimensions in July 1895, when President Grover Cleveland informed the British Government that it was in effect invading Venezuelan territory and thus violating the Monroe Doctrine! He threatened to call the matter to the attention of Congress if Great Britain did not agree to arbitration of the boundary dispute. When the British failed to take this threat seriously, Cleveland asked Congress for authority to appoint an American commission that would determine the boundary and to "resist by every means" any British attempt to seize territory the commission assigned to Venezuela. This woke up the British, and they quickly agreed to arbitration, which incidentally awarded them most of the disputed territory.

232 **Alaskan Boundary Controversy,** 1903. This conflict involved the line separating Canada and the southeastern Alaskan panhandle. The issue was whether the line followed the extremely convoluted coast (which would deprive Canada of access to the sea along the entire length of the panhandle) or ran in a relatively straight line, leaving the heads of the estuaries under Canadian sovereignty. The territory was mostly wilderness, but was thought to contain valuable gold deposits, and public opinion was such that politicians in both Canada and the United States were unwilling to "surrender" any of their claims. However, Great Britain still controlled the Dominion of Canada's foreign relations, and the British were eager to avoid another boundary dispute with the headstrong Americans. They agreed to the appointment of a six-man tribunal of "impartial jurists of repute" to determine the line. Three were to be Americans, two Canadians, and one British. In effect none was impartial, and the Briton, Lord Alverstone, sided with the Americans. The angry Canadians refused to sign the award, which they said "ignored the just rights of Canada." But once settled, the boundary ceased to be a problem of any importance in Canadian-American relations.

Street life, Nome, Alaska, around 1901. CULVER PICTURES, INC.

THIRD PARTIES

We have, and have had since political parties first appeared in the 1790s, a two-party system. Only on rare occasions—1860 and 1912 are the outstanding examples—have more than two parties had even a remote chance of winning the presidency or capturing a majority of either house of Congress in an election. Yet along with an almost infinite number of splinter organizations devoted to advancing one or another particular cause, there have been a large number of significant "third" parties, and sometimes these have changed the course of history. Here are the most important examples.

233 Workingmen's Party. Thought by some to be the first "labor" party in the world, it was organized by trade union leaders in Philadelphia in 1828. It spread to New York City a year later. It was more a general reform organization (calling, for example, for free public schools and antimonopoly legislation) than a party concerned strictly with issues related to wages, hours, and working conditions. The New York branch attracted the attention of the Utopian re-formers Robert Dale Owen (see numbers 424–25) and Frances Wright (see number 426), and their "support" had a good deal to do with the party's lack of electoral success.

234 Antimasonic Party. This organization grew out of the distrust of the Masonic order (see number 654). It developed in New York and Pennsylvania, and a number of important anti-Jackson politicians were attracted to it. In 1831 the Antimasons held the first presidential nominating convention, choosing William Wirt as their candidate. Wirt, who had served as Attorney General in the Cabinet of James Monroe, won 7 votes in the electoral college in the 1832 election. By the end of the decade the movement had died out, its leaders having become Whigs.

235 Liberty Party. This antislavery organization ran James G. Birney for President in 1840 and again in 1844, on which occasion he polled about 62,000 votes. In 1848 it merged with the

236 Free Soil Party. This broader-based and less radical organization stood not for abolition but for the exclusion of slavery from the territories and a ban on the admission of new slave states. Its candidate was former President Martin Van Buren, who received more than 290,000 votes. Many "Van Buren Democrats" voted for the Free Soil Party because the Democratic candidate, Lewis Cass, had led the swing from Van Buren to Polk at the 1844 presidential convention (see number 552).

Free Soil Party banner for candidates Martin Van Buren and Charles F. Adams.
CULVER PICTURES, INC.

237 American Party. This organization grew out of a secret, so-called "patriotic" society, the Order of the Star-Spangled Banner. (Members were called "Know-Nothings" because when questioned about the society, they were instructed to answer "I don't know" or "I know nothing." Know-Nothings found the influx of European immigrants in the 1830s and 1840s alarming;

they would support only native-born candidates for office and favored requiring a long period of residence before a foreigner could become a citizen. By 1854, the organization was fielding candidates for office under the American Party banner. It soon won control of several state governments and elected a number of representatives to Congress. In 1856, the party nominated ex-President Millard Fillmore, but despite winning more than 20 percent of the popular vote, Fillmore carried only Maryland, with its 8 electoral votes. Many American Party voters then moved on to

238 **The Constitutional Union Party.** This organization, founded on the eve of the Civil War, was concerned chiefly with trying to avoid the disruption of the country over slavery. It ran ex-Senator John Bell of Tennessee for President in 1860, on a platform which declared that it was "the part of patriotism and of duty to recognize no political principle other than the Constitution of the Country, the Union of the States, and the enforcement of the laws." Bell carried Tennessee, Virginia, and Kentucky, a region where voters were sharply divided and acutely conscious that, if

a civil war erupted, the fighting was most likely to occur in their neighborhood.

239 **Greenback Labor Party.** This party emerged in response to the deflationary cycle that followed the Civil War. Its supporters favored the issuance of paper money unbacked by gold, and they particularly opposed the withdrawal from circulation of unbacked "greenback" currency issued during the Civil War. Although Congress made the greenbacks convertible into gold in 1879, Greenback Labor presidential candidates received more than 3 percent of the popular vote in 1880, and a bit more than half that many in 1884.

240 **People's or Populist Party.** This was another party that arose in response to economic problems caused by the post–Civil War deflation. Founded in 1892 by representatives of the Farmers' Alliances of the South and Midwest and the Knights of Labor, the party ran James B. Weaver for President in 1892 on a platform calling for a graduated income tax, nationalization of the railroads, a "sub-treasury plan" designed to boost farm prices, and the unlimited coinage of silver in order to increase the money supply. Weaver received more than

a million votes (22 votes in the electoral college). Four years later, amid bitter controversy, the Populists combined with the Democrats in support of William Jennings Bryan. After his defeat, it soon disappeared from the scene.

241 **Socialist Labor Party.** This was a Marxist-oriented party, founded in 1877 and dedicated to the idea that the "industrial emancipation of labor must be achieved by the working classes themselves, independent of all parties but their own." For years it was torn by factional disputes, but in 1900 it joined with other socialist groups to form the

1904 campaign poster for Eugene V. Debs.
LIBRARY OF CONGRESS.

242 **Socialist Party.** Their presidential candidate was Eugene V. Debs (see number 982). Debs polled fewer than 100,000 votes in 1900, but he ran again in 1904, 1908, and 1912, his total rising in the last of these years to

900,000—or 6 percent of the total cast, a percentage never again approached by any Socialist Party presidential candidate.

243 Progressive Party. This was Theodore Roosevelt's "Bull Moose" Party, founded in 1912 by Republicans opposed to the re-election of President William Howard Taft. Roosevelt, campaigning for his New Nationalism (see number 414), polled over 4 million votes and won 88 electors—both totals much larger than Taft's. But the Republican split made the Democrat, Woodrow Wilson, an easy winner. Rather than repeat that debacle, Roosevelt refused to run as a Progressive in 1916, and the party died. But a second

244 Progressive Party emerged in 1924, when Wisconsin Senator

Robert La Follette campaigning from train in La Valle, Wisconsin, October 1900. STATE HISTORICAL SOCIETY (WISCONSIN).

Robert M. La Follette, with the backing of the Socialist Party and the American Federation of Labor, ran for President on a neo-Populist platform calling for the direct election of the President, nationalization of the railroads, and other reforms. La Follette carried only Wisconsin, but nationally he received 4.8 million votes.

245 Union Party. This party, which ran North Dakota Congressman William Lemke for President in 1936, was supported by a mixture of radicals of the left and right— by supporters of the recently assassinated Huey Long (see number 516), of Dr. Francis E. Townsend's Old Age Revolving Pension scheme, of Father Charles E. Coughlin's National Union for Social Justice, and by outright fascist followers of Gerald L. K. Smith.

246 Progressive Party. The third party of this name was created in 1948 by supporters of former Vice President Henry A. Wallace, who had been "dumped" as Franklin Roosevelt's running mate by the Democrats four years earlier in favor of Harry Truman. The Progressives opposed Truman's tough stance in the Cold War, calling for cooperation with the

Supporters await Henry A. Wallace's arrival for the Founding Convention of the Progressive Party, July 1948. WIDE WORLD PHOTOS.

Soviet Union rather than confrontation. Wallace fared poorly in the election, receiving 1.1 million votes, less than 2.5 percent of the total. There was another "third" party in 1948, the

247 States' Rights, or "Dixiecrat" Party. This was made up of southern Democrats who disliked the domestic policies of President Truman. Their candidate, Senator J. Strom Thurmond of South Carolina, got almost exactly the same number of popular votes as Wallace, but he won 39 electoral votes and carried four states in the Deep South.

248 American Independent Party. This was the organization of Governor George C. Wallace of Alabama, who first came to national attention in 1963 when he personally prevented two black students from registering at the University of Alabama until forced to yield by federal troops. Wallace, who combined his opposition to desegregation with support of many liberal economic policies, received nearly 10 million popular votes and 46 electoral votes in the 1968 presidential election. He sought the presidency again four years later as a Democrat, but had to withdraw from the campaign after he was paralyzed by the bullet of a would-be assassin.

PART II
IDEAS

NOTABLE QUOTATIONS

249 "[Smoking tobacco is] lothsome to the eye, hatefull to the Nose, harmefull to the braine, dangerous to the Lungs, and in the blacke stinking fume thereof, neerest resembling the horrible Stigian smoke of the pit that is bottomlesse." King James I in "A Counter-Blast to Tobacco," 1604.

Tobacconist's label, 1730.
CULVER PICTURES, INC.

250 "No person in this Colony shall be molested or questioned for the matters of his conscience to God, so he be loyal and keep the civil peace. . . . Forced worship stincks in Gods nostrils." Roger Williams of Rhode Island, 1670.

251 "The first Planters of these Colonies were a chosen Generation of Men. . . . *New England* was a true *Utopia*. But, alas, the Children and Servants of those old Planters must needs afford many degenerate Plants, and there is now risen up a Number of People otherwise inclined." Cotton Mather, *Enchantments Encountered,* 1693.

Engraving of Cotton Mather.
CULVER PICTURES, INC.

252 "Man, as he stands in relation to man simply, hath liberty to do what he lists; it is a liberty to do evil as well as good. This liberty is incompatible and inconsistent with authority. . . . But if you will be satisfied to enjoy such civil and lawful liberties, such as Christ allows you, then will you quietly and cheerfully submit unto that authority which is set over you . . . for your good." John Winthrop, "Speech on Liberty," 1645.

253 "Being thus arrived in a good harbor, and brought safe to land, they [the Pilgrims] fell upon their knees and blessed the God in Heaven who had brought them over the vast and furious ocean . . . again to set their feet on the firm and stable earth, their proper element." William Bradford, *Of Plymouth Plantation,* c. 1630.

254 "Every British subject born on the continent of America, or in any other of the British dominions, is by the law of God and nature, by the common law, and by act of Parliament . . . entitled to all the natural, essential, inherent, and inseparable rights of our fellow subjects in Great Britain." James Otis, protesting the Sugar Act of 1764 in *The Rights of the British Colonies Asserted and Proved.*

Portrait of James Otis
MUSEUM OF FINE ARTS, BOSTON.

255 "Compelling the colonies to pay money without their consent would be rather like raising contributions in an enemy's country than taxing Englishmen for their own benefit." Benjamin Franklin, 1764.

256 "Colonies and plantations in *America* have been, are, and of right ought to be subordinate unto, and dependent upon the imperial crown and Parliament of *Great Britain*." Declaratory Act, 1766.

257 "Let us [colonists] behave like dutiful children, who have received unmerited blows from a beloved parent. . . . Where shall we find another Britain?" John Dickinson, *Letters from a Farmer in Pennsylvania to the Inhabitants of the British Colonies,* 1768.

Title page of Dickinson's *Letters from a Farmer in Pennsylvania,* from a 1771 woodcut by Paul Revere. COURTESY OF THE NEW YORK PUBLIC LIBRARY.

258 "The New England colonies are in a state of rebellion. Blows must decide whether they are to be subject to this

country, or independent." King George III, 1774.

259 "Kings are the servants, not the proprietors of the people." Thomas Jefferson, *A Summary View of the Rights of British America,* 1774.

Drawing of Thomas Jefferson. MARYLAND HISTORICAL SOCIETY.

260 "O! ye that love mankind! Ye that dare oppose not only tyranny but the tyrant, stand forth!" Thomas Paine, urging the colonists to declare their independence in *Common Sense,* 1776.

King George III reacts to Thomas Paine's writings. LIBRARY OF CONGRESS.

261 "RESOLVED: That the United Colonies are, and of right ought to be, free and independent States, that they are absolved from all allegiance to the British Crown, and that all political connection between them and the State of Great Britain is, and ought to be, totally dissolved." Richard Henry Lee, delegate from Virginia to the Second Continental Congress, June 7, 1776. This resolution resulted in the drafting and adoption of the Declaration of Independence.

262 "I only regret that I have but one life to lose for my country." Nathan Hale, just before being hanged as a spy by the British in 1776. The statement was recorded by a British soldier who was present at the execution.

263 "If America preserves her freedom, she will be an asylum for the oppressed and persecuted of every country; her example and success will encourage the friends and rouse the spirit of liberty through other nations. . . ." Simeon Howard, a Massachusetts minister, 1780.

264 "The times that tried men's souls are over and the greatest and completest revolution the world ever knew gloriously and happily accomplished." Thomas Paine, 1783.

265 "There is something noble and magnificent in the perspective of a great Federal Republic, closely linked in the pursuit of a common interest, tranquil and prosperous at home, respectable abroad. But there is something proportionably diminutive and contemptible in the prospect of a number of petty states, with the appearance only of union, jarring, jealous, and perverse, without any determined direction, fluctuating and unhappy at home, weak and insignificant by their dissensions in the eyes of other nations." Alexander Hamilton, 1782.

266 "What then is the American, this new man? . . . I could point out to you a man, whose grandfather was an Englishman, whose wife was Dutch, whose son married a French woman, and whose present four sons have now four wives of different nations. *He* is an American. . . . Here individuals of all nations are melted into a new race of men, whose labours and posterity will one day cause great change in the world." Michel Guillaume de Crèvecoeur, *Letters from an American Farmer*, 1782.

267 "America is an independent empire, and ought to assume a national character. Nothing can be more ridiculous, than a servile imitation of the manners, the language, and the vices of foreigners." Noah Webster, *Sketches of American Policy*, 1785.

Engraving of Noah Webster.
COURTESY OF THE NEW-YORK HISTORICAL SOCIETY.

268 "Let us compare every constitution we have seen with those of the United States of America, and we shall have no reason to blush for our country. On the contrary, we shall feel the strongest motives to fall upon our knees, in gratitude to heaven for having been graciously pleased to give us birth and education in that country, and for having destined us to live under her laws!" John Adams, *A Defence of the Constitutions of Government of the United States of America*, 1787–88.

A scene in Shays's rebellion, 1780s. *POPULAR HISTORY OF THE UNITED STATES*, VOL. 4 1881, WILLIAM CULLEN BRYANT, COURTESY OF THE NEW YORK PUBLIC LIBRARY.

269 "I hold it, that a little rebellion, now and then, is a good thing, and as necessary in the political world as storms are in the physical. . . . It is a medicine necessary for the sound health of government." Thomas Jefferson, letter to James Madison, January 30, 1787, discussing Shays's rebellion (see number 849).

270 "The tree of liberty must be refreshed from time to time, with the blood of patriots and tyrants. It is its natural manure." Thomas Jefferson on the same subject, in a letter to William Stephens Smith, November 13, 1787.

271 "As I enter the Building, I stumble at the Threshold," Samuel Adams, 1787, after examining the Preamble of the Constitution, which reads, "We the people . . .

establish this CONSTITUTION," rather than (as he would have wished it to read), "We the States . . ."

272 "My movements to the chair of Government will be accompanied by feelings not unlike those of a culprit who is going to the place of his execution." George Washington, contemplating his inauguration as President of the United States in a letter to Henry Knox, April 1, 1789.

Lithograph commemorating Washington's reception at Trenton, N.J., April 1789, on his way to the inauguration.
LIBRARY OF CONGRESS.

273 "As a man is said to have a right in his property, he may equally be said to have a property in his rights." James Madison, 1792.

274 "The principle of society with us is the equal rights of all. . . . Nobody shall be above you, nor you above anybody, *pell-mell* is our law." Thomas Jefferson, 1801.

275 "There is on the globe one single

spot, the possessor of which is our natural and habitual enemy. It is New Orleans." President Thomas Jefferson, in a letter to Robert R. Livingston, American minister to France, expressing concern that if France controlled New Orleans it could block the access of the farmers of the Mississippi Valley to the markets of the world, 1802. This concern led to the purchase of the entire Louisiana Territory from France. (See number 213.)

276 "I can give you no direction. You have made a noble bargain for yourselves, and I suppose you will make the most of it." French foreign minister Talleyrand to American diplomat Robert R. Livingston when asked about the boundaries of Louisiana, just purchased by the United States for about $15 million, 1803.

277 "Asking one of the States to surrender part of her sovereignty is like asking a lady to surrender part of her chastity." John Randolph of Roanoke, c. 1805.

278 "Sell [our] country! Why not sell the air, the clouds, and the great sea? Did not the Great Spirit make them all for the use of his children?" The Shawnee

chief Tecumseh, speaking to General William Henry Harrison, 1810.

Oil portrait thought to be Shawnee leader Tecumseh.
CHICAGO NATURAL HISTORY MUSEUM.

279 "England is a proud and lofty nation that disdaining to wait for danger, meets it half way. Haughty as she is, we once triumphed over her, and if we do not listen to the councils of timidity and despair, we shall again prevail. . . . But if we fail, let us fail like men, lash ourselves to our gallant tars, and expire together in one common struggle, fighting *'for seamen's rights and free trade.'*" Henry Clay, speaker of the House of Representatives, 1813.

280 "Our country! In her intercourse with foreign nations may she always be in the right and always successful, right or wrong."· Captain Stephen Decatur, commander of the frigate *United States* in the

War of 1812, and hero of the war against the Barbary pirates, 1816.

281 "It would be more candid, as well as more dignified, to avow our principles explicitly . . . than to come in as a cockboat in the wake of the British man-of-war." Secretary of State John Quincy Adams, urging President James Monroe to reject a British proposal that the two nations issue a joint statement opposing European efforts to reassert control over the newly independent republics of South America, 1823.

John Quincy Adams, photographed by Matthew Brady around 1847.
CULVER PICTURES, INC.

282 "The American continents, by the free and independent condition which they have assumed and maintained, are henceforth not to be considered as subjects for future colonization by any European pow-

ers." James Monroe, enunciating the Monroe Doctrine in his annual message to Congress, 1823.

Monroe Doctrine, *Puck*'s 1901 commentary.
CULVER PICTURES, INC.

283 "The mass of mankind has not been born with saddles on their backs, nor a favored few booted and spurred, ready to ride them legitimately, by the grace of God." Thomas Jefferson, letter to Roger C. Weightman, 1826.

284 "The whites want slaves, and want us for their slaves, but some of them will curse the day they ever saw us. As true as the sun ever shone in its meridian splendor, my colour will root some of them out of the very face of the earth. They shall have enough of making slaves of, and butchering, and murdering us in the manner which they have." David Walker, *Appeal . . . to the Coloured Citizens of the World,* 1829.

285 "The politicians of New York are not so fastidious as some gentlemen are, as to disclosing the

principles on which they act. They boldly preach what they practice. . . . If they are defeated, they expect to retire from office. If they are successful, they claim, as a matter of right, the advantages of success. They see nothing wrong in the rule that to the victor belongs the spoils of the enemy." Senator William L. Marcy, defending President Jackson's appointment of Martin Van Buren as minister to Great Britain, 1831.

286 *"I will be* as harsh as truth, and as uncompromising as justice. . . . I am in earnest—I will not equivocate—I will not excuse—I will not retreat a single inch—AND I WILL BE HEARD." William Lloyd Garrison in *The Liberator,* 1831.

William Lloyd Garrison banner.
THE MASSACHUSETTS HISTORICAL SOCIETY, PHOTO BY GEORGE M. CUSHING, JR.

287 "The practical liberty of America is found in its great space and small population. Good land, dog-cheap everywhere, and for nothing, if you will go for it, gives as much elbow room to every man as he chooses to take. Poor laborers, from every country in Europe, hear of this cheap land. . . . They come, they toil, they prosper. This is the real liberty of America." George Flower, *History of the English Settlement in Edwards County, Illinois,* c. 1860.

Nineteenth-century immigration poster. LANDAUER COLLECTION, THE NEW-YORK HISTORICAL SOCIETY.

288 "Nothing can exceed their activity and perseverance in all kinds of speculation, handicraft, and enterprise which promise a profitable pecuniary result. . . . Such unity of purpose, such sympathy of feeling can, I believe, be found nowhere else, except, perhaps, in an ant's nest." Frances Trollope, *Domestic Manners of the Americans,* 1832.

289 "Any man's son may become the equal of any other man's son; and the consciousness of this is certainly a spur to that coarse familiarity, untempered by any shadow of respect, which is assumed by the grossest and the lowest in their intercourse with the highest and most refined. . . . Strong, indeed, must be the love of equality in an English breast, if it can survive a tour through the Union." Frances Trollope, *Domestic Manners of the Americans,* 1832.

290 "Secession, like any other revolutionary act, may be morally justified by the extremity of oppression; but to call it a constitutional right is confounding the meaning of the terms. . . . The laws of the United States must be executed. I have no discretionary power on the subject." President Andrew Jackson, responding to the nullification of the Tariff Acts of 1828 and 1832 by South Carolina, 1832. (Also see numbers 19, 177).

291 "In the United States they have neither war, nor pestilence, nor literature, nor eloquence, nor fine arts, nor revolutions. . . . They enjoy there the most insipid happiness that may be imagined."

Alexis de Tocqueville, *Democracy in America,* 1835.

292 "I ask not for the great, the remote, the romantic; what is doing in Italy or Arabia; what is Greek art, or Provençal minstrelsy; I embrace the common, I explore and sit at the feet of the familiar. . . . If the single man plant himself indomitably on his instincts, and there abide, the huge world will come round to him." Ralph Waldo Emerson, "The American Scholar," 1837.

Author's card for Ralph Waldo Emerson, 1888. COLLECTION OF HERBERT J. SIEGAL, PENNSYLVANIA.

293 "Members of Congress would repose themselves by our fireside. Mr. Clay, sitting upright on the sofa, with his snuffbox ever in his hand, would discourse for many an hour in his even, soft, deliberate tone on any one of the great subjects of American policy. . . . Mr. Calhoun, the cast-

iron man, who looks as if he had never been born and never could be extinguished, would come in sometimes to keep our understandings upon a painful stretch for a short while. . . . His speech abounds in figures, truly illustrative, if that which they illustrate were but true also." Harriet Martineau, *A Retrospect of Western Travel*, 1838.

294 "They won't let me alone about slavery. A certain judge in St. Louis went so far yesterday that I fell upon him. . . . I told him that I could sympathize with men who admitted it to be a dreadful evil, but frankly confessed their inability to devise a means of getting rid of it; but that men who spoke of it as a blessing, as a matter of course, as a state of things to be desired, were out of the pale of reason." Charles Dickens, while on tour in America in 1842.

295 "I am the most unfortunate man in the history of parties; always run by my friends when sure to be defeated, and now betrayed when I, or anyone, would be sure of election." Henry Clay, after failing to win the 1840 Whig nomination. (He had previously run for President in 1824 and 1832.) True to form, when Clay was nominated again in 1844, he lost to James K. Polk.

Henry Clay cigar holder, 1884 campaign. STANLEY KING COLLECTION, PHOTO BY PAULUS LEESER.

Train travelers' buffalo hunt, nineteenth century. CULVER PICTURES, INC.

296 "It is the nature of the Buffalo & all other kinds of game to recede before the approach of civilization, and the injury complained of is but one of those inconveniences to which every people are subjected by the changing & constantly progressive spirit of the age." Commissioner of Indian Affairs William Medill, responding to complaints of the Sioux that white immigrants were killing and driving off the game on which they depended, c. 1846.

297 "The parties that made the Constitution aimed to cheat and defraud the slave, who was not himself a party to the compact or agreement." Frederick Douglass, "The Constitution and Slavery," 1849.

Frederick Douglass. PRIVATE COLLECTION.

298 "The Constitution regulates our stewardship. . . . But there is a higher law than the Constitution, which regulates our authority." Senator William H. Seward of New York, during the debate on the Compromise of 1850.

299 "If a man does not keep pace with his companions, perhaps it is

because he hears a different drummer." Henry Thoreau, *Walden,* 1854.

300 "We provide for each slave, in old age and in infancy, in sickness and in health, not according to his labor, but according to his wants. . . . A southern farm is the beau ideal of Communism." George Fitzhugh, *Sociology for the South,* 1854.

Engraving of Thomas Hart Benton. CULVER PICTURES, INC.

301 "The famous Madame Roland, when mounting the scaffold, apostrophized the mock statue upon it with this exclamation: 'Oh Liberty! how many crimes are committed in thy name!' After what I have seen in my thirty years of inside and outside views in the Congress of the United States, I feel qualified to paraphrase the apostrophe, and exclaim: 'Oh Politics! how much bamboozling is prac-

ticed in thy game!' " Thomas Hart Benton, *Thirty Years' View,* 1854.

302 "If Kansas wants a slave-State constitution she has a right to it: if she wants a free-State constitution she has a right to it. It is none of my business which way the slavery cause is decided. I care not whether it is voted down or voted up." Senator Stephen A. Douglas of Illinois, during the debate on Kansas's Lecompton Constitution, 1857.

303 "In all social systems there must be a class to do the menial duties, to perform the drudgery of life. That is, a class requiring but a low order of intellect and but little skill. Its requisites are vigor, docility, fidelity. Such a class you must have, or you would not have that other class which leads to progress, civilization, and refinement. It constitutes the very mud-sill of society and of political government; and you might as well attempt to build a house in the air, as to build either one or the other, except on this mud-sill." Senator James H. Hammond of South Carolina, 1858.

304 "I believe that to have interfered as I have done in behalf of His

despised poor, is no wrong, but right. Now, if it is deemed necessary that I should forfeit my life for the furtherance of the ends of justice, and mingle my blood with the blood of millions in this slave country whose rights are disregarded by wicked, cruel, and unjust enactments, I say let it be done." John Brown, before being sentenced to be hanged for his part in the raid on Harpers Ferry, 1859.

John Brown and companions at the arraignment, *Harper's Weekly,* November 12, 1859. CULVER PICTURES, INC.

305 "We the people of the Confederate States, each State acting in its sovereign and independent character, in order to form a permanent federal government . . . do ordain and establish this Constitution," Preamble of the Confederate Constitution, 1861.

306 "If I could save the Union without freeing *any* slave, I would do it; and if I could save it by freeing *all* the slaves, I would do it; and if I could do it by freeing some and leaving others alone, I would do

that. . . . I have here stated my purpose according to my *official* duty, and I intend no modification of my oft-expressed *personal* wish that all men, everywhere, could be free." Abraham Lincoln, replying to the appeal of editor Horace Greeley (August 1862) that he emancipate the slaves.

307 "I sincerely wish that war was an easier and pleasanter business than it is, but it does not admit of holidays." Abraham Lincoln to a civilian who had requested that a division of Kentucky troops be sent to that state, 1862.

Poncas family group, Arkansas City, Kansas.
CULVER PICTURES, INC.

308 "War usually springs from a sense of injustice. The best possible way to avoid war is to do no act of injustice. When we learn that the same rule holds good with Indians, the chief difficulty is removed. But it is said that our wars with them have been almost constant. Have we been uniformly unjust? We answer unhesitatingly, yes." Report of the Commissioner of Indian Affairs, 1868.

309 "I repose in this quiet and secluded spot, not from any natural preference for solitude, but, finding other cemeteries limited by charter rules as to race, I have chosen this, that I might illustrate in my death the principles which I advocated through a long life—Equality of Man before his Creator." Epitaph of Congressman Thaddeus Stevens, written by himself, 1868.

310 "As the British Constitution is the most subtle organism which has proceeded from the womb and the long gestation of progressive history, so the American Constitution is, so far as I can see, the most wonderful work ever struck off at a given time by the brain and purpose of man," William E. Gladstone, *North American Review,* 1878.

311 "Every man that lowered our flag was a Democrat. Every man that bred bloodhounds was a Democrat. Every preacher that said that slavery was a divine institution was a Democrat. Every man that shot a Union soldier was a Democrat. Every wound borne by you Union soldiers is a souvenir of a Democrat." Robert G. Ingersoll "waving the bloody shirt" (see number 75) during the 1880 presidential campaign.

312 "Reformers . . . are the worst possible political advisers—upstarts, conceited, foolish, vain, without knowledge of measures, ignorant of men, shouting a shibboleth. . . . They are noisy but not numerous, pharisaical but not practical, ambitious but not wise, pretentious but not powerful!" Senator James G. Blaine, 1883.

Reformers' view of Senator Blaine, *Puck,* 1880s. COURTESY OF THE NEW-YORK HISTORICAL SOCIETY.

313 "Our organization does not consist of idealists. . . . We do not control the production of the world. That is controlled by the employers. . . . I look first to the trade I represent; I look first to cigars."

Adolph Strasser, president of the Cigar Makers' Union, 1883.

Cigar trade card.
CULVER PICTURES, INC.

314 "There is in all the past nothing to compare with the rapid changes now going on in the civilized world. . . . The snail's pace of crawling ages has suddenly become the headlong rush of the locomotive, speeding faster and faster. This rapid progress is primarily in industrial methods and material powers. But industrial changes imply social changes and necessitate political changes. Progressive societies outgrow institutions as children outgrow clothes." Henry George, *Social Problems,* 1883.

315 "The ordinary American voter does not object to mediocrity. He has a lower conception of the qualities requisite to make a statesman than those who direct public opinion in Europe have. . . . He sees no need for originality or profundity, a fine culture or a wide knowledge." James Bryce, "Why Great Men Are Not Chosen President," 1888.

316 "I admire the splendid complacency of my countrymen, and I find something exhilarating and inspiring in it. We are a nation which has struck *ile,* but we are also a nation that is sure the well will never run dry." James Russell Lowell, *Political Essays,* 1888.

317 "Count me out. The civilians of the U.S. should, and must, buffet with this thankless office, and leave us old soldiers to enjoy the peace we fought for, and think we earned. . . . I will not accept if nominated and will not serve if elected." General William Tecumseh Sherman, referring to the suggestion that he run for President in 1884.

Andrew Carnegie and his wife, 1910. CULVER PICTURES, INC.

318 "The man of wealth [should] consider all surplus revenues which come to him simply as trust funds, which he is called upon to administer . . . to produce the most beneficial results for the community." Andrew Carnegie, "Wealth," 1889.

319 "To those of my race who depend on bettering their condition in a foreign land or who underestimate the importance of cultivating friendly relations with the Southern white man, who is their next-door neighbor, I would say: 'Cast down your bucket where you are.'" Booker T. Washington, speaking at the Atlanta Cotton States and International Exposition, 1895 (see number 181).

***Puck* cover, December 31, 1890.**
PUCK, DECEMBER 31, 1890.

320 "Please remain. You furnish the pictures and I'll furnish the war." William Randolph Hearst, publisher of the New York *Journal,* to the artist Frederic Remington, whom he had sent to Cuba to draw pictures of the Cuban revolution, then in progress, 1898.

321 "I said [last September] that nothing would induce me to be a candidate for the Presidency. Since then, however, I have had the leisure and inclination to study the matter, and have reached a different conclusion. . . . If the American people want me for this high office, I shall be only too willing to serve them. . . . Since studying this subject I am convinced that the office of President is not such a very difficult one to fill." Admiral George Dewey, in an interview with a correspondent of the New York *World,* April 1900.

Photograph of Admiral George Dewey. THE NATIONAL ARCHIVES.

322 "Th' Supreme Coort follows th' iliction returns," Finley Peter Dunne ("Mr. Dooley"), 1901.

323 "I beg of you not to be discouraged. The rights and interests of the laboring man will be protected and cared for—not by the labor agitators, but by the Christian men to whom God in his infinite wisdom has given the control of the property interests of this country." George F. Baer, president of the Philadelphia and Reading Coal and Iron Company, responding to a letter urging him to try to find a solution to a coal strike, 1902 (see number 983).

Cartoon from the *Minneapolis Times,* 1902.
CULVER PICTURES, INC.

324 "[Mr. Washington] apologizes for injustice. He belittles the emasculating effects of cast distinctions, and opposes the higher training and ambitions of our brightest minds. . . . The way for people to gain their reasonable rights is not by voluntarily throwing them away." W. E. B. Du Bois, "Of Mr. Booker T. Washington and Others," 1903.

Dr. W. E. B. Du Bois.
LIBRARY OF CONGRESS.

325 "Don't bluster. Don't flourish a revolver, and never draw unless you intend to shoot." Theodore Roosevelt on foreign policy, c. 1900. This was a "cowboy" version of an African proverb that Roosevelt admired: "Speak softly and carry a big stick; you will go far."

326 "What this country needs is a really good five-cent cigar." Woodrow Wilson's Vice President, Thomas R. Marshall, in an aside while presiding over the Senate during an interminable speech by a senator who was spelling out the "needs" of the country.

327 "In the course of my life I have tried Boston on all sides: I have . . . tried it drunk and tried it sober; and, drunk or sober, there's nothing in it—save Boston!" Charles Francis Adams, Jr., *Autobiography,* 1916.

328 "I have known, and know tolerably well, a good many 'successful' men—'big' financially—men famous during the last half-century; and a less interesting crowd I do not care to encounter. Not one that I have ever known would I care to meet again, either in this world or the next. . . . A set of mere money-getters and traders, they were essentially unattractive and uninteresting." Charles Francis Adams, Jr., *Autobiography,* 1916.

329 "The example of America must be the example not merely of peace because it will not fight, but of peace because peace is the healing and elevating influence of the world, and strife is not. There is such a thing as a man being too proud to fight." Woodrow Wilson, "Address to Newly Naturalized Citizens," 1915.

330 "I have seen the future; and it works." The journalist Lincoln Steffens, in a letter written shortly after returning from a visit to the Soviet Union, 1919. Many years later, in his *Autobiography,* Steffens

remembered having put this idea slightly differently in a conversation in 1919 with Bernard Baruch: "I have been over into the future, and it works."

Bolshevik poster hailing the coming worldwide socialist revolution. PRIVATE COLLECTION

331 "As democracy is perfected the office [of President] represents, more and more closely, the inner soul of the people. We move toward a lofty ideal. On some great and glorious day the plain folks of the land will reach their heart's desire at last, and the White House will be adorned by a downright moron." H. L. Mencken, on presidential candidates Warren G. Harding and James M. Cox, 1920.

332 "We in America have had too much experience of life to fool ourselves into pretending that all men are equal in ability, in character, in intelligence,

in ambition. That was part of the claptrap of the French Revolution. We have grown to understand that all we can hope to assure to the individual through government is liberty, justice, intellectual welfare, equality of opportunity, and stimulation to service." Herbert Hoover, *American Individualism,* 1922.

333 "The general prosperity of the country, in spite of bad farm years, is in direct proportion to the number of automobiles." Henry Ford, *Today and Tomorrow* (1926).

"Hatching" automobiles, September 7, 1927. CULVER PICTURES, INC.

334 "[Democracy] came into the world as a cure-all, and it remains primarily a cure-all to this day. Any boil upon the body politic, however vast and raging, may be relieved by taking a vote. . . . As for me, I have never encountered any actual evidence, convincing to an ordinary jury, that *vox*

populi is actually *vox Dei*." H. L. Mencken, *The Future of Democracy* (1926).

335 "When men who are willing and able to work and want to work are unable to obtain work, we need not be surprised if they steal before they starve. Certainly I do not approve of stealing, but if I had to make a choice between stealing and starving, I would surely not choose to starve—and in that respect I do not think I am unlike the average individual." Daniel Willard, president of the Baltimore & Ohio Railroad, 1928.

Unemployed man looking for work in Detroit, 1930s.
DETROIT NEWS.

336 "Franklin Roosevelt is no crusader. He is no tribune of the people. He is no enemy of entrenched privilege. He is a pleasant man who, without any important qualifications for the office, would very much like to be President." Political commentator Walter Lippmann, 1932.

337 "The royalists of the economic order have conceded that political freedom was the business of government, but they have maintained that economic slavery was nobody's business. . . . Today we stand committed to the proposition that freedom is no half-and-half affair. If the average citizen is guaranteed freedom of opportunity in the polling place, he must have freedom of opportunity in the marketplace." Franklin D. Roosevelt, accepting the Democratic nomination for a second term as President, 1936.

338 "Businessmen have a different set of delusions from politicians; and need, therefore, different handling. They are, however, much milder than politicians, at the same time allured and terrified by the glare of publicity. . . . You could do anything you like with them, if you would treat them (even the big ones) not

as wolves and tigers, but as domestic animals by nature, even though they have been badly brought up and not trained as you would wish." British economist John Maynard Keynes, in a letter to President Franklin D. Roosevelt, 1938.

339 "I have said this before, but I shall say it again and again and again; your boys are not going to be sent into any foreign wars." Franklin D. Roosevelt during the 1940 presidential campaign.

340 "The main element of any United States policy toward the Soviet Union must be that of long-term, patient, but firm and vigilant containment of Russian expansive tendencies." "X" (George F. Kennan), "The Sources of Soviet Conduct," 1947.

341 "Puritanism is the haunting fear that someone, somewhere, may be happy." H. L. Mencken, 1949.

342 "Old soldiers never die; they just fade away." General Douglas MacArthur, addressing a joint session of Congress after being relieved of his command by President Truman during the Korean War, 1951.

343 "In the councils of government, we must guard against the acquisition of unwarranted influence, whether sought or unsought, by the military-industrial complex. The potential for the disastrous rise of misplaced power exists and will persist." President Dwight D. Eisenhower, 1961.

John F. Kennedy and Jacqueline Kennedy, 1961 inauguration. SAN FRANCISCO PUBLIC LIBRARY, NEW CALL-BULLETIN COLLECTION.

344 "Let every nation know, whether it wish us well or ill, that we shall pay any price, bear any burden, meet any hardship, support any friend, oppose any foe in order to assure the survival and the success of liberty." President John F. Kennedy, Inaugural Address, 1961.

345 "A billion here and a billion there and pretty soon you are talking about real money." Attributed to Senator Everett M. Dirksen of Illinois.

346 "Will it play in Peoria?" Presidential assistant John D. Ehrlichman, 1968. Peoria, Ehrlichman explained to the journalist William Safire, stood for any place "removed from the media centers on the coasts, where the national verdict is cast."

John Ehrlichman appearing before the Senate Watergate Committee, 1973. UPI/BETTMANN NEWSPHOTOS.

347 "If when the chips are down, the world's most powerful nation—the United States of America—acts like a pitiful, helpless giant, the forces of totalitarianism and anarchy will threaten free nations and free institutions throughout the world." President Richard M. Nixon, explaining his decision to send American troops into Cambodia, 1970.

348 "We ought to let him hang there. Let him twist slowly, slowly in the wind." John D. Ehrlichman, 1973, explaining to White House legal adviser John Dean that nothing should be done to help acting FBI Director L. Patrick Gray, whose confirmation as director by the Senate was under attack.

349 "The very purpose of having a written Constitution is to provide safeguards for certain rights that *cannot* yield to public opinion. That is why our Constitution created an independent judiciary." Chief Justice Warren E. Burger, 1973.

Chief Justice Warren E. Burger, 1973. WIDE WORLD PHOTOS.

350 "People have got to know whether or not their President is a crook. Well, I'm not a crook. I've earned everything I've got." Richard M. Nixon, 1973.

351 "What you say, do, and advocate in respect to religion shows that you do not understand the

religious clauses of the First Amendment. . . . You urge adoption of a constitutional amendment to authorize prayer in the public schools. The adoption of such an amendment would drastically alter the First Amendment, which commands the government to be strictly neutral in respect to religion and leaves the task of teaching religion to children to the homes and churches of our land. The government must keep its hands off religion if our people are to enjoy religious freedom." Ex-Senator Sam Ervin to President Ronald Reagan, 1985.

MISQUOTATIONS: THINGS THAT WERE *NOT* SAID

352 "Why don't you speak for yourself, John?" There is no record that Myles Standish asked John Alden to propose to Priscilla Mullens or any other female Pilgrim in his behalf, and since John and Priscilla may have been married as early as 1621, the story told by Henry Wadsworth Longfellow in "The Courtship of Miles Standish" is no doubt an example of poetic license.

353 "Caesar had his Brutus; Charles the First his Cromwell; and George the Third . . ." (Response of the Speaker of the Virginia House: "Treason!") Patrick Henry, attacking the Stamp Act in the Virginia House of Burgesses, 1765. Henry apparently said something like this, though no copy of his actual speech exists. But he almost surely did not add, as tradition has it: "*may profit by this example.* If *this* be treason, make the most of it." The evidence that he said these words consists of the recollections of eyewitnesses, which were not recorded until half a century later. The only contemporary written account claims that "Henery," when interrupted by the Speaker, "said that if he had afronted the speaker, or the house, he was ready to ask pardon, and he would show his loyalty to his majesty, King G. the third, at the Expense of the last drop of his blood."

354 The "Mecklenburg Declaration of Independence," supposedly adopted by a committee of citizens of Mecklenburg County, North Carolina, in 1775—more than a year before the real Declaration—did not take place. The Mecklenburgers did adopt a series of patriotic resolutions reorganizing the government and declaring that anyone who in the future accepted a "Commission from the Crown" be "deemed an Enemy of his Country." However, they also included a resolution suspending the resolutions if "*Great-Britain* [would] resign its unjust and arbitrary Pretentions with Respect to America," which was far from a declaration of independence.

Engraving of Alexander Hamilton. COURTESY OF HENRY FRANCIS DU PONT WINTERTHUR MUSEUM.

355 "The people are a Great Beast." Alexander Hamilton. Hamilton made many disparaging remarks about the capacities of the lower orders, but not, so far as is known, this one. Such comments were common at the time among educated people. For example, Jefferson: "Lions and tigers are mere lambs compared with men."

356 "Entangling alliances." This phrase

is often incorrectly said to come from George Washington's Farewell Address (see number 405). Washington warned not against "entangling" alliances but against both "passionate attachments" and "inveterate antipathies" to particular foreign countries. It was Thomas Jefferson who said, in his first inaugural (see number 406), "Peace, commerce, and honest friendship with all nations, entangling alliances with none."

357 "Millions for defense, but not one cent for tribute." Charles Cotesworth Pinckney was supposed to have said this in 1797, when he and two other American diplomats, who were trying to negotiate a commercial treaty with France, were asked for a bribe by three agents of Foreign Minister Talleyrand. What Pinckney did say to the greedy Frenchmen, who were known only as X, Y, and Z, was "No! No! Not a sixpence!" The "millions for defense" phrase was coined later by Virginia Congressman Robert Goodloe Harper, at a dinner honoring John Marshall, another of the Americans involved in the incident. A play on this more grandiloquent expression, "Millions for Expense, but Not One Cent for Efficiency," was used during

the New Deal by critics of Harry Hopkins (see numbers 153, 364), head of the New Deal relief program.

358 "John Marshall has made his decision: *now let him enforce it!*" Supposedly said by President Andrew Jackson about the case of *Worcester* v. *Georgia* (1832), in which the Supreme Court, speaking through Chief Justice Marshall, had ruled that the state of Georgia did not have jurisdiction over the Cherokee Indians living within its borders. Jackson would have had no possible reason for saying this because there was nothing for him to enforce. However, Jackson's biographer, Robert Remini, points out that Jackson may have said "sportively" in private conversation that if called on to "support the decree of the Court," he would "call on those who have brought about the decision to enforce it."

Chief Justice John Marshall.
THE NATIONAL ARCHIVES.

359 "I wish some of you would tell me the brand of whiskey that Grant drinks. I would like to send a barrel of it to every one of my other generals." Lincoln was supposed to have said this to a group of temperance workers who had complained to him of Grant's drinking. Lincoln, however, denied having made the remark, saying, "That would have been very good if I had said it," and on another occasion, "No, I didn't happen to say it—but it's a good story, a hardy perennial. I've traced that story as far back as George II and General Wolfe. When certain persons complained to George that Wolfe was mad, George said, 'I wish he'd bite some of the others!' "

360 "Damn the torpedoes! Full speed ahead!" What Admiral David Farragut actually said when he ordered his ships to enter Mobile Bay in 1864, despite the danger that the harbor might have been mined by the Confederates, was more precise. To Percival Drayton, the commander of his flagship, USS *Hartford,* he said, "Damn the torpedoes! Four bells [i.e., full speed]! Captain Drayton, go ahead!" To James E. Jouett, commander of the gunboat *Metacomet,* which was lashed to the *Hartford,* he said, "Jouett, full speed!"

361 "The only good Indian is a dead Indian." Attributed to General Philip H. Sheridan, who in fact said something almost as objectionable, "The only good Indians I ever saw were dead."

Photograph of General Philip Sheridan. THE NATIONAL ARCHIVES.

362 "Lafayette, we are here." This was thought to be said by General John J. Pershing upon setting foot on French soil with advance units of the American Expeditionary Force in 1917; it was actually said by an aide, Charles E. Stanton.

363 "Prosperity is just around the corner." Though it was repeatedly attributed to Herbert Hoover, the ex-President always denied having used the phrase. Actually there was nothing fatuous in the statement, even if Hoover did make it. Well into 1931 most people believed that the Depression would be short. Hoover claimed that his enemies were twisting a statement

he made in 1930: "I am convinced we have passed the worst and with continued effort we will rapidly recover."

364 "We shall tax and tax, and spend and spend, and elect and elect." Supposedly said by Harry Hopkins, New Deal relief administrator, before the 1938 congressional elections. Hopkins denied having made the statement. What had apparently happened was that he had been asked by a friend he had run into at the racetrack about government policy; he had responded by saying that to stimulate the economy it would be necessary to spend more and that this would require additional taxation. He added that he expected most people on relief to vote Democratic, and felt that the Democrats would win the election.

BUT WE'VE GOT SOMETHING TO SHOW FOR IT!

The *New World Telegram* sizes up the New Deal, August 23, 1934. COURTESY OF THE FRANKLIN D. ROOSEVELT LIBRARY, HYDE PARK.

365 "What's good for General Motors is good for the country." What Charles E. Wilson (see number 148), former head of General Motors, actually said in testifying before the Senate committee considering his nomination to be Eisenhower's Secretary of Defense in 1953 was a bit different: "I thought that what was good for our country was good for General Motors and vice versa."

COMMENTS ABOUT WOMEN BY MEN

"Indians Fishing," Theodore de Bry. CULVER PICTURES, INC.

366 "The men bestow their times in fishing, hunting, warres, and such man-like exercises, scorning to be seen in any woman-like exercise, which is the cause that the women be very painefull, and the men often idle. The women and children doe the rest of the worke." John Smith, describing the Indians of Virginia, 1607.

367 "The appointment of a woman to office is an innovation for which the public is not prepared, nor am I." President Thomas Jefferson, responding to a suggestion of Secretary of the Treasury Albert Gallatin, 1807.

368 "The majority of women (happily for them) are not much troubled with sexual feeling of any kind." Dr. William Acton.

369 "I do not wish to see the day come when the women of my race in my state shall trail their skirts in the mire of partisan politics. I prefer to look to the American woman as she always has been, occupying her proud estate as the queen of the American home, instead of regarding her as a ward politician." Congressman Frank Clark of Florida, 1915.

Supporters of Victoria Woodhull for President storm the capitol for votes. COLLECTION OF AMERICAN HERITAGE.

370 "The physiological peculiarities of a woman even in single life,

and the disorders consequent on them, cannot fail frequently to interfere with the regular discharge of her duties as physician. . . . The delicate organization and predominance of the nervous system render her peculiarly susceptible to suffer, if not to sink, under the fatigue and mental shocks which she must encounter in her professional round. Man, with his robust frame and trained self-command, is often barely equal to the task." Philadelphia County Medical Society, 1867.

371 "To purchase woman suffrage at the expense of the Negro's rights is to pay a shameful price." William Lloyd Garrison, Jr., 1903.

Photograph of William Lloyd Garrison. LIBRARY OF CONGRESS.

372 "When spinsters can support themselves with more physical

comforts and larger leisure than they would [could?] as wives; when married women may prefer the money they can earn and the excitement they can find in outside employment to the bearing and rearing of children; when they can conveniently leave their husbands should it so suit their fancy—the conditions are clearly unfavorable to marriage and the family." Psychologist James McKeen Cattell, 1909.

***Puck* glimpses the future, March 29, 1899.** *PUCK*, MARCH 29, 1899.

COMMENTS ON MEN AND WOMEN BY WOMEN

373 "[Men] denied us the means of knowledge and then reproached us for the want of it. . . . They doomed the sex to servile or frivolous employment on purpose to degrade their minds, that they themselves might hold unrivalled the power and preemptions they usurped." Priscilla Mason, salutatorian at the graduation exercises of the Young Ladies Academy of Philadelphia, 1793.

374 "Women may, if they exert their talents and the opportunities nature has furnished, obtain an influence in society. . . . They may enjoy the luxuries of wealth, without enduring the labors to acquire it; and the honors of office, without feeling its cares; and the glory of victory, without suffering the dangers of battle." Editor Sarah Josepha Hale, in *Ladies Magazine*, 1830.

Mrs. Dawson.—Well, here's the bill from the dressmaker, for my new Fall dresses!
Dawson (as he recovers from the shock). — Thanks, dear; they've gone!

Puck views marital economics, 1893. *PUCK*, 1893.

375 "For the first time in this country woman's labor had a money value. She had become not only an earner and a producer, but also a spender of money, a recognized factor in the political economy of her time." Harriet Robinson, describing her experi-

ences as a factory worker in Lowell, Massachusetts, in *Loom and Spindle, or Life Among the Early Mill Girls,* 1898.

Seamstresses and working women, Watertown, Wisconsin, around 1890. COURTESY OF THE STATE HISTORICAL SOCIETY OF WISCONSIN.

376 "Southern women are I believe all at heart abolitionists. I will stand to the opinion that the institution of slavery degrades the white man more than the Negro and exerts a most deleterious effect upon our children." Ella Thomas, a Georgian, writing in her journal, 1858.

377 "The mind has no sex but what habit and education give it." Frances Wright, letter to the Marquis de Lafayette, c. 1825.

378 "Let us not teach, that virtue consists in the crucifying of the affections and appetites, but in their judicious government! Let us not attach ideas of purity to monastic chastity, impossible to man or woman without consequences

fraught with evil." Frances Wright, "Explanatory Notes, Respecting the Nature and Objects of the Institution of Nashoba," 1828.

379 "There is a vulgar persuasion, that the ignorance of women, by favoring their subordination, insures their utility. Tis the same argument employed by the ruling few against the subject many in aristocracies; by the rich against the poor in democracies; by the learned professions against the people in all countries." Frances Wright, c. 1829.

Sojourner Truth, 1864 photograph. CULVER PICTURES, INC.

380 "The man over there says women need to be helped into carriages and lifted over ditches and have the best place everywhere. Nobody helps me into carriages and over puddles, or gives me the best place—and ain't I a woman? I have ploughed and planted and gathered into barns, and no man could head me—and ain't I a woman?" Sojourner Truth, speaking at a Women's Rights Convention, 1851.

381 "Men and women are CREATED EQUAL. . . . All I ask our brethren is that they take their feet from off our necks and permit us to stand upright on the ground which God destined for us to occupy." Sarah Grimké, *Letters on the Equality of the Sexes and the Condition of Woman,* 1838.

382 "The history of mankind is a history of repeated injuries and usurpations on the part of man toward woman, having in direct object the establishment of an absolute tyranny over her." Elizabeth Cady Stanton and Lucretia Mott, "Declaration of Senti-

Photograph of Elizabeth Cady Stanton. LIBRARY OF CONGRESS.

Engraving of Lucretia Mott. LIBRARY OF CONGRESS.

ments," presented at the Woman's Rights Convention, Seneca Falls, New York, 1848.

Victoria Woodhull CULVER PICTURES, INC.

383 "Women have the same invaluable right to life, liberty, and the *pursuit* of happiness that men have. Why have they not this right politically as well as men? Women consti-

tute a majority of the people of this country—they hold vast portions of the nation's wealth and pay a proportionate share of the taxes. . . . The American nation, in its march onward and upward, cannot publicly choke the intellectual and political activity of half its citizens by narrow statutes." Victoria Woodhull, testifying before the House Judiciary Committee, 1871.

384 "The marriage institution, like slavery and monarchy, and many other things which have been good or necessary in their day, is now *effete,* and in a general sense injurious. . . . I mean by marriage, in this connection, any *forced* or *obligatory tie* between the sexes." Victoria Woodhull, in *Woodhull and Claflin's Weekly,* 1872.

385 "The true feminist, no matter how far to the left she may be in the revolutionary movement, sees the woman's battle as distinct in its objectives and different in its methods from the worker's battle. . . . The whole of woman's slavery is not summed up in the profit system, nor is her complete emancipation assured by the downfall of capitalism. If we should graduate into communism tomorrow . . . man's attitude to

his wife would not be changed." Crystal Eastman, 1920.

386 "If our husbands, and fathers, and brethren are ready to prostrate themselves before the swift-running car of the mighty Juggernaut which slavery hath set up—we hope the women of our country, untrammeled by the love of gain, will exert a countervailing influence." Maria A. Sturgis, "Address to Females of the State of Ohio," 1836.

387 "There is no foundation in reason or expediency, for the absolute and slavish subjection of the wife to the husband, which forms the foundation of the present legal relations. Were woman, in point of fact, the abject thing which the law, in theory, considers her to be when married, she would not be worthy the companionship of man." Lucretia Mott, 1849.

388 "Men call us angels, and boast of the deference they pay to our weakness! They give us their seats in church, in cars and omnibusses, at lectures and concerts, and in many other ways show us great respect where nothing but form is concerned. . . . But at the same time they are defraud-

ing us of our just rights by crowding us out of every lucrative employment, and subjecting us to virtual slavery." Amelia Bloomer, 1851.

Engraving of Amelia Bloomer.
COURTESY OF THE
NEW-YORK HISTORICAL SOCIETY.

389 "The reason why women effect so little & are so shallow is because their aims are low. Marriage is the prize for which they strive; if foiled in that they rarely rise above the disappointment. . . . We feel we have powers which are crushed, responsibilities which we are not permitted to exercise. . . . Because we feel this so keenly we now demand an equal education with man to qualify us to become co-workers with him in the great arena of human life." Sarah Grimké, "Education of Women," 1852–57.

390 "You white folks spose cause you white, and we all black, that us donno noffin, and you knows eberyting. Now missus, youse one bery good white woman, come down from de great North, to teach poor we to read, and sich as that; but . . . does ye suppose I gwine to give up all my rights to ye, just cause youse a Yankee white woman? Does ye know missus that we's free now? Yas, free we is, and us ant guine to get down to ye, any more than to them ar rebs." A Georgia freedwoman, 1866.

1892 engraving of Charity Still, twice escaped from slavery.
CULVER PICTURES, INC.

391 "I suppose I am about the only colored woman that goes about to speak for the rights of colored women. I want to keep the thing stirring, now that the ice is cracked. What we want is a little money. You men know that you get as much again as women, when you write, or for what you do. When we get our

rights, we shall not have to come to you for money, for then we shall have money enough in our own pockets; and maybe you will ask us for money. But help us now until we get it." Sojourner Truth, 1867.

392 "This Government is menaced with great danger. . . . That danger lies in the votes possessed by males in the slums of the cities, and the ignorant foreign vote. . . . There is but one way to avert that danger—cut off the vote of the slums and give to woman, who is bound to suffer all, and more than man can, of the evils his legislation has brought upon the nation, the power of protecting herself that man has secured for himself—the ballot." Carrie Chapman Catt, 1894.

Liberty comments on votes for women, *Life*, October 28, 1920. CULVER PICTURES, INC.

393 "My first medical consultation was a curious experience. In a severe case of pneumonia in an elderly lady I called in consultation a kind-hearted physician of high standing. . . . This gentleman, after seeing the patient, went with me into the parlour. There he began to walk about the room in some agitation, exclaiming, 'A most extraordinary case! Such a one never happened to me before; I really do not know what to do!' I listened in surprise and much perplexity, as it was a clear case of pneumonia and of no unusual degree of danger, until at last I discovered that his perplexity related to *me,* not to the patient, and to the propriety of consulting with a lady physician!" Dr. Elizabeth Blackwell, *Pioneer Work in Opening the Medical Profession to Women,* 1895.

394 "To the man, the whole world was his world, his because he was male; and the whole world of woman was the home, because she was female. She had her prescribed sphere, strictly limited to her feminine occupations and interests; he had all the rest of life, and . . . having it, insisted on calling it male." Charlotte Perkins Gilman, 1904.

395 "The real antagonism is not that which exists or is supposed to exist between the sexes; but between the capitalist class and the proletariat. Women are victims of class distinctions more than of sex distinctions, and when I perceived this fact I changed my course of action." Lena Morrow Lewis, "Experiences as a Socialist Propagandist," 1907.

396 "A woman's body belongs to herself alone. It does not belong to the United States of America or any other government on the face of the earth." Margaret H. Sanger, *Woman Rebel,* 1914.

Margaret Sanger, January 4, 1917. UPI/BETTMANN NEWSPHOTOS.

397 "It is utterly false that love results from marriage. On rare occasions one does hear of a miraculous case of a married couple falling in love after marriage, but on close examination it will be found that it is a mere adjustment to the inevitable." Emma Goldman, 1917.

398 "Marriage is too much of a compromise; it lops off a woman's life as an individual. Yet renunciation too is a lopping off. We choose between the frying pan and the fire—both very uncomfortable." Sue Sheldon White in *The Nation,* 1927.

399 "The women of America will tell you, as they have told me often, that the New Deal is a square deal for them. . . . They have gained a new freedom because a just President in appointing them to high offices and places of distinction has given them more courage and faith in themselves." Congresswoman Mary T. Norton of New Jersey, 1936.

400 "In Germany, German women are governed by German men; in France, French women are governed by Frenchmen; and in Great Britain, British women are governed by British men; but in this country, American women are governed by every kind of man under the light of the sun. There is no race, there is no color, there is no nationality of men who are not the sovereign rulers of American women." National American Woman Suffrage Association president Anna Howard Shaw, 1914.

401 "Now do not misunderstand me; if Louisiana employs an understanding clause to preserve white supremacy and will grant woman suffrage, then I will not have a word to say against it." Kate M. Gordon, vice president, National American Woman Suffrage Association, 1915.

VOTES FOR WOMEN

You've called us the better half long enough, now make good your bluff.

Gentle persuasion from feminists, 1920.
CULVER PICTURES, INC.

402 "Men will cede to women only what by ceding gives them an assurance of power, like making an allowance to a wife or educating a daughter to citizenship, or they will cede only what they consider has ceased to give mastery—just as they are now ceding the vote. . . . Even the woman movement we call feminism has not succeeded by and large in giving women any control over men. It has only changed the distribution of women . . . removing vast numbers of women from the class supported by men to the class working for them." Elsie Clews Parsons, *Social Rule,* 1916.

403 "With women as half the country's elected representatives, and a woman President once in a while, the country's *machismo* would be greatly reduced. . . . I'm not saying that women leaders would eliminate violence. We are not more moral than men; we are only uncorrupted by power so far." Gloria Steinem, 1970.

FAMOUS SPEECHES

404 **Jonathan Edwards's "Sinners in the Hands of an Angry God" sermon,** 1741, was preached during the Great Awakening (see number 641) when he assured listeners that only by strict adherence to the Puritan faith could they hope to avoid the eternal tortures of Hell. "There is no want of power in God to cast wicked men into Hell at any moment," he warned. "O sinner! consider the fearful danger you are in; it is a great furnace of wrath, a wide and bottomless pit."

The Reverend Jonathan Edwards. LIBRARY OF CONGRESS.

405 **George Washington's Farewell Address,** 1796, in which he announced his intention to retire at the end of his second term as President and stressed the importance of national unity as the "main pillar" of the nation's independence, peace, and prosperity. He criticized what he called the "baleful effects" of partisan political squabbling and urged the people to avoid both "inveterate antipathies" and "passionate attachments" to any foreign nation.

406 **Thomas Jefferson's First Inaugural Address,** 1801, which contains his famous reference to the United States as "the world's best hope" and his praise of "wise and frugal government, which shall restrain men from injuring one another, [and] shall leave them otherwise free to regulate their own pursuits." Jefferson's electoral victory over John Adams marked the first real change of party control, and made his promise to respect the rights of the Federalist minority seem the most important point in his address.

407 **Daniel Webster's "Second Reply to Hayne,"** 1830, in which he called the American flag "the gorgeous ensign of the republic" and concluded with the sentence—memorized by generations of school children—"Liberty *and* Union, now and forever, one and inseparable." Webster's grandiloquence was much admired by contemporaries, but the speech, delivered during a senatorial debate on states' rights, was actually important because of its powerful refutation of South Carolina Senator Robert Y. Hayne's passionate but confused argument that the separate states were the ultimate repository of sovereignty in the American political system.

408 **Webster's "Seventh of March" speech,** 1850, urging support of the Compromise of 1850 (see number 178) in order to prevent a sectional split over the question of slavery in the territories. "I wish to speak to-day, not as a Massachusetts man, nor as a Northern man, but as an American," he began, and he went on to urge Northerners to accept a stronger fugitive slave law and Southerners to give up all thought of secession. "Peaceable secession! Peaceable secession! . . . Heaven forbid! Where is the flag of the republic to remain? Where is the eagle still to tower!"

Daniel Webster addressing the U.S. Senate in 1850. COURTESY OF THE NEW-YORK HISTORICAL SOCIETY.

409 **Abraham Lincoln's "House Divided" speech,** 1858, delivered on the occasion of his nomination as the Republican candidate for senator from Illinois. This was probably Lincoln's most radical statement about the implications of the slavery question, the one in which he predicted that "this government cannot endure permanently half slave and half free." It got him into a cer-

tain amount of trouble with conservative Northerners, especially when opponents quoted the remark out of context in order to suggest that Lincoln was an abolitionist. Lincoln did not, in this speech or on any other occasion before the Civil War, call for the abolition of slavery.

410 **Lincoln's Gettysburg Address,** 1863, dedicating the National Soldiers' Cemetery at the Gettysburg battlefield. Contrary to legend, Lincoln did not write this famous speech, ending with the words "... that government of the people, by the people, for the people shall not perish from the earth" on the back of an envelope while riding on the train to Gettysburg. He worked out his main theme, that the war was being fought to protect democratic values, before leaving, and he put the words together at the home of his host, David Wills, after arriving at Gettysburg.

411 **Lincoln's Second Inaugural Address,** 1865, which contains the warning that the war might continue "until every drop of blood drawn with the lash, shall be paid by another drawn with the sword," and which closed with the line: "With malice toward none;

with charity for all; with firmness in the right, as God gives us to see the right, let us strive on to finish the work we are in. . . ."

Lincoln spars with Davis, 1865 commentary on the Civil War. COURTESY OF THE NEW-YORK HISTORICAL SOCIETY.

412 **William Jennings Bryan's "Cross of Gold" speech,** 1896, at the Democratic National Convention, which he attended as a delegate from Nebraska. Arguing for a plank in the party platform calling for the free coinage of silver, Bryan stressed the importance of agriculture in the nation's economy (he claimed that grass would grow in the streets of American cities if the farmers' interests continued to be neglected), and he ended with this sentence: "You shall not press down upon the brow of labor this crown of thorns, you shall not crucify mankind upon a cross of gold." The "you" Bryan was referring to was not the Republi-

cans but the Gold Democrats, those supporters of President Grover Cleveland who were opposed to the unlimited coinage of silver. The speech made a national figure of the thirty-six-year-old Bryan and led to his nomination for the presidency by the convention.

Bryan straddles the issues, 1896 cartoon from the *Washington Post.* LIBRARY OF CONGRESS.

413 **Albert J. Beveridge's "March of the Flag" speech,** 1899, an unabashed glorification of imperialism in general and the annexation of the Philippines in particular. At the time of this speech, Beveridge was running for the Senate from Indiana. He traced the territorial expansion of the United States step by step from 1789, when "timid souls" said "no new territory was needed," through Jefferson's purchase of Louisiana, the addition of Florida and Texas, the Mexican War ("the flag swept over the Southwest, over peerless California, past the Golden Gate to Oregon"), and so on, periodically characterizing these events as "the march of the flag," each time to thunderous applause. As a climax he said, "William McKinley plants the flag over the islands of the seas, outposts of commerce, citadels of national security, and the march of the flag goes on."

414 Theodore Roosevelt's "New Nationalism" speech, 1910, was delivered before a group of veterans at Osawatomie, Kansas. Roosevelt had gone to Africa on a hunting trip after completing his second term as President. Upon his return he had been caught up in an intraparty conflict between progressive and conservative Republicans. In this speech, in which he used the slogan "A Square Deal," he denounced "the sinister influence . . . of special interests" and came out in favor of "thoroughgoing and effective regulation" of big business rather than using the antitrust act to break up monopolistic corporations. It marked a turning point in Roosevelt's career—leading to his break with his protégé, William Howard Taft, and eventually to a split in the Republican Party that resulted in the election of Democrat Woodrow Wilson in the 1912 presidential election.

415 Woodrow Wilson's call for a declaration of war against Germany, 1917, which contains the famous line "The world must be made safe for democracy." The speech is remarkable for Wilson's insistence that the American people "have no quarrel with the German people. . . . We fight without rancor and without selfish object." Such forbearance, and Wilson's promise that victory in the conflict would result in "a universal dominion of right," helped win liberal support for the war effort; but of course they also contributed to postwar disillusionment when the President's idealistic hopes were not realized after victory was achieved.

416 Wilson's "Fourteen Points" address to Congress, 1918, outlining his plan for a nonvindictive treaty ending the war. "The day of conquest and aggrandizement is gone by," he announced, and he went on to list fourteen specific peace terms. These included freedom of the seas, an end to secret treaties, a reduction in armaments, national self-determination for all peoples, and "a general association of nations" that would guarantee the "political independence and territorial integrity of great and small states alike."

417 Franklin D. Roosevelt's First Inaugural Address, 1933, remembered for the line, "the only thing we have to fear is fear itself," for Roosevelt's promise "to put people to work," and perhaps for his use of the phrase "good neighbor" when referring to foreign policy. It was an extraordinarily effective speech, but it also contained a good deal of windy political foolishness and a considerable amount of bad advice. For example, the President felt it necessary to point out that "happiness lies not in the mere possession of money"; he promised to balance the federal budget and urged state and local governments to reduce expenditures "drastically." He also claimed that there was an "overbalance of population" in the nation's cities.

418 Franklin D. Roosevelt's "Quarantine" speech, 1937, in which he warned that the "very foundations of civilization" were being threatened by the aggressions of the Fascist powers, and called upon "peace-loving nations" to try to check them. "When an epidemic of physical disease starts to spread, the community approves and joins in a quarantine . . . to protect the health of the community."

Senator Joseph McCarthy packs his briefcase, May 25, 1950.
UPI/ BETTMANN NEWSPHOTOS.

419 Joseph R. McCarthy's speech on Communists in government, 1950, delivered before the Women's Republican Club of Wheeling, West Virginia. McCarthy blamed the State Department for the loss of classified information to the Soviets. He is reported to have said, "I have here in my hand a list of 205—a list of names that were known to the Secretary of State as being members of the Communist Party and who nevertheless are *still working and shaping . . . policy.*" No copy of

what McCarthy actually said on that occasion exists, and he never exposed any actual Communist in the State Department, but the speech made him a national figure and produced the phenomenon known as "McCarthyism."

420 Richard M. Nixon's "Checkers" speech, 1952, delivered during his campaign for the vice presidency, in which he defended having received $18,000 from a group of supporters to defray "political expenses that I did not think should be charged to the taxpayers." After summarizing his personal assets and liabilities and saying that instead of a mink, his wife owned only "a respectable Republican cloth coat," Nixon suggested that a number of Democrats ought to be equally revealing about their finances. He then reminded his listeners that 600 million people "had been lost to the Communists" under President Truman and closed by asking

Nixon and Checkers, 1952.
UPI/ BETTMANN NEWSPHOTOS.

people to let the Republican National Committee know "whether . . . I should stay on or whether I should get off" the ticket. The "Checkers" of the speech was a cocker spaniel given the Nixon children by a man in Texas, about which Nixon said, "Regardless of what they say about it, we're gonna keep it."

421 Martin Luther King's "I have a dream" speech, 1963, delivered before a crowd of 200,000 at the climax of the March on Washington for Jobs and Freedom. King appealed to the better instincts of whites and blacks alike, repeating the quoted phrase time and again, each time describing his aspirations and each time drawing a powerful emotional response from the crowd.

Martin Luther King, Jr., addresses the crowds in Washington, D.C., 1963.
NEW YORK *DAILY NEWS* PHOTO.

AMERICAN UTOPIAS

Between the Revolution and the Civil War, a remarkable

interest in social and religious experimentation developed in the United States. This is not surprising when one recalls that the nation's institutions were still relatively new, its society plastic when compared with that of Europe. It was, after all, a New World, a place where anything could happen. Indeed,

422 **Utopia,** the imaginary island where Sir Thomas More placed the ideal community he created in 1516, was located in the New World, off the coast of South America.

More than a hundred "utopias" were founded in the United States before 1861. Because the country was large and sparsely populated, land was cheap. As a result, much of this experimentation was centered in self-contained communities whose members could put unconventional ideas into practice, in most cases undisturbed by their neighbors. (The communes of the 1960s were superficially similar, but because land was no longer so cheap and open space at a premium, the communes were more likely to have neighbor problems.) Among the most interesting of the early-

nineteenth-century settlements were the

423 **Shaker communities,** the first founded by "Mother" Ann Lee near Albany, New York, in the 1770s. Mother Ann, who had had four stillborn children and who almost died in childbirth, became convinced that "cohabitation of the sexes" was bad business; she and her followers practiced celibacy. (She also believed that the millennium was at hand and that Christ had returned to earth and quite literally resided in her person.) After her death the Shaker movement ex-

A Crown of Fortitude
Mother from Ann.

A Trumpet of Declaration
from
Father Joseph.

panded, becoming a joyful and profoundly emotional religion whose celibate practitioners lived together in harmony and produced the remarkable furniture, simple and beautiful, which is so highly prized today.

424 **Harmony,** founded in western Pennsylvania in 1804 by a German immigrant, George Rapp. The Rappites were also celibate and hardworking. They pooled their wealth and prospered greatly. But "Father" Rapp ruled Harmony with an iron hand—anyone who committed a sin during the day was required to confess to Rapp before going to bed—and he moved the entire community, more or less on a whim, first to Indiana, then back to Pennsylvania. After he died in 1847 the community began to shrink, but it did not finally disappear until 1905. In 1824 Rapp sold the Indiana property for $150,000 to Robert Owen, an English industrialist, who founded

425 **New Harmony,** a socialist community of some nine hundred persons, which was, according to Owen's son, "a heterogeneous collection of radicals . . . honest latitudinarians, and lazy theorists, with a sprinkling of unprincipled sharpers thrown in." Owen's socialist experiment did not work. There was much "grumbling, carping, and murmuring" about members suffering from the "disease of laziness." Owen soon abandoned the community, selling the land to the settlers at bargain prices.

Robert Dale Owen, founder of New Harmony.
THE SMITHSONIAN INSTITUTION.

426 **Nashoba** was established by Frances Wright, a friend of the Owens who was much influenced by the elder Owen's ideas. In 1825 Wright purchased Nashoba, a plantation in Tennessee. She installed there a small group of slaves, her idea being that by living in a friendly, supervised atmosphere they could learn skills and pay off their cost by their labor. They were then to be freed and set up on their own somewhere outside the United

Frances Wright, founder of Nashoba. COURTESY OF THE NEW YORK PUBLIC LIBRARY.

States. The community was a failure, both financially and in its plan for helping the slaves to earn their freedom. Wright freed the slaves anyway and shipped them off to a new life in Haiti. She then settled for a time in New Harmony, where she advocated doing away with the legal institution of marriage, and indeed of monogamy (see number 378). This led to much trouble for her, the least of which was the nickname "Priestess of Beelzebub."

427 **Brook Farm.** Another "Owenite" community, but the antithesis of Wright's Nashoba, was founded in 1841 by well-known Boston transcendentalists led by George Ripley, a Unitarian minister. The residents of Brook Farm sought a "union between intellectual and manual labor." They created a cross between a co-op and a joint stock company, a commu-

nity in which all work was paid for at the same rate and (in theory) members were to earn 5 percent a year on their investments. Things did not work out as planned, but most Brook Farmers appeared to be enjoying themselves. Nathaniel Hawthorne, who owned stock in Brook Farm and lived there briefly, called it "a daydream, and yet a fact."

428 **Hopedale,** another experiment in socialism-*cum*-religion, was founded in Massachusetts by Universalist minister Adin Ballou, at about the same time as Brook Farm. Ballou believed it was literally possible to create the kingdom of heaven on earth. Members of his community, who purchased shares for fifty dollars, were guaranteed work, and all shared equally in what was produced. All members—"irrespective of sex, color, occupation, wealth, rank, or any other natural or adventitious peculiarity"—were treated the same, and all were pledged to oppose "all things known to be sinful against God or human nature." Hopedale grew slowly and by 1853 was a going concern. But by that time two members had bought up nearly all the stock. They decided to liquidate the organization and devote its assets to a conventional Hopedale Manufacturing Company. Without capital the community gradually withered away.

Residents on the grounds of the Oneida Community. AMERICAN ANTIQUARIAN SOCIETY, WORCESTER, MASSACHUSETTS.

429 **Oneida** was founded by John Humphrey Noyes in 1848 in New York. Noyes was a "Perfectionist," one who believed that when once "converted," a person could be free of sin and totally happy. At Oneida he hoped to combine perfectionism with socialism. He invented and practiced "complex marriage," a system where all the men were married to all the women, but he combined it with "male continence"— sexual relations between individuals were supposed to be regulated by the group. Children were raised in community nurseries. Competition of any kind was frowned upon, and stress was placed on all sorts of community activities. Wrongdoers were subjected to "mutual criticism" by a committee

headed by Noyes. Oneida prospered, manufacturing high-quality silverware, and eventually Noyes dropped both socialism and complex marriage. In 1880, Oneida became a corporation.

430 **Nauvoo** was the Illinois community created by the Mormons, the followers of Joseph Smith, in 1839. Smith, who claimed to have discovered and translated a sacred text (the Book of Mormon), was a handsome, outgoing man whose religious ideas encouraged people to enjoy life to the full, but he ruled Nauvoo with an iron hand. The community prospered, but ran into opposition from nearby nonbelievers when Smith instituted "celestial marriage," the practice of polygamy, himself accumulating a very large number of wives. He also created a private army, the Nauvoo Legion, and announced his intention of running for President of the United States. Smith made many enemies in and out of his community, and in 1844 he

President Joseph Smith's family, March 15, 1904.
LIBRARY OF CONGRESS.

was arrested and lynched before he could be brought to trial. The Mormons then entered upon their epic march westward under a new leader, Brigham Young, who brought them to Utah, where they founded Salt Lake City and became by far the most enduring of the ideal communities.

431 **Icaria,** the brainchild of French socialist Étienne Cabet, a man far different from Joseph Smith, took over much of the property of the Mormons in Nauvoo. Cabet, who was much influenced by the Owenites, had written a widely read utopian tale, *Voyage en Icarie,* which won him a wide following in France. He obtained a huge tract of land in Texas, intending to found a community there. Upon reaching New Orleans with several hundred followers, he discovered that the land was too remote for development. He therefore took his group to Nauvoo in 1849. Settling in an already established community, the hard-working Icarians prospered, farming and running various small businesses, including a distillery, though they did not themselves drink. Eventually, however, the group split in two and their communal way of life was abandoned.

PART III
People

FAMOUS FAMILIES

The Constitution provides that "no Title of Nobility shall be granted by the United States," in part out of a general distaste for royalty and its appurtenances and in part, no doubt, to discourage all forms of hereditary privilege. This has not, however, prevented many "dynasties" from developing in America. Here are some of the best known.

The Adamses

432 **Samuel Adams** (1722–1803), organizer of the Sons of Liberty and the Boston Tea Party, signer of the Declaration of Independence, governor of Massachusetts.

Samuel Adams.
CULVER PICTURES, INC.

433 **John Adams** (1735–826), cousin of Samuel, one of the drafters of the Declaration of Independence, a negotiator of the peace treaty ending the Revolution, first Vice President and second President of the United States.

434 **Abigail Smith Adams** (1744–1818), the wife of John, manager of the family properties during long periods when he was away on public business. Popular with modern feminists, especially for having urged John to "remember the ladies" while helping to create the new nation.

Abigail Adams, painting by Benjamin Blyth. MASSACHUSETTS HISTORICAL SOCIETY.

435 **John Quincy Adams** (1767–1848), the son of John and Abigail, diplomat, senator, sixth President of the United States, and, late in life, a member of the House of Representatives.

436 **Charles Francis Adams** (1807–86), the son of J.Q., vice presidential candidate of the Free Soil Party in 1848, congressman, minister to Great Britain during the Civil War, editor of the papers of John and John Quincy.

Charles Francis Adams as depicted in *Vanity Fair*, October 5, 1872. LIBRARY OF CONGRESS.

437 **Charles Francis Adams, Jr.** (1835–1915), the son of Charles, Union officer in Civil War, historian, railroad executive, public official.

438 **Henry Adams** (1838–1918), second son of Charles, Sr., his-

Henry Adams. MASSACHUSETTS HISTORICAL SOCIETY.

torian (see number 530), editor, teacher, novelist, author of *The Education of Henry Adams.*

439 **Brooks Adams** (1848–1927), another son of Charles, Sr., historian, philosopher, professional pessimist.

Brooks Adams, 1870.
HARVARD UNIVERSITY LIBRARY.

There are descendants of these Adamses too numerous to mention, and also an almost unlimited number of unrelated Adamses of some importance, such as:

• Alva Adams (1850–1922), governor of Colorado.
• Charles Adams (c. 1845–95, b. Karl Adam Schwanbeck), Indian agent, minister to Bolivia.
• Charles Kendall Adams (1835–1902), president of Cornell and the University of Wisconsin.
• Henry Carter Adams (1851–1921), economist.

• Herbert Baxter Adams (1850–1901), professor, founder of the American Historical Association.
• John Adams (1947–), composer.
• Maude Adams (1872–1953), actress.
• Sherman Adams (1899–), adviser to President Eisenhower.
• William Wirt Adams (1819–85), Confederate brigadier.

The Harrisons

Another two-President family:

440 **Benjamin Harrison** (1726–91), Virginia planter and politician, member of the Continental Congress, signer of the Declaration of Independence, governor of Virginia.

441 **William Henry Harrison** (1773–1841), the son of Benjamin, army officer, governor of Indiana Territory, hero of the Battle of Tippecanoe (see number 538), and the Battle of the Thames (where Tecumseh fell), congressman, senator, ninth President of the United States.

442 **John Scott Harrison** (1804–78), son of President William Henry Harrison, congress-

man, father of President Benjamin Harrison, the only person to be both the child and the parent of a President.

443 **Carter Henry Harrison** (1825–93), distant cousin of John Scott Harrison, real estate operator, congressman, mayor of Chicago for five terms, assassinated by a disappointed office seeker.

Carter Henry Harrison.
CULVER PICTURES, INC.

444 **Benjamin Harrison** (1833–1901), son of John Scott Harrison, a Civil War brigadier general, lawyer, senator, twenty-second President of the United States.

Benjamin Harrison with his daughter and grandchildren.
BENJAMIN HARRISON HOME.

445 **Carter Henry Harrison, Jr.,** (1860–1953), son of Carter Henry Harrison and, like his father, a five-term mayor of Chicago.

446 **William Henry Harrison** (1896–1962), four-term congressman from Wyoming in the 1950s and early 1960s.

As with the Adamses, there are also many important unrelated Harrisons, such as:

- Constance Cary Harrison (1843–1920), novelist, playwright.
- Gabriel Harrison (1818–1902), actor.
- George Paul Harrison (1841–1922), Confederate brigadier general, congressman.
- Henry Baldwin Harrison (1821–1901), governor of Connecticut.
- Peter Harrison (1716–75), architect.

The Emory Harrisons and sons, 1955. UPI/BETTMANN NEWSPHOTOS.

The third and so far the only other family to produce two Presidents is

The Roosevelts

447 **Theodore Roosevelt** (1831–1919), historian, rancher, soldier, assistant secretary of the Navy, governor of New York, Vice President, and twenty-fourth President of the United States.

Theodore Roosevelt and grandchild. AMERICAN MUSEUM OF NATURAL HISTORY.

448 **Alice Roosevelt Longworth** (1869–1931), daughter of Theodore, wife of Congressman Nicholas Longworth, longtime observer and commentator on Washington social and political affairs (see number 152).

449 **Franklin Delano Roosevelt** (1882–1945), distant cousin of Theodore, assistant secretary of the Navy, governor of New York, four-term

President of the United States.

Franklin Delano Roosevelt, 1937. UPI/BETTMANN NEWSPHOTOS, COURTESY OF FRANKLIN D. ROOSEVELT LIBRARY

450 **Anna Eleanor Roosevelt Roosevelt** (1884–1962), niece of Theodore, wife of Franklin, social worker, columnist, delegate to the United Nations, human rights activist.

Anna Eleanor Roosevelt. LIBRARY OF CONGRESS.

451 **Theodore Roosevelt, Jr.** (1887–1944), son of Theodore, assistant secretary of the Navy, soldier in both World Wars, governor of Puerto Rico, governor general of the Philippines.

452 **James Roosevelt** (1907–), son of Franklin and Anna Eleanor, congressman, member of the UN Economic and Social Council.

453 **Elliot Roosevelt** (1910–), son of Franklin and Anna Eleanor, mayor of Miami Beach, Florida.

454 **Franklin Delano Roosevelt, Jr.** (1914–1988), son of Franklin and Anna Eleanor, congressman, undersecretary of Commerce.

Here are some other American dynasties:

The Fishes

455 **Nicholas Fish** (1758–1833), Revolutionary War soldier, public official, unsuccessful Federalist candidate for the House of Representatives and for lieutenant governor of New York, named his eldest son after his friend and wartime comrade, Alexander Hamilton, little knowing what he was beginning.

456 **Hamilton Fish** (1808–93), Whig congressman from New York, lieutenant governor and governor of New York, United States senator, Secretary of State under President Grant. He named his son

457 **Hamilton Fish** (1849–1936). This Hamilton Fish served as speaker of the New York Assembly, Republican congressman from New York, assistant treasurer of the United States. He named his son

458 **Hamilton Fish, Jr.** (1888–). The first Hamilton Fish, Jr., was a twelve-term Republican congressman from New York, noted pre–World War II isolationist, prominent anti-Communist. He named his son

459 **Hamilton Fish, Jr.** (1926–). The second Hamilton Fish, Jr., is a ten-term (so far) Republican congressman from New York. He named his son

Hamilton Fish, 1941.
WIDE WORLD PHOTO.

460 **Hamilton Fish III** (1951–). He has been publisher of *The Nation* since 1978 and is a Democrat.

The Rockefellers

461 **John D. Rockefeller** (1839–1937), organizer of the Standard Oil trust, founder of the University of Chicago, billionaire, *bête noire* of Henry Demarest Lloyd (see number 799) and other antimonopolists. Also founder of the Rockefeller Institute for Medical Research, the Rockefeller Foundation "to promote the well-being of mankind," and other charitable organizations, and long-time Baptist Sunday school superintendent of Cleveland.

John D. Rockefeller, 1937.
WIDE WORLD PHOTOS.

462 **William Rockefeller** (1841–1922), brother of John D., oilman, Wall Street promoter, founder of the National City Bank, public utility magnate, and railroad man, *bon vivant.*

463 **John D. Rockefeller, Jr.** (1874–

1960), son of John D., founder of Rockefeller University and the Cloisters Museum, builder of Riverside Church and Rockefeller Center in New York City, restorer of Colonial Williamsburg and other historic sites, contributor of the property on which the United Nations headquarters is located, teetotaller.

John D. Rockefeller, Jr.
CULVER PICTURES, INC.

464 **Abby Aldrich Rockefeller** (1874–1948), the wife of John D., Jr., and daughter of Senator Nelson Aldrich of Rhode Island; benefactor and one of the founders of the Museum of Modern Art.

465 **John D. Rockefeller III** (1906–78), son of John D., Jr., president of the Rockefeller Brothers Fund, Lincoln Center for the Performing Arts, and the Asia Society.

466 **Blanchette Hooker Rockefeller** (1909–), wife of John D. III, art collector, president of the Museum of Modern Art.

Abby Aldrich Rockefeller and Blanchette Hooker Rockefeller.
UPI/BETTMANN NEWSPHOTOS.

Nelson Aldrich Rockefeller.
UPI/BETTMANN NEWSPHOTOS

467 **Nelson Aldrich Rockefeller** (1908–79), son of John D., Jr., coordinator of the Office of Inter-American Affairs, assistant secretary of state, undersecretary in the Department of Health, Education, and Welfare, four-term Republican governor of New York, Vice President of the United States.

468 **Laurance S. Rockefeller** (1910–), son of John D., Jr., and Abby, philanthropist, businessman, conservationist.

469 **Winthrop Rockefeller** (1912–73), son of John D., Jr., and Abby, Republican governor of Arkansas, closely involved in development of Colonial Williamsburg.

470 **David Rockefeller** (1915–), son of John D., Jr., and Abby, international banker, chairman of Chase Manhattan Bank, philanthropist, public official.

471 **John D. Rockefeller IV** (1937–), son of John D. III and Blanchette, Democratic governor of West Virginia, diplomat.

John D. Rockefeller IV.
UPI/BETTMANN NEWSPHOTOS.

472 **Michael Rockefeller** (1938–61?), son of Nelson. An anthropologist, he disappeared while on a field trip in New Guinea.

The Longs

473 **Huey P. Long** (1893–1935) was known as "the Kingfish." Louisiana railroad commissioner and public service commissioner, governor of Louisiana, United States senator; assassinated (see numbers 130, 245).

Senator Huey P. Long and Rose M. Long, 1934.
WIDE WORLD PHOTOS.

474 **Rose M. Long** (c.1892–1958), the wife of Huey, United States senator, filling the vacancy created by Huey's assassination.

475 **George S. Long** (1883–1958), the brother of Huey, member of the Oklahoma state legisla-ture, United States congressman.

476 **Earl K. Long** (1895–1960), the brother of Huey and George, lieutenant governor of Louisiana, governor of Louisiana for three terms. Mentally unbalanced in his later years.

Earl K. Long. WIDE WORLD PHOTOS.

477 **Blanche R. Long** (1904–), wife of Earl, member Louisiana State Tax Commission, Democratic National Committee member from Louisiana.

478 **Russell B. Long** (1918–), son of Huey, United States senator from Louisiana for eight terms.

479 **Gillis W. Long** (1923–85), cousin of Russell, United States congressman from Louisiana for seven terms.

480 **Speedy O. Long** (1928–) was so called because he was born more than two months prematurely, cousin of Russell and Gillis, congressman from Louisiana for five terms.

Speedy O. Long.
WIDE WORLD PHOTOS.

The Johnsons

If it is difficult to keep the famous and near-famous members of the Adamses and other such families straight, the famous people named Johnson are even more difficult to master. Neither of the two President Johnsons, Andrew (1808–75) and Lyndon (1908–73), nor any of the following is related to *any* of the others:

481 **Sir William Johnson** (1715–74), soldier, Indian agent and advisor.

482 William Johnson (1771–1834), U.S. Supreme Court justice.

483 Richard Mentor Johnson (1780–1850), congressman, soldier (said to have dispatched Tecumseh at the Battle of the Thames), Vice President of the United States under Martin Van Buren.

484 Eastman Johnson (1824–1906), artist, painter of portraits and of genre scenes such as "Old Kentucky Home."

Eastman Johnson, self-portrait. COURTESY OF THE MUSEUM OF FINE ARTS, BOSTON, EMILY L. AINSLEY FUND.

485 Tom Loftin Johnson (1854–1911), street railroad magnate, municipal reformer, four-term mayor of Cleveland.

486 Byron "Ban" Johnson (1864–1931), founder and president of the American League, organizer of baseball's World Series.

487 Hiram W. Johnson (1866–1945), reformer, governor of California, United States senator.

488 James Weldon Johnson (1871–1938), poet, editor, diplomat, author of *The Autobiography of an Ex-Colored Man.*

James Weldon Johnson. COURTESY OF YALE UNIVERSITY LIBRARY.

489 Jack A. Johnson (1878–1946), the first black heavyweight boxing champion of the world.

Jack Johnson. LIBRARY OF CONGRESS.

490 Hugh S. Johnson (1882–1942), an army officer, businessman, troubleshooter, administrator of the New Deal's National Recovery Administration (NRA). Sometimes known as "Old Ironpants."

491 Walter Johnson (1887–1946), big league pitcher, winner of 414 games, charter member of the Baseball Hall of Fame.

There were also numerous "Johnstons" (see numbers 879, 880), but we won't go into that here.

The Joneses

Considering how many people bear the name, there is no Jones "dynasty," and even unrelated famous Joneses are rather rare. There is, of course,

John Paul Jones, painting by C. W. Peale. INDEPENDENCE NATIONAL HISTORICAL COLLECTION.

492 John Paul Jones (1747–92) was the sailor, whose *Bon Homme*

Richard (see number 896) defeated HMS *Serapis* in a mighty battle during the Revolution, but he was not a real Jones, having been born John Paul. He added Jones to his name in 1773, after having killed an unruly sailor in Tobago, an affair which compelled him to "remain incog-[nito]" for some time.

Of the "real" Joneses, here are the most historically significant:

493 **Mary Harris "Mother" Jones** (1830–1930), radical labor leader.

Mary Harris "Mother" Jones.
CULVER PICTURES, INC.

494 **Samuel M. "Golden Rule" Jones** (1846–1904), mayor of Toledo, Ohio, an important Progressive Era reformer.

495 **Jesse Holman Jones** (1874–1956), head of the Reconstruction Finance Corpora-tion and sometime Secretary of Commerce under Franklin Roosevelt.

496 **Robert Tyre "Bobby" Jones, Jr.,** (1902–1971), grand-slam golfer, founder of the Masters' Tournament.

Robert Tyre Jones, Jr.
UNITED STATES GOLF ASSOCIATION.

497 **James Jones** (1921–77), novel-ist, author of *From Here to Eternity.*

498 **Lindley "Spike" Jones** (1911–65), the band leader best known for his raucous spoof of Adolf Hitler, "Der Führer's Face."

The Smiths

There has been no Smith "dynasty" either, but a fair number of important people have borne that name. Consider:

499 **John Smith** (c. 1579–1631), the fabulous adventurer, hard-nosed savior of the colony of Jamestown, himself saved by the equally fabulous Indian princess Pocahontas.

Captain John Smith.
CULVER PICTURES, INC.

500 **Sophia Smith** (1796–1870), founder of Smith College.

Sophia Smith.
SMITH COLLEGE ARCHIVES.

501 **Gerrit Smith** (1797–1874), philanthropist, supporter of votes for women, prison reform, temperance, Irish independence, and the abolition of slavery, in the last of which causes he helped finance John Brown's raid on Harpers Ferry.

Gerrit Smith.
CULVER PICTURES, INC.

502 **Joseph Smith** (1805–44), creator of the Mormon religion, author or discoverer (as you will have it) of the Book of Mormon, ruler—until he was assassinated—of the Mormon community of Nauvoo, Illinois (see number 430).

503 **James Smith** (1851–1927), Democratic boss of New Jersey who recognized the talents of Woodrow Wilson and, by arranging for his nomination for governor of New Jersey in 1910, put him on the road to the White House. Smith lived to regret his action.

504 **Alfred Emanuel Smith** (1873–1944), four-term governor of New York, Democratic candidate for President in 1928, who performed a somewhat similar role in the career of Franklin Roosevelt, with a similar result.

505 **Preserved Smith** (1880–1941), historian, author of major biographies of Martin Luther and Erasmus and of the still-read *Age of the Reformation* (1920).

506 **Bessie Smith** (1894–1937) was a blues singer extraordinary.

Bessie Smith, 1925.
CULVER PICTURES, INC.

507 **Walter Bedell Smith** (1895–1961), chief of staff of General Eisenhower in World War II, Truman's ambassador to the Soviet Union, director of the CIA.

508 **Gerald L. K. Smith** (1898–1976), minister, orator, Depression-era radical who said that everyone should have "a real spending money, beefsteak and gravy, Chevrolet, Ford in the garage, new suit, Thomas Jefferson, Jesus Christ, red, white, and blue job." Later he became a fascist.

509 **David Smith** (1906–65), sculptor, considered by many authorities to be the finest American sculptor of this century.

510 **Horton Smith** (1908–63), golfer, winner of the first and third Masters' and of countless other tournaments.

ASSASSINS

511 **John Wilkes Booth** shot Abraham Lincoln in Washington, D.C.'s Ford's Theater in April 1865. Booth was a rabid Confederate sympathizer who believed that slavery was "one of the greatest blessings . . . that God ever bestowed upon a favored nation."

Photo of John Wilkes Booth.
COLLECTION OF FREDERICK HILL MESERVE.

512 **Charles J. Guiteau** shot President James A. Garfield at Union Station in Washington, D.C., in July 1881—not, as has often been claimed, because he was a disappointed office seeker, but on the order (he insisted) of "the Deity." Guiteau had, however, been seeking a State Department post, and he was an admirer of New York Senator Roscoe Conkling, leader of the Stalwart faction (see number 98), who had clashed with Garfield over patronage questions.

513 **Leon F. Czolgosz,** an anarchist, shot William McKinley in 1901 while McKinley was shaking hands on a reception line at the Pan-American Exposi-

tion in Buffalo. Czolgosz claimed to be against all government and said, "I didn't believe one man should have so much services and another man should have none." It is almost certain that neither Garfield nor McKinley would have died of their wounds had modern medical techniques been available.

514 **John F. Schrank** shot Theodore Roosevelt as the latter was leaving a hotel in Milwaukee on his way to make a speech during the 1912 presidential campaign. Though fired at point-blank range, the bullet passed through a folded copy of Roosevelt's hour-long speech and his glasses case before lodging just short of his lung. (If he had been less long-winded, he might well have been killed.) Roosevelt insisted on going ahead with his speech before being taken to a hospital. He also insisted that Schrank was not insane, since Schrank had shot him in a state that had no death penalty. "I may gravely question," Roosevelt later wrote an English friend, "if he had a more unsound brain than Senator La Follette or Eugene Debs." In fact, Schrank was clearly psychotic. He claimed that the ghost of William McKinley had told him that he had been assassinated by Roosevelt and

asked him "to avenge my death."

515 **Joseph Zangara** attempted to shoot Franklin D. Roosevelt during a Miami political rally in February 1933, two weeks before Roosevelt's inauguration. He missed, but the bullet mortally wounded Mayor Anton J. Cermak of Chicago, who was standing beside Roosevelt at the rally. "I do not hate Mr. Roosevelt personally," Zangara explained. "I hate all Presidents, no matter what country they come from, and I hate all officials and everybody who is rich."

Joseph Zangara arrested in Miami in 1933.
WIDE WORLD PHOTOS.

516 **Dr. Carl A. Weiss** shot and killed Senator Huey P. Long of Louisiana in the state capitol at Baton Rouge on September 8, 1935. Weiss was immediately gunned down by Long's bodyguards—his

head and body were literally riddled with bullets—so he made no statement about his reason for shooting Long. He was a son-in-law of an anti-Long judge whose election district had just been gerrymandered, but Long's biographer, T. Harry Williams, concluded that "Weiss was a sincere and idealistic young man who agonized over the evils he believed Huey Long was inflicting on his class and his state. . . . He was willing to be a martyr."

517 **Oscar Collazo and Griselio Torresola** attempted to shoot their way into Blair House in Washington, D.C., where President Harry S Truman was staying, in November 1950. In an exchange of fire with guards, Torresola and one guard were killed. Collazo was wounded, but recovered. The attackers were Puerto Rican nationalists, and Collazo claimed that they hoped by the attack "to awake an American public essentially ignorant of the situation in Puerto Rico." They expected that a revolution might break out in America if Truman were killed and that one result might be Puerto Rican independence.

518 **Lee Harvey Oswald**'s motive for shooting John F. Kennedy in 1963 cannot be determined; nor for that matter can his responsibility for the murder be settled beyond question, since he was himself killed by one Jack Ruby before he could be brought to trial.

Lee Harvey Oswald in the custody of the Dallas police, November 22, 1963.
WIDE WORLD PHOTOS.

519 **Sirhan B. Sirhan** shot and killed presidential candidate Robert F. Kennedy in a Los Angeles hotel in 1968 because of Kennedy's outspoken support of Israel. Sirhan, a Jordanian who had been born in Jerusalem, had begun to think of killing Kennedy even before the New York senator entered the 1968 presidential campaign. Sirhan was convicted of murder and sentenced to death, but the sentence was reduced to life imprisonment when the Supreme Court declared capital punishment laws unconstitutional.

520 **John W. Hinckley, Jr.,** shot and seriously wounded Ronald Reagan and three members of his party in March 1981 outside a Washington, D.C., hotel because Hinckley wished to impress Jodie Foster, an actress for whom he had developed a secret passion after seeing her in a movie. The day of the shooting he wrote, but did not mail, a letter to her, saying, "The reason I'm going ahead with this attempt now is because I just cannot wait any longer to impress you." Hinckley, who was acquitted on the grounds of insanity, is also alleged to have told someone in Texas that "as far as he was concerned, [all] politicians should be eliminated."

FAMOUS BLACK LEADERS AND "TROUBLEMAKERS"

During their lifetimes, the following important blacks were looked upon by most white people as no less menacing than the most heartless of assassins. With one exception, duly noted below, none of these "troublemakers" ever killed anyone. On the contrary, all of them were, and are recognized by modern scholars to have been, dedicated fighters for racial equality.

521 Paul Cuffe (1759–1817), was a self-made merchant sailor. Although he was the first American black to achieve substantial wealth, he nevertheless became convinced that only by getting out of the country could black people hope to achieve a decent existence. He became the first American black nationalist, and in 1815 he transported a group of American blacks to Sierra Leone, in Africa. As his biographer says, "American racism forced him to accept the racist doctrine of separation as the ultimate solution."

522 Denmark Vesey (1767–1822), a slave who purchased his freedom after winning a lottery, organized an elaborate uprising among South Carolina slaves. However, the authorities got wind of the scheme when some of the conspirators lost their nerve, and Vesey and thirty-five other blacks were hanged, despite the fact that no actual uprising had taken place.

523 Sojourner Truth (1797–1883) was a leading black abolitionist in the decades before the Civil War, unusual in that she campaigned for women's rights as well as for the ending of slavery (see number 391).

1861 woodcut depicting the discovery of the fugitive Nat Turner. LIBRARY OF CONGRESS.

524 Nat Turner (1800–31) really was a troublemaker for whites. Turner, a Virginia slave, was a deeply religious person who believed that he had "been ordained for some great purpose by the Almighty." Assuming that he had a divine mission to destroy the institution of slavery, he and a group of his followers, striking without warning, murdered more than fifty whites before being captured and executed.

525 Frederick Douglass (1817–95), a Baltimore slave, escaped to New York on a ship in 1838. He became an abolitionist

Frederick Douglass is flanked by Hiram R. Revels and Blanche K. Bruce in lithograph commemorating black leaders. CULVER PICTURES, INC.

and developed an extraordinary ability as a speaker. He published an abolitionist paper, the *North Star*. During the Civil War he helped raise black regiments and in later life continued to campaign for full equality for blacks and other disadvantaged groups.

526 Marcus M. Garvey (1887–1940), an ardent black nationalist, founded the Universal Negro Improvement Association. By the mid-1920s the association had nearly a million members and Garvey had created the Black Star Steamship Line and other all-black businesses. He hoped to establish an independent black nation in Africa, the success of which would compel whites to accept blacks as equals. He was a poor businessman, however. His companies failed, and eventually he was deported to his native Jamaica.

Marcus Garvey en route to a rally, 1921.
UPI/BETTMANN NEWSPHOTOS

527 **Malcolm X** (1925–65), born Malcolm Little, was a "hustler" who was converted to the Black Muslim movement while in prison. He became one of the most radical Muslim critics of white America, a black nationalist who opposed integration of any sort on the ground that all white people were devils. He began to moderate his position after extensive travels in Asia and Africa. His career was cut short when he was assassinated by Black Muslims after he had begun to criticize other Muslim leaders.

Malcolm X speaks out for integration, 1963.
UPI/BETTMANN NEWSPHOTOS.

GREAT HISTORIANS

528 **George Bancroft,** because his ten-volume *History of the United States* (1834–74)—based on archives in America and Europe—was the first detailed account of the period from the founding of the colonies to the end of the Revolution. Bancroft was also an important public official, serving as Secretary of the Navy and minister to Great Britain in the Polk Administration and minister to Prussia after the American Civil War.

George Bancroft, Brady photograph. LIBRARY OF CONGRESS.

529 **Francis Parkman,** because his multivolume history of France's exploration and colonization of North America and of the Franco-British struggle for control of the continent (1851–92) is one of the most gripping narrative histories in the English language. Although Parkman had many prejudices (he considered Indians untrustworthy savages and Catholics by nature undemocratic), his enormous work, completed despite years of fragile health and near blindness, is both beautifully written and factually accurate.

530 **Henry Adams** (one of *the* Adamses, see number 438), because his *History of the United States during the Administrations of Jefferson and Madison* (1889–91) is still a major source for the period. In addition, Adams taught at Harvard, where he sponsored the first history Ph.D.'s granted by the university, and wrote other important works of history, two novels, and his autobiography, *The Education of Henry Adams* (1918).

Frederick Jackson Turner, 1906.
HENRY E. HUNTINGTON LIBRARY AND ART GALLERY.

531 **Frederick Jackson Turner,** because his essay "The Significance of the Frontier in American History" (1893), which stressed the way the frontier experience had affected American development, was a major influence on the writing of all American history for more than half a century.

532 **Charles A. Beard,** because his controversial *An Economic Interpretation of the Constitution* (1913) put an end to the view of the Founding Fathers as demigods by emphasizing that the Constitution they created benefited them financially. Beard is also important because his *Rise of American Civilization* (1927), written with his wife Mary, provided a gripping narrative account of American development that stressed economic, intellectual, and social aspects of the subject.

Allan Nevins.
LOS ANGELES TIMES PHOTO.

533 **Allan Nevins,** because besides training more than a hundred

Ph.D.'s and writing dozens of excellent historical works —which won him two Pulitzer prizes, a National Book Award, and numerous other honors—he was a lifelong advocate of the writing of good popular history.

534 **Samuel Eliot Morison,** because of the universal elegance of his many important books, ranging from his volumes on the great explorers (most notably *Admiral of the Ocean Sea,* his life of Columbus), through his *Maritime History of Massachusetts* and his biographies of John Paul Jones (see number 492) and Matthew Calbraith Perry, to his fifteen-volume *History of U.S. Naval Operations in World War II.* Besides these works dealing with the sea, Morison wrote an influential textbook, the *Oxford History of the United States,* as well as a history of Harvard (his alma mater) and many other books.

IMPORTANT INDIANS

535 **Pocahontas** (c.1596–1617) While she is famous because of her role in saving the life of John Smith, Pocahontas is more important as the wife of John Rolfe, the person who introduced the cultivation of tobacco in Virginia.

By her marriage and by her conversion to Christianity, she helped preserve peace between the colonists and the local Indians. In 1616, Rolfe took her to England, where people saw in her evidence that the New World could be "civilized" and made a welcoming place for settlers.

Pocahontas intercedes for
Captain Smith.
CULVER PICTURES, INC.

536 **Squanto** (?–1622). According to the leader of the Pilgrims, William Bradford, Squanto was "a spetiall instrument sent by God for their good beyond their expectation." He had been kidnapped and taken to Europe in 1615 by an early explorer. There he learned English. Later he returned to America as pilot of a ship and decided to remain in his native land. Squanto was indeed a godsend for the Pilgrims. As Bradford explained, "he directed them how to set their corne, wher to take fish . . . and was also their pilott to bring them to unknowne places for their profitt, and never left them till he dyed."

537 Pontiac (c. 1720–69). Pontiac, chief of the Ottawa, sometimes called "the Indian Hannibal," had been a minor thorn in the side of the British in the Ohio Valley during the French and Indian War. After the war, however, Pontiac—whose intelligence was of a high order, and who was a brilliant orator—organized what whites called a "conspiracy" (1763–64) in a desperate attempt to drive white settlers back across the Appalachians. "We must exterminate from our land this nation whose only object is our death," he announced at a great Indian gathering near Detroit. He won some early victories, but in the end his forces were worn down by sheer numbers, and in 1766 he finally made peace with the British.

538 Tecumseh (1768–1813). This Shawnee chief organized what was probably the most formidable Indian military alliance of American history. A truly charismatic leader (General William Henry Harrison called him "one of

those uncommon geniuses who spring up occasionally to produce revolutions"), Tecumseh roused nearly all the tribes east of the Mississippi in a campaign to drive back the whites and to expunge all signs of their civilization from Indian culture (see number 278). His force was defeated by Harrison at the Battle of Tippecanoe (see number 56) in 1811. Two years later, at the Battle of the Thames, Tecumseh was killed.

539 Tenskwatawa (1768–c.1834). "The Prophet" (also sometimes called "the Open Door"), an Indian religious leader, was Tecumseh's brother. He claimed to see visions, burned rivals as witches, and practiced mystic rites which won him a wide following. Like Tecumseh, the Prophet urged the Indians to give up alcohol, European tools and clothing, and to return to their traditional way of life. He was also, however, headstrong and a poor soldier. It was he who precipitated the disastrous Battle of Tippecanoe, despite the fact that Tecumseh, who was absent at the time, had warned him not to engage in battle with the whites.

540 Sequoyah (c. 1770–1843), a

Cherokee craftsman who had been crippled in a hunting accident, developed a written alphabet or "syllubulary" for the Cherokee language, which enabled many Cherokee speakers to learn to read and write.

Sequoyah poses with his Cherokee syllabary for Charles Bird King's lithograph. ARCHIVES AND MANUSCRIPT DIVISION OF THE OKLAHOMA HISTORICAL SOCIETY.

541 Sacagawea (c. 1786–1812) was the wife of a Canadian who lived with the Hidatsa Indians in what is now North Dakota. In 1805, the Lewis and Clark expedition hired her husband as an interpreter, and she served as an interpreter and informal ambassador to the Shoshone and other tribes as the explorers made their way through the Rocky Mountain wilderness. Her role was romanticized and much exaggerated in later years, but, together with Pocahontas, she is probably the best known of all Indian women.

542 Black Hawk (1767–1838). This

Sauk chief believed, probably correctly, that his tribe had been tricked by the whites into surrendering their lands east of the Mississippi. He joined in the confederation organized by Tecumseh and participated in many battles during the War of 1812. In 1831, he organized a new Indian confederation and attempted to invade his old homeland in Illinois from Iowa. The resulting Black Hawk War was a minor affair that ended with Black Hawk's capture in August 1832. He was taken to Washington, D.C., held in prison briefly, and then returned to Iowa, where he passed the rest of his days uneventfully. The Black Hawk War is probably best known because Abraham Lincoln, then an aspiring politician, served in it as a captain of volunteers. The closest Lincoln saw of combat, however, was when he came across the bodies of five whites who had been killed and scalped in a skirmish.

543 Sitting Bull

(c. 1834–90). Although famous as the victor (along with Crazy Horse and Rain-in-the-Face) in the Battle of the Little Big Horn (see number 939), the Sioux Chief Sitting Bull should better be remembered for his uncompromising opposition to the "assimilationists,"

those who sought to convert Indians to the ways of the whites. For this reason he was enormously popular among the tribes. Because white Americans were eager to see the leader of the men who had annihilated an entire army unit, in 1885, he spent some time touring with Buffalo Bill's Wild West Show, drawing huge crowds. But Sitting Bull never changed his attitude. "I hate all the white people," he said on one occasion. "You are thieves and liars. You have taken away our land and made us outcasts."

Sitting Bull. CULVER PICTURES, INC.

544 Joseph

(c. 1840–1904). As a warrior, this Nez Percé chief was more of a strategist than he was a fighter; indeed, he sought to avoid conflicts with the whites. But in 1877, when the Nez Percé were ordered to move from their homeland to a small reservation in Idaho, some

Chief Joseph (center) is photographed with friends.
COURTESY OF LAWRENCE E. GICHNER.

of his warriors rebelled and killed a number of whites. Facing overwhelming numbers, Joseph sought to escape with his people across a thousand miles of wilderness to Canada, where Sitting Bull had taken refuge after the Battle of the Little Big Horn. He executed a series of brilliant maneuvers, repeatedly avoiding capture by the army units that pursued them. But he was finally forced to surrender. As he turned over his gun to General O. O. Howard, he made a now-famous speech. "I am tired of fighting," he said. "It is cold and we have no blankets. . . . Hear me, my chiefs! I am tired; my heart is sick and sad. From where the sun now stands, I will fight no more."

545 Geronimo

(c. 1829–1909).

Goyathlay, called by the Mexicans Geronimo (Jerome), was a Chiricahua Apache. His story, like so many of these others, involved resistance to white pressure. When the Chiricahuas were ordered in 1876 to move from their lands in Arizona to a reservation in New Mexico, he and a number of others fled instead to Mexico, where they lived by stealing livestock, which they sold in the United States. Over the next years, he was in and out of trouble with the American authorities. Then, in 1885, he conducted a series of bloody raids on both sides of the border. He was finally captured in Arizona in September 1886. Eventually he abandoned his efforts to destroy the whites, joined the Dutch Reformed Church, and spent much of his last years, like Sitting Bull, as an attraction at various public events. One of the greatest of Indian guerrilla warriors, Geronimo was, in the historian Alvin Josephy's words, "the last of all the Indian patriots. . . . Dearest to them were their freedom and their attachment to their land."

Geronimo. THE NATIONAL ARCHIVES.

FAMOUS INDISCRETIONS

This is the Place to affix the STAMP.

Pennsylvania Journal **of 1765 reacts to the Stamp Act.** LIBRARY OF CONGRESS.

546 **The Stamp Act,** passed by Parliament in 1765 at the instigation of Prime Minister George Grenville. Grenville assumed that taxing colonial legal documents, newspapers, playing cards, and other kinds of printed matter would be a painless way to meet "the expenses of defending, protecting, and securing" the American colonies. Instead, the act resulted in widespread indignation, rioting, and the adamant refusal of the public to buy or use the stamps. Taxation without representation, the colonists insisted, was tyranny.

547 **The Declaratory Act,** passed by Parliament in 1766 at the same time that the unenforceable Stamp Act was repealed. This law "declared" that the colonies were "subordinate" to Great Britain and that Parliament "had, hath, and of right ought to have, full power and authority to make laws . . . to bind the colonies and people of *America,* subjects of the crown of *Great Britain,* in all cases whatsoever." Since it had just been demonstrated that Parliament did not have such power, the law served no useful purpose and further angered the Americans.

British criticism of inflammatory colonial policy, *Westminster Magazine,* **December 1774.** THE BRITISH MUSEUM.

548 **Lord North's decision** to retain the tax on tea imported into the colonies. The Tea Act of 1773, designed to aid the financially troubled British East India Company, made tea much cheaper in America by eliminating both the British tea tax and most of the middlemen involved in importing tea. Company officials asked North to have the American tax removed as well, because the Americans were boycotting tea because they objected in principle to being taxed by Parliament. But Lord North insisted on keeping the tax in order to preserve a principle of his own: that Parliament had the right to tax the colonies without their consent. He thought that Americans would swallow their principle in order to get the tea at a bargain price. The result was the Boston Tea Party, and soon thereafter the outbreak of the Revolution.

Broadside of 1773.
LIBRARY OF CONGRESS.

Edmond Charles Genet.
LIBRARY OF CONGRESS.

549 **Citizen Genet's flouting of Washington's proclamation of neutrality** in the war raging in Europe, 1794. Edmond Charles Genet, the first French minister to the United States, attempted to outfit privateers in America to attack British shipping and to organize attacks on Spanish possessions in North America. There was wide popular support in the United States for France after the outbreak of the French Revolution and the deposition of King Louis XVI, and Genet, who was a most attractive young man, was received in America enthusiastically. This turned his head. When Washington ordered him to cease outfitting privateers, he appealed to public opinion over the President's head and continued his nonneutral activities. Washington was furious and demanded his recall, which action the public accepted without a murmur.

The French Government had moved further to the left, and Genet's replacement arrived with orders for his arrest. Genet, who was intelligent, an ardent admirer of America, and an adaptable person, decided to stay where he was. He bought a farm on Long Island, married the daughter of the governor, George Clinton, and became an American citizen. Thus despite his indiscretion, all turned out well for him.

550 **The Mazzei Letter,** written by Thomas Jefferson to Philip Mazzei, an Italian friend, in 1796. In the letter Jefferson criticized the Federalists in a way that ex-President George Washington found personally offensive when the letter was published in America in 1797. As Genet had discovered a few years earlier, it was politically disadvantageous to displease George Washington.

551 **Thomas Jefferson's decision** to ask Congress to pass the Embargo Act, 1807. This law made it illegal for American ships to sail to foreign ports and allowed foreign vessels to clear American ports only if empty. Jefferson believed this would put an end to the impressment of American seamen (see number 15) and compel Great Britain and France, which were at war, to agree to stop violating the rights of neutral vessels on the high seas. The law had little effect on the Europeans, but in the United States it caused great economic damage, was extremely unpopular, and was widely violated. It was repealed in 1809.

552 **The Hammet Letter** was written by Martin Van Buren to Congressman William H. Hammet of Mississippi in 1844. Hammet had asked Van Buren if he favored the annexation of the Republic of Texas. In his answer, which he released to the press, Van Buren, who had previously agreed with the probable Whig presidential candidate, Henry Clay, to try to keep the Texas question out of the campaign, expressed the opinion that annexation would lead to war with Mexico and that he was, therefore, opposed to taking Texas until Mexico's consent was obtained. This policy angered many southern Democrats and cost Van Buren the presidential nomination at the 1844 Democratic National Convention. However, it did Clay no good, because in

553 **The Raleigh Letter,** published the

same day as the Hammet Letter, Clay took the same position, hedging only to the extent that he said he opposed annexation "at this time." After he was nominated by the Whigs, Clay published two

554 **Alabama Letters,** one saying he had no personal objection to annexation, the second that he would be glad to see Texas annexed if it could be accomplished peaceably. These remarks alienated both pro- and antiannexation factions and contributed to the election of the Democrat, James K. Polk.

555 **The Fugitive Slave Act,** 1850. Since relatively few slaves ever escaped (most of those that did came from border states where slavery was relatively unimportant), and since a fugitive slave act was already on the books, this part of the Compromise of 1850 (see number 407) was of almost no benefit to slave owners. But the law was extremely harsh. It authorized federal marshals to compel "bystanders" to join in posses to hunt down fugitives, denied arrested blacks the right to testify in their own defense, and provided that fugitives could be sent back to the South without a jury trial. Northern opposi-

tion was so great that the law was extremely difficult to enforce—only about three hundred slaves were returned to their owners between 1850 and the secession of the southern states in 1860–61. Its chief result was to increase intersectional bad feeling.

1850 lithograph lampoons Webster's support of the Fugitive Slave Act. WORCESTER ART MUSEUM, GOODSPEED COLLECTION.

556 **Senator Stephen A. Douglas's introduction of the Kansas-Nebraska Bill,** 1854. To win southern support for what looked like a routine measure providing a territorial government for the land west of Missouri and Iowa, Douglas agreed to divide the region into two territories and to repeal the part of the Missouri Compromise (see number 176) that banned slavery in the area north of Latitude 36°30′. The bill left settlers "perfectly free to form and regulate their domestic institutions in their own way." This superficially democratic concept, the brainchild of Senator Lewis Cass of Michigan, was known as popular sovereignty. But by making it possible for slaves to be brought to an area from which the institution had previously been excluded, the bill outraged thousands of Northerners. Its passage probably destroyed Douglas's chances of ever being President, and it marked a major step down the road to the Civil War.

557 The Freeport Doctrine, 1858. This was not a true indiscretion, but a desperate effort by Senator Douglas to extricate himself from the corner he had painted himself into by putting the popular sovereignty idea in the Kansas-Nebraska Act. In the Dred Scott case (see number 202), the Supreme Court ruled that Congress could not prevent slaveholders from bringing their human property into a territory. During their joint debate at Freeport, Illinois, Abraham Lincoln asked Douglas how, in the light of this decision, the people of a territory could exclude slavery before statehood was achieved. "Slavery cannot exist," Douglas replied, "unless it is supported by local police regulations." This helped Douglas in the Illinois senatorial contest, but by arguing that "it matters not what way the Supreme Court may hereafter decide," he practi-

cally destroyed his chances of winning southern support for his bid for the Democratic presidential nomination in 1860.

558 The Mulligan Letters were written by Republican Congressman James G. Blaine, connected Blaine with a favor he had done for the Little Rock and Fort Smith Railroad in 1869, while he was speaker of the House of Representatives. Later, it appeared, officials of the Little Rock line secretly gave Blaine the right to sell bonds of the company at a fat commission. When these letters, some of which contained the postscript "burn this letter," were published in 1884, they seriously damaged Blaine's campaign for the presidency.

559 The "Burchard Break" was another indiscretion that cost Blaine dearly in 1884. Speaking at a rally of pro-Blaine clergymen in New York, the Reverend Samuel D. Burchard referred to the Democratic Party as "the party whose antecedents are rum, Romanism, and Rebellion." When Blaine, who was on the platform but apparently was not paying close attention to the speaker, failed to repudiate this remark in his own speech, the Democrats charged him with being anti-Catholic.

Blaine lost New York State, and with it the presidency, by fewer than 1,200 votes. He later characterized Burchard as "an ass in the shape of a preacher."

Blaine loses the match, 1884 election campaign.
LIBRARY OF CONGRESS.

560 The de Lôme Letter was written by Depuy de Lôme, the Spanish minister to the United States, to a friend in Cuba in 1898. During this time, American feeling was against Spain because of the harsh way it was trying to put down the Cuban revolution. In the letter de Lôme referred to President McKinley as a *"politicastro"* (small-time politician) and a "seeker after the plaudits of the crowd." The letter was stolen and a translation published in the *New York Journal*. De Lôme was forced to resign, but more important, by exacerbating the already strong public feeling against Spain, the letter became a contributory cause of the Spanish-American War.

561 **William Howard Taft's antitrust suit against the United States Steel Corporation,** 1911. This was an indiscretion not because the U.S. Supreme Court eventually decided the case against the government but because the Taft Administration focused in its argument in the suit on U.S. Steel's absorption of the Tennessee Coal and Iron Company, a deal that had been unofficially authorized by President Theodore Roosevelt. Roosevelt had done so during the panic of 1907 (see number 976) because he had been assured that the action was necessary to prevent the collapse of an important banking house. The suit made him appear to be either a supporter of monopoly or (far worse) a dupe of the steel corporation. He had already become estranged from Taft, who had been his personal choice as his successor, but the steel suit left him determined to run for President again himself, a decision that doomed Taft's chances of being re-elected.

562 **Woodrow Wilson's "Appeal"** to the public to elect a Democratic Congress, October 1918. While it was not unusual for a President to urge voters to send members of his party to Congress, Wilson accused the Republicans of behaving in a partisan manner during the Great War, which was then in its final stage, and this offended many people. By making the election a test of his own leadership, and insisting that he could not properly deal with the problems of the peace without a Democratic Congress, he was profoundly embarrassed and politically damaged when the Republicans won control of both the House and the Senate in November.

A TICKLISH MOMENT FOR THE FAMILY DISCIPLINE

ARE YOU GOING TO EAT THAT OATMEAL OR AREN'T YOU!?!

DEMOCRATIC SENATE

Cartoon commentary on a recalcitrant Senate, 1916.
JAY N. "DING DARLING," *DES MOINES REGISTER.*

563 **Herbert Hoover's decision to use the Army to evict the "Bonus Expeditionary Force,"** 1932. About twenty thousand veterans had gathered in Washington, D.C., to "demand" that Congress authorize immediate payment of the World War I Adjusted Compensation Bonus, which was not due until 1945. When Congress did not do so, about two thousand of the veterans refused to leave their ramshackle camp at Anacostia Flats on the edge of the city. After the local police informed him that it could not "maintain law and order except by the free use of firearms," President Hoover issued instructions to the military to "surround the affected area and clear it without delay." Army Chief of Staff General Douglas MacArthur, going beyond these orders, decided to "break the back of the B.E.F.," which he did by driving the men from the camp with cavalry, infantry, tanks, and tear gas, and then by burning it to the ground. Fortunately no one was killed, but President Hoover, who had not intended that the veterans be treated so brutally, was made to appear a heartless autocrat.

564 **Harry Truman's letter to music critic Paul Hume,** 1950. The President, after reading Hume's unfavorable review in the *Washington Post,* of his daughter Margaret's singing, wrote Hume an intemperate letter—calling him, among other things, an "eight-ulcer man on four-ulcer pay" and threatening to make him need "a new nose, a lot of beefsteak for black eyes, and perhaps a supporter below!" The publication of the letter made Truman look foolish as well as vulgar, but with the passage of time it has probably improved Truman's reputation because it shows him as being loyal to his daughter and willing to say what he really thought, regardless of the political consequences.

565 **U-2 Affair,** 1960. In May 1960 President Dwight Eisenhower announced that an American high-altitude U-2 reconnaissance plane had been shot down over the Soviet Union. It was, the President claimed, a weather plane that had wandered off course. The plane had actually been photographing military installations. Contrary to American assumptions, the pilot, Francis Gary Powers, had not been killed in the crash and had admitted the true purpose of his mission to the Russians. When the Soviet authorities trumpeted this information to the world, Eisenhower had to confess that he had not told the truth. This was most embarrassing.

566 **George McGovern's** **"endorsement" of Thomas Eagleton,** 1972. Shortly after McGovern selected Senator Thomas Eagleton of Missouri as his running mate in the 1972 presidential election, he was informed that Eagleton had in the past received electric shock treatments for severe depression. When word of this got out, McGovern announced that he stood behind Eagleton "1,000 percent." Then, almost immediately, he succumbed to political pressure and "dumped" Eagleton. This caused both his decisiveness and his reputation for integrity to be called into question, weakening his already slim chances of defeating President Richard Nixon in the election.

Senator Thomas F. Eagleton accepts the nomination for Vice President, 1972.
UPI/BETTMANN NEWSPHOTOS.

567 **Richard Nixon's** **Cover-Up of the Watergate Affair,** 1973. The burglary of the Democratic Party headquarters in Washington by agents of the Republican Committee to Re-elect the President (CREEP) would not, in itself, have been particularly important if Nixon had not attempted to conceal his personal connection with the crime. The incident did not prevent his landslide victory in the 1972 presidential election. But although he promised a thorough investigation, accepted the resignation of several White House officials who were involved, and agreed to the appointment of an independent special prosecutor, he persistently denied his own involvement. When the prosecutor, Archibald Cox, sought White House documents related to the scandal, Nixon had him discharged. Calls for the President's resignation—even for his impeachment—followed.

Nixon hugs daughter Julie just before his resignation speech, 1974. OLLIE ATKINS/PRESIDENT NIXON'S PRESIDENTIAL PAPERS/NATIONAL ARCHIVE.

568 Richard Nixon's White House Tapes. Among the evidence sought by Cox, and by the prosecutor who replaced him, Leon Jaworski, were tapes that the President had made of his White House conversations with his advisers. Aside from whether or not he was wise to have installed the taping system, his failure to turn it off while discussing the Watergate break-in and the resulting investigations, and failing that, his not having had the tapes erased, was an indiscretion of monumental proportions. Finally he had to release the tapes, and they contained statements clearly demonstrating that he had sought to conceal the truth. This "smoking gun" connecting him with the cover-up made his resignation inevitable.

569 Ronald Reagan's decision to sell arms to Iran, 1986. This decision was made in hopes of obtaining freedom for Americans who had been taken hostage by pro-Iranian terrorists in Lebanon, in 1986. But because the sale was carried out in secret, and despite Reagan's oft-repeated insistence that he would never make concessions to terrorists, when it came to light it undermined Reagan's credibility and blurred his image as the Teflon President (see number 160).

570 Aiding the Nicaraguan "Contras," 1987. President Reagan's popularity suffered a more serious blow when it was revealed that the money obtained by selling arms to Iran had been used to supply Nicaraguan anti-Communist rebel troops (the Contras) with weapons, despite the fact that Congress had banned such arms deliveries. It could be argued that selling arms to Iran might have been in the national interest, but supplying weapons to the Contras was patently illegal. Reagan's insistence that it was done by members of the White House staff (including White House Security Adviser Admiral John Poindexter) without his knowledge further weakened him politically, since it suggested that he was either lying or incompetent.

POLITICAL BOSSES
New York State

Throughout American history, the state of New York had been famous for the political ingenuity (if not the integrity) of the party managers it has produced. Consider, for example:

571 Matthew L. Davis (1773–1850), ally of Aaron Burr (he was one of Burr's seconds at his duel with Alexander Hamilton). While Grand Sachem of Tammany Hall, Davis was convicted of swindling several million dollars, but he obtained a new trial and was acquitted.

572 Thurlow Weed (1797–1882), editor of the *Albany Evening Journal* and "dictator" of the New York Whig Party in the pre–Civil War decades, has been described by a biographer as "the wizard of the lobby." He was an inveterate enemy of the Albany Regency and the mentor of William H. Seward (see numbers 38, 299). "Others formulated the principles and Weed secured the votes."

573 William Marcy Tweed (1823–78), Grand Sachem of Tammany Hall and boss of the New York State Democratic Party in the late 1860s and early 1870s. Tweed was master of the "Tweed Ring" and of numerous techniques for extracting personal profit from city construction projects. He was exposed by *Harper's Weekly* and the *New York Times,* caricatured brutally by the cartoonist

William Marcy "Boss" Tweed.
CULVER PICTURES, INC.

Thomas Nast, and convicted of graft. He died in jail.

574 Thomas Collier Platt (1833–1910), Republican congressman and senator, known as the "easy boss" because of the seemingly effortless way he controlled the New York Republican Party in the late nineteenth century. Platt handpicked most party candidates and dispensed patronage with cold-blooded efficiency. His one monumental mistake came when he promoted the nomination of then-Governor Theodore Roosevelt as the party vice presidential candidate in 1900. He did so in order to get the popular Roosevelt, who threatened his control of the New York party, out of the state and into a traditionally powerless office. Alas for Boss Platt, the as-sassination of William McKinley (see number 513) made Roosevelt the President and marked the beginning of the end of Platt's influence in the state.

575 Richard Croker (1841–1922), rose from being a prize-fighter and fireman to become Grand Sachem of Tammany Hall in 1886. After that, "for sixteen years his word was law in the Democratic organization of New York City." By obtaining the stock of construction companies dependent on city contracts, he amassed enough wealth to buy a large farm and a stable of race-horses. After his candidate for mayor was defeated by a reform slate in 1901, Croker spent most of his time in Great Britain. One of his horses won the 1907 English Derby.

576 Charles Francis Murphy (1858–1924), a saloon keeper, was Grand Sachem of Tammany Hall from 1902 until his death. Although superficially unprepossessing, he had a brilliant political mind, so brilliant that he was able to control the organization without resorting to corrupt practices. Before World War I, Murphy advanced the careers of Alfred E. Smith and Robert F. Wagner, but he clashed with young Franklin D. Roosevelt, then a member of the state Senate. An intuitive, unflamboyant type, unusual among politicos, Murphy raised Tammany, a biographer has written, to "the highest point of its prestige and power."

577 Timothy D. "Big Tim" Sullivan (1862–1913) was the "uncrowned king" of the Lower East Side of New York City around the turn of the century. "Big Tim," also known as "the Big Feller," was both an extremely efficient collector of graft and a lavish distributor of political largess. He supplied thousands of poor people with turkey dinners and gifts each Christmas, distributed shoes to school children on his birthday, and sponsored picnics and other public entertainments for constituents, rich and poor alike. He was mentally unbalanced in his later years and died under mysterious circumstances. His funeral was attended by 215,000 people.

578 Carmine De Sapio (1908–), leader of Tammany from 1949 to 1961, was the first person of Italian descent to hold this powerful position. He initiated important internal reforms in the Tammany organization, opening leadership posts to blacks and Hispanics and women. However, in 1969 he was convicted in a bribery case, which put an end to his political career. He served seventeen months in prison.

Other States

New York, while outstanding in the field, has never had a monopoly of the state and local political boss market. Here are a half-dozen other examples:

579 **Abraham Ruef** (1864–1936), a lawyer, dominated San Francisco politics in the first decade of this century through his control of the Union Labor Party. He extracted huge fees from various corporations in return for franchises and other favors. In 1909 he was convicted of bribing municipal officials and served five years in San Quentin prison.

580 **Thomas J. Pendergast** (1872–1945) began as a protégé of his brother, the Democratic boss of Kansas City, Missouri. After his brother retired, Thomas increased his influence, first in the suburbs and then throughout the state. During the New Deal, which he supported vigorously, he even exerted considerable influence in national Democratic affairs, but in 1939 he was found guilty of income tax invasion and jailed.

581 **Edward H. Crump** (1874–1954) was a successful insurance salesman and businessman who dominated the politics of Memphis, and to a lesser extent Tennessee, from 1909 until his death. During his long reign, he was elected mayor several times and served two terms in Congress. Crump gave Memphis an efficient government, but he used corrupt means to control elections.

"Big Boss" Crump throws a party for 50,000. State Fair Grounds, Memphis, Tennessee.
UPI/BETTMANN NEWSPHOTOS.

582 **James Michael Curley** (1874–1958) served in the Massachusetts legislature and in Congress before being elected mayor of Boston in 1914. He served two more terms as mayor in the 1920s, building up a powerful machine. Curley was governor of Massachusetts from 1935 to 1937, and during the 1940s served again in Congress and as mayor of Boston. In 1947 he was convicted of mail fraud and sent to prison. He refused, however, to resign as mayor and maintained his office while in jail. Edwin O'Connor's novel *The Last Hurrah* was based in part on Curley's career.

Mayor Curley files for re-election to a fifth term.
UPI/BETTMANN NEWSPHOTOS,

583 **Frank Hague** (1876–1956) first won power in Jersey City Democratic politics as a reformer. In 1917 he was elected mayor. Thereafter he controlled the local and state party into the 1940s, hand-picking candidates for governor and senator. He gave Jersey City efficient public services, but ran the city, as a biographer writes, "with a heavy, ruthless hand." He is famous for the line "I am the law." His power declined when he failed to make room for new ethnic groups in his predominantly Irish organization.

584 **Richard J. Daley** (1902–76), served in the Illinois legislature before being elected chairman of the Cook County (Chicago) Democratic Party in 1953. Two years later he was elected mayor of Chicago, a post he held for five terms. Like many other twentieth-century bosses, he provided efficient government and catered as much to the interests of business as to those of ordinary voters. His regime was credited (or blamed) for carrying crucial Illinois for John F. Kennedy by illegal means in the 1960 presidential election, and came in for almost universal criticism after the brutal suppression of anti-Vietnam War protesters at the 1968 Democratic Convention by the Chicago police. Daley's failure to make room in the organization for black leaders weakened his influence in the 1970s.

WOMEN PIONEERS

The contribution of pioneer women to the settlement of the West—the way they endured hardships, raised families, labored in the fields, and (on occasion) helped to fight Indians—is well known and widely appreciated. There have been, however, other kinds of women pioneers, and most of these individuals are not so well known. Here are a few who ought to be.

585 **Elizabeth (Eliza) Lucas Pinckney** (c. 1722–93), when only seventeen, took over the management of her father's three South Carolina plantations. She introduced to the colonies the cultivation of indigo, the source of a valuable blue dye. After the death of her husband, Charles Pinckney, she managed his extensive properties. When she died, President George Washington was one of her pallbearers.

Elizabeth Lucas Pinckney, 1802 painting by Malbone.
CAROLINA ART ASSOCIATION/GIBBS MUSEUM OF ART

586 **Hannah Adams** (1755–1831) was the first American woman to make a living by writing. She published a number of books on religious subjects and *A Summary History of New-England* (1799).

587 **Emma Willard** (1787–1870) founded the Troy (N.Y.) Female Seminary, the first American college-level educational institution for women, in 1821.

588 **Mary Lyon** (1797–1849) founded the Mount Holyoke Female Seminary in 1837. This was the first true women's college, with its own campus, endowment, and a board of trustees committed to its continuation beyond the life of the founder.

Mary Lyon, 1845 photograph.
COURTESY OF MOUNT HOLYOKE

589 **Pauline Wright Davis** (1813–76) was the first American to use a model of the female anatomy while lecturing on physiology. She was also the founder in 1853 of *Una,* the first American newspaper devoted primarily to the cause of women's rights.

590 **Maria Mitchell** (1818–89) was the first American woman astronomer, the discoverer of

Mitchell's Comet (1847), the first woman elected to the American Academy of Arts and Sciences (1848), a member of the first faculty of Vassar College, the first woman elected to the American Philosophical Society (1869), and a founder of the Association for the Advancement of Women (1873). Mitchell explained her many achievements by saying, "I was born of only ordinary capacity, but of extraordinary persistency." Don't you believe it.

Maria Mitchell in the observatory.
VASSAR COLLEGE LIBRARY

591 **Elizabeth Blackwell** (1821–1910) was the first woman in the United States to earn an M.D. degree—in 1849, from Geneva (N.Y.) Medical College—after having been turned down by Harvard, Yale, and most of the other medical schools in the country). In 1857 she founded the New York Infirmary for Women and Children; she

played an important role in the establishment of the United States Sanitary Commission during the Civil War; in 1868 she founded the Women's Medical College in New York City. In later years she was a pioneer in sex education, writing *The Human Element in Sex* (1884) and campaigning against the double standard.

592 **Antoinette Brown** (1825–1921) studied theology at Oberlin College but was not granted a degree because of her sex. (Oberlin finally gave her an honorary D.D. in 1908.) However, in 1853 she was ordained as a Congregationalist minister, the first woman minister in the United States. She later became a Unitarian.

593 **Myra Bradwell** (1831–94) founded, managed, and edited the *Chicago Legal News* in 1868, which soon became the most prominent legal journal in the West. She also qualified for admission to the Illinois bar. When admission was denied because of her sex, she carried her case to the U.S. Supreme Court, but lost. Finally, in 1882, she persuaded the Illinois legislature to pass a law banning the exclusion of anyone from any profession on the basis of sex.

594 **Victoria Claflin Woodhull** (1838–1927) in 1868 joined her sister Tennessee Claflin Cook (1846–1923), and together they became the first female New York stockbrokers. Victoria Woodhull was also (in 1871) the first woman to testify before a congressional committee, on which occasion she campaigned vigorously for women's suffrage. In 1872 she was the candidate of the Equal Rights Party for President of the United States (see number 384).

Victoria Woodhull and Tennessee Cook at work on Broad Street.
AMERICAN HERITAGE COLLECTION.

595 **Elsie De Wolfe** (1865–1950) gave up a successful career as an actress to become the first woman professional interior decorator in 1905. Her "anti-Victorian" style, featuring bright colors and much light, was described in her book *The House in Good Taste* (1913). She is also said to have been among the first women to fly and to dance the fox trot.

596 **Alice Hamilton** (1869–1970), an-

other early woman doctor, created the field of industrial medicine and was a leader in publicizing the dangers of lead poisoning and other industrial hazards. In 1919 she became the first female professor at Harvard. (She was not, however, permitted to march at commencement and was not even allotted her quota of faculty football tickets.) Her *Industrial Poisons in the United States* (1925) was the first textbook on this subject.

597 **Katharine Bement Davis** (1860–1935), a pioneer in prison reform before World War I, conducted the first broad survey of women's sexual behavior, *Factors in the Sex Life of Twenty-two Hundred Women* (1929).

Katharine Bement Davis.
VASSAR COLLEGE LIBRARY.

598 **Mary (Molly) Dewson** (1874–1962) was a pioneer in the mobilization of women as a force in partisan politics and as executives in the federal bureaucracy. She began this work during the 1928 presidential campaign of Al Smith, continuing it during Franklin Roosevelt's 1930 campaign for the governorship of New York, during his campaign for the presidency in 1932, and thereafter. As head of the women's division of the Democratic Party, she was responsible for recruiting large numbers of women for government jobs and in training women campaign workers.

599 **Katharine Dexter McCormick** (1875–1966), an advocate of birth control, provided the financial support needed for the development of the first effective oral contraceptive (see number 968).

600 **Mary McLeod Bethune** (1875–1955) became, after a long

Mary McLeod Bethune at the White House in 1944.
UPI/BETTMANN NEWSPHOTOS.

career as an educator, the founder of the National Council of Negro Women and then, in 1936, the first black woman to head a federal agency, the Division of Negro Affairs of the National Youth Administration. She was also a founder of the so-called "Black Cabinet," a group of New Deal officials working to persuade various government agencies to pay more attention to the interests of blacks.

601 **Margaret H. Sanger** (1879–1966) invented the term "birth control" in 1914 and founded the first birth control clinic in the United States in 1916. In 1921, she organized the American Birth Control League, forerunner of the Planned Parenthood Federation, and two years later opened the Birth Control Research Bureau, which became the model for hundreds of local birth control clinics.

602 **Frances Perkins** (1880–1965) was the first woman appointed to the New York State Industrial Commission (1919). Later she was the industrial commissioner of the state. In 1933, when President Franklin Roosevelt made her Secretary of Labor, she be-

came the first woman member of a President's Cabinet.

Frances Perkins photographed by Clara Sipprell around 1945.
NATIONAL PORTRAIT GALLERY, SMITHSONIAN INSTITUTION.

603 **Jeannette Rankin** (1880–1973) became the first woman member of Congress when she was elected as Montana's sole member of the House of Representatives in 1916. Being a pacifist, she voted against declaring war on

Jeannette Rankin, 1918.
BROWN BROTHERS.

Germany in 1917 and was not a candidate for re-election. In 1940, however, she was again elected to Congress. When she again voted against declaring war after Pearl Harbor, she became the only person of either sex to have voted against American participation in both World Wars.

604 **Ruth Bryan Owen** (1885–1977), although benefiting politically from the fact that she was a daughter of William Jennings Bryan, was a pioneer in many ways. She was the first woman elected to Congress from a southern state (Florida, in 1928) and the first woman member of an important congressional committee (Foreign Affairs). In 1933, President Roosevelt named her minister plenipotentiary to Denmark, making her the first American woman to hold a high diplomatic post.

605 **Ruth Benedict** (1887–1948), anthropologist, developed the theory, particularly influential in the decades before and after World War II, that distinctive cultures produce people with one dominant type of personality. She was

also, as her biographer in *Notable American Women* writes, the first woman to become "the preeminent leader of a learned profession," a distinction symbolized by her election as president of the American Anthropological Association in 1947.

606 **Sandra Day O'Connor** (1930–) was the first woman associate justice of the United States Supreme Court.

Associate Justice Sandra Day O'Connor, 1981.
UPI/BETTMANN NEWSPHOTOS.

607 **Geraldine Ferraro** (1935–), Democratic candidate for vice president in 1984, was the first woman nominated for national office by a major party.

PART IV
What'ses

WHAT'S NEW?

Ever since Europeans began referring to North and South America as the *New* World and naming places there after places in the old country, as in New England, *Nieuw* Netherlands, and *Nova España*, the idea of newness has had positive associations for most Americans. One thinks immediately of the New Deal and John F. Kennedy's New Frontier, but here are some other examples:

608 **New Harmony.** The utopian settlement in Indiana, founded by Robert Owen (see number 233).

609 **New South.** A term used after the Civil War by southern publicists and boosters of industrial development as a kind of shorthand for modernization and economic expansion. The leading advocate of the movement was Henry Grady, editor of the *Atlanta Constitution,* whose speeches and editorials reached wide audiences in the North as well as in the South. The term is still used by southern business interests and others interested in distancing themselves from the bad old days of racial segregation.

610 **New Nationalism.** Theodore Roosevelt's program (see number 243) for regulating big business and expanding the role of the federal government in economic and social matters.

Teddy Roosevelt steers in a new direction, 1907.
CULVER PICTURES, INC.

611 **New Freedom.** The program of Woodrow Wilson in the 1912 presidential campaign, a counter to Roosevelt's New Nationalism. The country was to rely on competition rather than government regulation to protect the public against economic exploitation. Monopolistic corporations should be broken up into their component parts by strict enforcement of an-

Evaluation of Wilson's New Freedom, 1914.
CULVER PICTURES, INC.

titrust laws. Then the competition of the "freed" smaller companies would keep costs and prices down and profits reasonable.

612 **New Negro.** A term used in the decade after World War I by black intellectuals of the Harlem Renaissance, who stressed racial pride and independence from white influences. In *The New Negro* (1925), the philosopher Alain Locke urged blacks to exchange "the status of beneficiary and ward for that of a collaborator and participant in American civilization."

Cover of *Life* during the Coolidge era, July 1, 1926. COURTESY OF THE NEW-YORK HISTORICAL SOCIETY.

613 **New Era.** The Republican description of the mid-1920s, the years of "Coolidge Prosperity" when wages, profits, and stock prices were on the rise, interest rates were low, and business leaders seemed the embodiment of wisdom and good citizenship. During the New Era, ad man Bruce Barton described Jesus Christ in all seriousness as the "founder of modern business." The New Era was followed by the Great Depression (see number 647).

614 **New Left.** A name taken by radicals in the 1960s, mostly young, who bitterly opposed racism, the Vietnam War, corporate power, and "middle class" morality. The term was used as a pejorative by many people, but the big exception to the generalization that "new" equals "good" was

Antiwar demonstrators at the Pentagon, October 21, 1967.
UPI/BETTMANN NEWSPHOTOS

615 **The New Immigration.** This term was used by opponents of unrestricted immigration to distinguish the change that occurred in the flow of European immigrants to the United States beginning in the 1880s. Whereas previously the majority of Europeans had come from north-

ern and western sections of the continent, the "new" immigrants came from southern and eastern parts of Europe. People who made the distinction claimed that the newcomers were either "unfit" or incapable of being assimilated into the "American melting pot."

WHAT'S OLD

But "old" is also nearly always good. Consider the following:

616 **Old Hickory.** Andrew Jackson was dubbed this because of both his physical and characterological toughness. The name dates from his days as an Indian fighter during the War of 1812.

Label depicting Andrew Jackson.
CULVER PICTURES, INC.

617 **Old Tippecanoe.** General William Henry Harrison, so called after his victory over the Indians at the Battle of Tippecanoe (see number 538).

618 **Old Rough and Ready.** General Zachary Taylor, the name having been given to him by his troops during his long career in the Army because of his rough-hewn appearance and his informal yet confidence-building way of dealing with enlisted men.

619 **Old Man Eloquent.** John Quincy Adams, the name given him during his service in the House of Representatives (1831–48), where he spoke repeatedly and fervently on behalf of freedom of speech and petition.

620 **Old Bullion.** Senator Thomas Hart Benton of Missouri, so called because of his vehement opposition to all forms of paper money.

621 **Old Brains.** Civil War Union General Henry W. Halleck, because of his reputation as a strategist and as an expert on the work of the French military authority, Henri Jomini.

622 **Old Pete.** Confederate General James Longstreet (see number 882), so called by his men probably because of his combination of energy, imperturbability, and evident concern for their welfare.

623 Old Jack. Another name for General "Stonewall" Jackson (see number 878) despite the fact that at the time of his death he was less than forty years old.

624 Old Ironsides. See number 898.

625 Old Guard. A name given to conservative Republicans. It originated after the 1880 presidential convention, at which three hundred-odd supporters of former President U. S. Grant held out for their man through thirty-six ballots. After the convention finally nominated James A. Garfield, one of the group gave each of them a medal bearing the phrase "Old Guard" as a memento.

The Republican National Convention at Chicago in June 1880. LIBRARY OF CONGRESS.

626 Old Northwest. The area bounded by the Appalachian Mountains, the Great Lakes, and the Mississippi and Ohio rivers, organized as the Northwest Territory in 1787 and eventually divided into the states of Ohio, Indiana, Illinois, Michigan, and Wisconsin.

627 Old Dominion. The royal colony of Virginia, so called because, after the restoration of Charles II to the English throne in 1660, the seal of Virginia was changed to indicate that it was no mere possession—but was, like England, Ireland, and Scotland, a "dominion" of the King.

"The English Empire of America," 1728 map. THE METROPOLITAN MUSEUM OF ART.

Exceptions to the idea that old is good are:

628 The Old Patroon. Stephen Van Rensselaer, congressman from New York, general in the War of 1812, and owner of vast Hudson Valley landholdings, so called because he was a great-great-great-grandson of the first patroon, Kiliaen Van Rensselaer, who had obtained a Charter of Privileges of Patroons from the Dutch West India Company in 1629. The Old Patroon was actually the last patroon (see number 852).

629 Old Fuss and Feathers. General Winfield Scott, like his contemporary Zachary Taylor, a successful soldier (more so as an organizer and strategist than as a battlefield leader). Scott earned this nickname by being extremely vain and something of a blusterer.

General Winfield Scott. THE NATIONAL ARCHIVE.

630 The Nine Old Men. The name given to members of the Supreme Court during the first Administration of Franklin

113

Roosevelt, after a majority of the justices had declared unconstitutional the National Industrial Recovery Act, the Agricultural Adjustment Act, other important New Deal measures, and many state laws dealing with social and economic problems. It was the title of a widely read book on the Court published in 1936 by Drew Pearson and Robert S. Allen.

WHAT'S UP? (PLANS)

631 **Albany Plan.** In 1754, the British government organized a meeting of delegates from New York, Pennsylvania, Maryland, the New England colonies, and the Six Nations of the Iroquois Confederation in Albany, in an attempt to work out an orderly way of dealing with white-Indian relations. At the gathering, Benjamin Franklin proposed the creation of "one general government . . . in America," consisting of a President-General chosen by the King and a council elected by "the representatives of the people of the several colonies." This government was to "make peace or declare war with Indian Nations," regulate Indian trading, and otherwise control matters of common interest. Neither Parliament nor the separate colonies were will-

ing to go along with this scheme.

632 **New Jersey Plan.** This was William Paterson's "small state" plan advanced at the Constitutional Convention in 1787. It called for revising the Articles of Confederation by strengthening the powers of the central government. The new system was to be run by a one-house legislature with equal representation for each state. It was rejected by the delegates of the larger states.

William Paterson. COURTESY OF CULVER PICTURES, INC.

633 **Virginia Plan.** This plan, drafted at the convention by Edmund Randolph of Virginia, dealt with the representation problem by creating a two-house "National Legislature"; one branch was to be elected by the people of each state, the other chosen by these representatives from "persons nominated by the [state] leg-

islatures." The National Legislature was empowered "to legislate in all cases to which the separate states are incompetent" and to "negative" [sic] state laws it considered unconstitutional. Differences between these plans were resolved by the Great Compromise (see number 174).

THE HERCULES OF THE UNION.

General Scott slays the dragon of secession. LIBRARY OF CONGRESS.

634 **Anaconda Plan.** This was General Winfield Scott's (see number 629) strategy for defeating the South by attrition and with a minimum of bloodshed. According to the plan, before the Confederates could mobilize, the Army should occupy key points on the Mississippi from southern Illinois to the Gulf of Mexico. At the same time, the Navy should blockade southern ports. Then the government should simply sit back and wait. Scott expected that this policy of strangulation would cause pro-Union sentiment to develop in the South. This strategy might well have worked, but Lincoln, and most other Northerners, were unwilling to adopt such a passive approach.

635 Dawes Plan. This scheme was devised in 1924 by a committee of the Allied Reparations Commission chaired by Charles G. Dawes (see number 126). It was aimed at enabling Germany to resume paying the reparations it owed to the victorious Allies. Annual payments were scaled down, and the United States lent Germany $200 million to stabilize its currency, which was ravaged by the Great Inflation of 1922–23. The plan did not solve the reparations problem, but it did result in Dawes sharing the 1925 Nobel Peace Prize.

636 Young Plan. Five years later, another commission was appointed, headed by Owen D. Young, chairman of the General Electric Company, who had also participated in the negotiations leading to the Dawes Plan. The Young Plan reduced Germany's obligation to $27 billion, payable over fifty-nine years. However, the outbreak of the Great Depression caused Germany to default again, and reparations and the related debts owed the United States by its World War I allies were never paid.

637 Swope Plan. Gerard Swope, long-time president of General Electric and thus a close associate of Owen D. Young, put this scheme forward in 1931 as a way of dealing with the spreading economic depression. He suggested that the firms in each industry be organized into trade associations and given the power to fix prices and allocate markets. The plan included setting up subsidized unemployment insurance and pension plans for employees, and the whole system was to be supervised by the federal government. Some of the ideas in the Swope Plan were adopted in the legislation creating the New Deal National Recovery Administration in 1933.

638 Marshall Plan. This plan was a scheme for financing the economic recovery and political stability of Europe after World War II. Following its proposal by Secretary of State George C. Marshall in a speech at Harvard in June 1947, Great Britain, France, and other Western European nations developed a four-year recovery plan which Congress financed to the tune of $13 billion (see number 196). Although they were offered the opportunity, the countries of the Soviet bloc refused to participate, but for the Western European countries the Marshall Plan was a smashing success. As Marshall predicted, it restored "the confidence of the European people in the economic future of their own countries."

Cartoon by Little, June 11, 1948, *The Nashville Tennessean.* CULVER PICTURES, INC.

639 Huston Plan. In 1970, Tom Charles Huston, an aide of President Richard M. Nixon, set up with the President's approval an "Interagency Group on Domestic Intelligence and Internal Security" to conduct electronic monitoring, break-ins, and mail intercepts of suspected domestic radicals and foreign diplomats. However, when J. Edgar Hoover of the FBI objected strongly to this competition with his agency, President Nixon canceled the operation.

"GREAT" THINGS

Statue of "The Pilgrim" by
J. Q. A. Ward.
CULVER PICTURES, INC.

640 The Great Migration. The emigration during the 1630s of some sixty thousand persons from England to the New World. Some left for economic reasons, but the bulk were Puritans offended by the policies of King Charles I and Bishop William Lord, which they considered too close to Roman Catholicism. Between ten and twenty thousand of the migrants came to the New England colonies; others, settled in the Caribbean colonies and Bermuda.

641 The Great Awakening. This is the name given to the wave of religious enthusiasm that swept through the colonies in the 1740s. The movement was a response to the growing prosperity of the colonies and to their religious diversity, which challenged strict Puritan concepts. Proponents of the Great Awakening stressed the tortures of Hell that awaited sinners, but also hinted that God was reasonable and would likely react favorably to those with good intentions.

642 The Second Great Awakening. This movement peaked in the 1820s and early 1830s. It was, if possible, even more emotional in character than the first, and more rejecting of predestination and other depressing religious ideas.

643 The Great War for the Empire. The name given to what is commonly known as the Seven Years' War by the historian Lawrence Henry Gipson in his monumental *The British Empire Before the American Revolution* (1936–68). Gipson's point was that what Americans know as the

French and Indian allies attack
Schenectady.
CULVER PICTURES. INC.

French and Indian War was part of a worldwide struggle between France and Great Britain for control of vast areas in America and Asia.

644 Great Compromise. Although "great" in the sense that the decision to give each state the same representation in the Senate and to apportion the seats in the House of Representatives on the basis of population enabled the Philadelphia Constitutional Convention to get on to more important matters (see number 174), the long-range significance of the agreement was less than the delegates imagined. In practice, most issues have divided the country on economic or geographical lines, not in terms of the size of the states.

645 Great Western. A wooden, steam-driven, British sidewheeler, the first regularly scheduled transatlantic steamer and the largest ever built when it was completed in 1837.

646 Great Eastern. Another path-breaking English-built vessel, this one made of iron, was the largest in the world when launched in 1858. It was nearly 700 feet in length and weighed 18,914 tons. In 1865–66, the American entrepreneur Cyrus Field used the *Great Eastern* to lay the first permanent transatlantic telegraph cable between England and the United States.

Painting of steamship *Great Eastern* by M. J. Deming.
SHELBURNE MUSEUM, SHELBURNE, VT.

647 **The Great Depression.** A worldwide period of deflation running from 1873 to 1897, marked in the United States by erratic, short-run changes in economic activity that caused much concern for economists, businessmen, and politicians. It should not be confused with the depression of the 1930s; from the modern perspective it was not a depression at all. Economic growth overall was extremely large (see number 650).

Economic choices, 1873.
LIBRARY OF CONGRESS.

648 **Great Northern Railway.** This last of the five nineteenth-century "transcontinental" lines ran from St. Paul, Minnesota, to Seattle, Washington. It was completed by James J. Hill in 1893 and was unique because it was built without the benefit of either federal land grants or watered stock and because it paid dividends regularly.

649 **The Great Gatsby** was a very highly regarded but (at the time) not very successful novel by F. Scott Fitzgerald, published in 1925.

Bonus marchers in Washington, D.C., 1932. CULVER PICTURES, INC.

650 **Great Depression of the 1930s.** Another worldwide period of falling prices, this one a genuine economic downturn marked by severe unemployment and declining production from 1929 to 1933, by very slow recovery from 1933 to 1937, and by an extremely severe "recession" in 1937–38. Full recovery only came after the outbreak of World War II in Europe.

651 **The Great Society.** President Lyndon B. Johnson's name for his program of social and economic reform. The program, enacted in 1964 and 1965, consisted of antisegregation legislation (the Civil Rights Act of 1964), a "War on Poverty" including vocational training (the Job Corps), federal aid to education, slum clearance, and health insurance (Medicare and Medicaid).

L.B.J.'s legislative program, *St. Louis Post Dispatch* view, December 8, 1963.
CULVER PICTURES, INC.

WHAT'S WRONG? (ANTI THINGS AND PEOPLE

It has not been uncommon for Americans, famous for being individualists, to be against things. There are many "antis" in our history.

652 **Antinomians.** The Puritans were not against as many things as they were said to be by H. L.

117

Mencken (see number 341), but they were people of strong opinions, especially in religious matters. Antinomianism was the belief that eternal salvation depended on faith and God's grace. It did not matter what you did; behavior was of no importance when it came to predicting who would and would not go to Heaven. The term was applied in the 1630s to the Massachusetts followers of Anne Hutchinson. Since the idea seemed a menace to the social order, orthodox Puritans objected strenuously; when Anne Hutchinson began to attract converts, she was banished from the colony. Antinomians should obviously be kept separate from *Arminians,* Puritans who believed that salvation could be achieved by "good works."

Anne Hutchinson, nineteenth-century print.
CULVER PICTURES, INC.

653 Antifederalists. People who opposed the ratification of the Constitution because they did not want a strong central government were known as Antifederalists; those who favored the Constitution were called Federalists. The Antifederalists were possessed of a vague fear that the stronger central government envisioned by the new system would undermine the independence of the states (see numbers 271, 277). The names of the two factions are confusing, since the Antifederalists actually wanted a federal system, whereas the Federalists were more sympathetic to a centralized, *national* government.

654 Antimasons. In the year of 1826, William Morgan, a Batavia, New York bricklayer, was arrested and charged with petty theft. He was never heard of again. Morgan was a member of the Masonic Order. Rumor had it that he was writing a book exposing the secrets of the order, and those predisposed to be suspicious of such secret societies assumed that the Masons had murdered him. An Antimasonic political party emerged as a result.

655 Antirent movement. See number 852.

656 Antibigamy Act. This law was passed in 1862; it was necessary because the Mormon practice of polygamy (they called it "celestial marriage") roused resentment and moral outrage in many non-Mormon quarters.

657 The Antimonopoly Party. In 1884, this party ran Benjamin Franklin Butler (see numbers 66, 75) for President on a ticket that called for the regulation of certain kinds of businesses and other economic reforms. Butler, who was in the midst of one of his many political shifts, was more interested in the defeat of the Democratic candidate, Grover Cleveland, than in getting elected himself. He was also the candidate of the Greenback Labor Party. He polled only 170,000 votes, however, and did not prevent Cleveland from being elected.

658 Antitrust Movement. The growth of large business enterprises in the late nineteenth century roused fears that competition would be stifled and consumers forced to pay higher prices for all kinds of goods. In particular, the domination of the refining of petroleum by John D. Rockefeller's Standard Oil Company caused great alarm. Since Standard Oil was organized as a trust company, the term "antitrust" came into being. It was soon applied to all large enterprises, most of which were actually corporations, not trusts—hence the name given the Sherman Antitrust Act of 1890 (see number 188), which declared "combinations in the form of trusts or otherwise" that *restrained trade* to be illegal.

Uncle Sam bounces the Coal Trusts, 1902.
CULVER PICTURES, INC.

659 **The Antisaloon League of America.** This organization, which was founded in 1895, sought to end the use of alcohol by political action. After the passage of the Prohibition Amendment, the League concentrated on enforcement. During the middle 1920s, it was dominated by Wayne Wheeler, who favored "even . . . calling out the Army and Navy" if necessary to stop the liquor traffic. The League campaigned vigorously for and against congressmen and had a large influence on many of them. "Wayne B. Wheeler has taken snuff, and the Senate, as usual, has sneezed," one "wet" senator complained.

660 **Anti-Imperialist League.** The United States's acquisition of colonies as a result of the Spanish-American War led to the founding of the Anti-Imperialist League. People as diverse in interest and point of view as Andrew Carnegie, Mark Twain, Samuel Gompers, and President Charles W. Eliot of Harvard were members. The League did not prevent the country from acquiring the Philippine Islands and other overseas possessions in 1898, but its opposition had much to do with discouraging the direct acquisition of territory in future years.

Aguinaldo: "Now, boys, sign this with me."

Anti-Imperialist League members Twain, Eliot, and Carnegie react to changes in the Philippines, 1901 cartoon.
CULVER PICTURES, INC.

661 **Anti-Injunction Act.** The Clayton Antitrust Act of 1913 had exempted labor unions from the restrictions on combinations in restraint of trade. However, conservative judges frequently issued injunctions prohibiting picketing and other such actions in labor disputes. In 1932 Congress passed the Norris-LaGuardia Anti-Injunction Act, banning the issuance of injunctions to prevent work stoppages, peaceful picketing, and similar union tactics.

662 **Anti-anticommunism.** This term emerged during the Cold War. Those who called themselves anti-anticommunists were left-leaning people who did not wish to identify themselves with the Communist Party but opposed the harassment of American Communists, the blanket condemnation of every action of the Soviet Government, and contempt for every aspect of Russian society.

663 **Antiballistic Missile Treaty.** This was another name for the 1972 Strategic Arms Limitation Treaty. (See number 224.)

119

PART V
Presidents, Pro And Con

1789–1860

George Washington

George Washington, 1796 portrait by Gilbert Stuart. THE PENNSYLVANIA ACADEMY OF FINE ARTS, BEQUEST OF WILLIAM BINGHAM, 1811.

664 "[Washington's] mind was great and powerful, without being of the very first order . . . and as far as he saw, no judgement was ever sounder. It was slow in operation, being little aided by invention, but sure in conclusion. . . . His integrity was most pure, his justice the most inflexible I have ever known, no motives of interest or consanguinity, of friendship or hatred, being able to bias his decision." Thomas Jefferson, 1814.

665 "All [Washington's] features were indicative of the most ungovernable passions, and had he been born in the forests . . . he would have been the fiercest man among the savage tribes." Gilbert Stuart, after first painting Washington's portrait, 1795.

666 "As to you, Sir, treacherous in private friendship (for so you have been to me, and that in a day of danger) and a hypocrite in public life, the world will be puzzled to decide whether you are an apostate or an impostor. . . . Elevated to the chair of the Presidency, you assumed the merit of everything to yourself, and the natural in gratitude of your constitution began to appear." Thomas Paine, 1796.

John Adams

667 "[Adams] is vain, irritable and a bad calculator of the force and probable effect of the motives which govern men. This is all the ill that can possibly be said of him. He is as disinterested as the being which made him: he is profound in his views: and accurate in his judgment except when knowledge of the world is necessary to form a judgment." Thomas Jefferson, 1787.

668 "[Adams] means well for his Country, is always an honest man, often a wise one, but sometimes, and in some things, absolutely out of his senses." Benjamin Franklin, 1783.

John Adams. CULVER PICTURES, INC.

669 "[Adams] does not possess the talents adapted to the *administration* of government, and . . . there are great and intrinsic defects in his character which unfit him for the office of chief magistrate. . . . He is often liable to paroxysms of anger, which deprive him of self-command and produce very outrageous behavior to those who approach him." Alexander Hamilton, 1800.

Thomas Jefferson

670 "[Jefferson] was a statesman: that is to say, a man capable of conceiving measures useful to the country and to mankind —able to recommend them to adoption, and to administer them when adopted. I have seen many politicians—a few statesmen—and, of these few, he their pre-eminent head." Thomas Hart Benton, 1854.

671 "I cannot live in this miserable, undone country, where . . . we are governed by the old red breeches of that prince of projectors, St. Thomas of Cantingbury; and surely, Becket himself never had more pilgrims at his shrine than the saint of Monticello." John Randolph of Roanoke, 1832.

1805 drawing of Thomas Jefferson. CULVER PICTURES, INC.

672 "It is with much reluctance that I am obliged to look upon [Jefferson] as a man whose mind is warped by prejudice and so blinded by ignorance as to be unfit for the office he holds. However wise and scientific as philosopher, as a politician he is a child and dupe of party." John Adams, 1797.

James Madison

Engraving of James Madison. CULVER PICTURES, INC.

673 "I do not know in the world a man of purer integrity, more dispassionate, disinterested, and devoted to genuine Republicanism; nor could I in the whole scope of America and Europe point out an abler head." Thomas Jefferson, 1812.

674 "Mr. Madison is wholly unfit for the storms of War. Nature has cast him in too benevolent a mould. Admirably adapted to the tranquil scenes of peace—blending all the mild and amiable virtues, he is not fit for the rough and rude blasts which the conflict of nations generate." Henry Clay, 1812.

675 "I think [Madison] a good man and an able man, but he has rather too much theory, and wants

that discretion which men of business commonly have. He is also very timid and seems evident to want manly firmness and energy of character." Fisher Ames, 1789.

James Monroe

676 "[Monroe] is a man whose soul might be turned wrong side outwards without discovering a blemish to the world." Thomas Jefferson, 1786.

Trade card, James Monroe. CULVER PICTURES, INC.

677 "Naturally dull and stupid; extremely illiterate; indecisive to a degree that would be incredible to one who did not know him; pusillanimous, and, of course, hypocritical; [Monroe] has no opinion on any subject, and will always be under the government of the worst men; pretends, I am told, to some knowledge of military matters, but never commanded a platoon, nor

was ever fit to command one." Aaron Burr, 1815.

678 "Tho' not brilliant, few men were [Monroe's] equals in wisdom, firmness and devotion to the country. He had a wonderful intellectual patience; and could above all men, that I ever knew, when called on to decide an important point, hold the subject immovably fixed under his attention, until he had mastered it in all its relations." John C. Calhoun, 1831.

John Quincy Adams

679 "I am a man of reserved, cold, austere, and forbidding manners: my political adversaries say, a gloomy misanthropist, and my personal enemies, an unsocial savage. With a knowledge of the actual defect in my character, I have not the pliability to reform it." John Quincy Adams, 1819.

680 "[Adams] was the ready vessel, always under sail when the duties of his station required it. . . . Punctual to every duty, death found him at the post of duty; and where else could it have found him, at any stage of his career, for the fifty years of his illustrious public life?" Thomas Hart Benton, 1848.

Lithograph of John Quincy Adams. CULVER PICTURES, INC.

681 "Mr. Adams' general personal demeanour was not prepossessing. He was on the contrary quite awkward, but . . . he was, in a small and agreeable party, one of the most entertaining table companions of his day." Martin Van Buren.

Andrew Jackson

682 "I never knew a man more free from conceit, or one to whom it was to a greater extent a

Andrew Jackson. CULVER PICTURES, INC.

pleasure, as well as a recognized duty, to listen patiently to what might be said to him upon any subject under consideration. . . . Neither, I need scarcely say, was [Jackson] in the habit of talking, much less of boasting, of his own achievements." Martin Van Buren.

683 "I feel much alarmed at the prospect of seeing General Jackson President. He is one of the most unfit men I know of for such a place. He has had very little respect for laws and constitutions, and is, in fact, an able military chief. His passions are terrible." Thomas Jefferson, 1824.

684 "General Jackson is the majority's slave; he yields to its intentions, desires, and half-revealed instincts, or rather he anticipates and forestalls them." Alexis de Tocqueville, 1836.

Martin Van Buren

685 "In point of mere intellectual force [Van Buren] must rank below the really eminent men with whom he was so long associated in public life. But he was able, industrious, and, in political management, clever beyond any man who has thus far appeared in American politics." James G. Blaine, 1884.

Martin Van Buren, Brady photo.
CULVER PICTURES, INC.

686 "[Van Buren] is not . . . of the race of the lion or the tiger; he belonged to a lower order— the fox; and it would be in vain to expect that he could command the respect or acquire the confidence of those who had so little admiration for the qualities by which he was distinguished." John C. Calhoun, 1836.

William Henry Harrison

687 "The President is the most extraordinary man I ever saw. He does not seem to realize the vast importance of his elevation. . . . He is as tickled with the Presidency as is a young woman with a new bonnet." Martin Van Buren, 1841.

688 "It is almost distressing to see [Harrison]. He is now in his 69th year, with the full share of infirmity belonging to that age, and very little of even the physical strength necessary to encounter the heavy responsibility belonging to his station; yet, as unconscious as a child of his difficulties and those of the country, he seems to enjoy his elevation as a mere affair of personal vanity." John C. Calhoun, 1841.

William Henry Harrison.
CULVER PICTURES, INC.

689 "I have not seen old 'Tip,' but all represent him as merry as a cricket, careless of the future, garrulous in the display of obscene stories, thoroughly intent with the spirit of lechery." William L. Marcy, 1841.

John Tyler

690 "Tyler is a political sectarian of the slave-driving, Virginian, Jeffersonian school, principled

John Tyler, photo by Handy.
CULVER PICTURES, INC.

against all improvement, with all the interests and passions and vices of slavery rooted in his moral and political constitution—with talents not above mediocrity, and a spirit incapable of expansion to the dimensions of the station upon which he has been cast by the hand of Providence." John Quincy Adams, 1841.

691 "[Tyler] looked somewhat worn and anxious, as well he might, being at war with everybody —but . . . his manner was remarkably unaffected, gentlemanly, and agreeable. I thought that in his whole carriage and demeanour, he became his station singularly well." Charles Dickens, 1842.

James K. Polk

692 "Polk is the leader of the Administration in the House, and is just

qualified for an eminent County Court lawyer.... He has no wit, no literature, no point of argument, no gracefulness of delivery, no eloquence of language, no philosophy, no pathos, no felicitous impromptus." John Quincy Adams, 1834.

693 "To extraordinary powers of labor, both mental and physical, [Polk] unites that tact and judgment which are requisite to the successful direction of such an office as that of Chief Magistrate of a free people." Andrew Jackson, 1844.

James Knox Polk.
CULVER PICTURES, INC.

694 "[Polk is] a blighted burr that has fallen from the mane of the warhorse of the Hermitage." Seargent S. Prentiss, 1844. (The "warhorse of the Hermitage" referred to was Andrew Jackson.)

Zachary Taylor

Engraving of Zachary Taylor in Mexico. CULVER PICTURES, INC.

695 "General Taylor's mind had not been enlarged and refreshed by reading, or much converse with the world. Rigidity of ideas was the consequence. ... In short, few men have ever had a more comfortable, labor-saving contempt for learning of every kind. Yet this old soldier and neophyte statesman had the true basis of a great character: —pure, uncorrupted morals, combined with indomitable courage." Winfield Scott, 1864.

696 "[Taylor] really is a most simpleminded old man. He has the least show or pretension about him of any man I ever saw; talks as artlessly as a child about affairs of state, and does not seem to pretend to a knowledge of any-

thing of which he is ignorant." Horace Mann, 1850.

Millard Fillmore

697 "I had not the advantage of a classical education, and no man should, in my judgement, accept a degree that he cannot read." Millard Fillmore, refusing an honorary degree offered by Oxford, 1855.

698 "Order and decorum, with all the proprieties that should govern high debate, were stamped upon his brow. Of him, taken together, it might be said . . . There 'indeed' is a man 'in whom is no guile.'" Alexander H. Stephens, 1870.

Millard Fillmore, Brady photo.
CULVER PICTURES, INC.

699 "Other Presidents may be forgotten; but the name signed to the Fugitive Slave Bill can never

be forgotten. . . . Better far for [Fillmore] had he never been born." Charles Sumner, 1850.

Franklin Pierce

700 "Pierce was . . . a small politician, of low capacity and mean surroundings, proud to act as the servile tool of men worse than himself but also stronger and abler. He was ever ready to do any work the slavery leaders set him." Theodore Roosevelt, 1886.

Franklin Pierce.
CULVER PICTURES, INC.

701 "Frank's a good fellow, I admit, and I wish him well . . . but when it comes to the hull Yewnited States, I dew say that in my jedgement Frank Pierce is a-goin to *spread durned thin.*" Unnamed resident of Concord, New Hampshire, 1852, quoted in John S. Wise, *Recollections of Thirteen Presidents.*

702 "[Pierce] has a subtle faculty of making affairs roll onward according to his will, and of influencing their source without showing any trace of his action. There are scores of men in the country that seem brighter than he is but [he] has the directing mind, and will move them about like pawns. . . . He is deep, deep, deep." Nathaniel Hawthorne.

James Buchanan

703 "Mr. Buchanan is an able man, but is in small matters without judgment and sometimes acts like an old maid." James K. Polk, 1849.

704 "Whatever may have been the effect of Mr. Buchanan's elevation to the presidency and of the possession of its overshadowing powers upon himself, he was, assuredly, before that occurrence a cautious, circumspect, and sagacious man." Martin Van Buren.

705 "Old James Buchanan . . . stands lowest, I think, in the dirty catalog of treasonable mischief-makers. For without the excuse of bad Southern blood . . . he has somehow slid into the position of boss-traitor and master-devil of the gang. He seems

James Buchanan.
CULVER PICTURES, INC.

to me the basest specimen of the human race ever raised on this continent." George Templeton Strong, 1861.

1861–1900

Abraham Lincoln

Abraham Lincoln.
CULVER PICTURES, INC.

706 "[Lincoln was] one of the very few white Americans who could converse with a Negro without anything like condescen-

sion and without anywise reminding him of the unpopularity of his color." Frederick Douglass.

707 "The greatness of Napoleon, Caesar or Washington is moonlight by the sun of Lincoln. His example is universal and will last thousands of years." Leo Tolstoy.

708 "[Lincoln] is the strong man of his party—full of wit, facts, dates, and the best stump-speaker, with his droll ways and dry jokes, in the West. He is as honest as he is shrewd. . . ." Stephen A. Douglas, 1858.

"[Lincoln's] appearance, his pedigree, his coarse low jokes and anecdotes, his vulgar similes and his frivolity, are a disgrace to the seat he holds. Other brains rule the country. *He* is made the tool . . . to crush out slavery, by robbery, rapine, slaughter, and bought armies." John Wilkes Booth, 1864.

Andrew Johnson

709 "Mr. Johnson was a Democrat of pride, conviction, and self-assertion—a man of the people, who not only desired no higher grade of classification, but could not be forced into its acceptance." Jefferson Davis, 1866.

710 "In Egypt, the Lord sent frogs, locusts, murrain, lice, and finally demanded the blood of the first-born of all the oppressors. . . . We have been oppressed by taxes and debts, and He has sent us worse than lice, and has afflicted us with Andrew Johnson." Thaddeus Stevens, 1866.

Andrew Johnson, Brady photo.
CULVER PICTURES, INC.

711 "[Johnson] never heeds any advice. He attempts to govern after he has lost the means to govern. He is like a General fighting without an army—he is like Lear roaring at the wild storm, bareheaded and helpless." William Tecumseh Sherman, 1868.

Ulysses S. Grant

712 "That, two thousand years after Alexander the Great and Julius Caesar, a man like Grant should be called—and

Ulysses S. Grant.
CULVER PICTURES, INC.

should actually and truly be —the highest product of the most advanced evolution, made evolution ludicrous. . . . The progress of evolution from President Washington to President Grant was alone evidence enough to upset Darwin." Henry Adams, 1918.

713 "[Grant's] imperturbability is amazing. I am in doubt whether to call it greatness or stupidity." James A. Garfield, 1876.

714 "Grant's whole character was a mystery even to himself—a combination of strength and weakness not paralleled by any of whom I have read in Ancient or Modern history." William Tecumseh Sherman.

Rutherford B. Hayes

715 "[Hayes's] administration was credit-

able to all concerned and was far better than four years of unrest which we should undoubtedly have had if Tilden had occupied the office of President. Sometimes we are disposed to doubt the guiding will of Providence in the history of mankind, but looking over the ground I feel that there never was in the history of the world an occasion where the interposition of a Higher Power was more manifest and more productive of good." Abram S. Hewitt, 1901. Hewitt was chairman of the Democratic National Committee during the Hayes-Tilden campaign for the presidency and one of the authors of the compromise that made Hayes President (see numbers 80, 180).

716 "President [Hayes], we are told, sits in his magisterial chair, serene, smiling, complacent, and confident that the best way to protect sheep from being devoured is to give them over to the custody of the wolves." William Lloyd Garrison, speaking of Hayes's "southern policy," 1878.

717 "The policy of the President has turned out to be a give-away from the beginning. He has nolled suits, discontinued prosecutions, offered concil-

Rutherford B. Hayes.
CULVER PICTURES, INC.

iation everywhere in the South while they have spent their time in whetting their knives for any Republican they could find." James A. Garfield, on the same subject, 1878.

James A. Garfield

718 "Who of us, having heard him here or elsewhere, speaking on a question of great national concern, can forget the might and majesty, the force and directness, the grace and beauty of his utterances? . . . He did not flash forth as a meteor; he rose with measured and stately step over rough paths and through years of rugged work." William McKinley, 1886.

719 "I am completely disgusted with Garfield's course. . . . Garfield has shown that he is not possessed of the backbone of an angleworm." Ulysses S. Grant, 1881.

Lithograph of James A. Garfield.
CULVER PICTURES, INC.

720 "The cynical impudence with which the reformers have tried to manufacture an ideal statesman out of the late shady politician [Garfield] beats anything in novel-writing." Henry Adams, 1881.

Chester A. Arthur

721 "I have but one annoyance with the Administration of President Arthur and that is, that, in contrast with it, the Administration of Hayes becomes respectable, if not heroic." Roscoe Conkling, 1883.

722 "I am but one in 55,000,000; still, in the opinion of this one-fifty-

Chester A. Arthur. CULVER
PICTURES, INC.

five millionth of the country's population, it would be hard to better President Arthur's Administration. But don't decide until you hear from the rest." Mark Twain, 1883.

723 "All [Arthur's] ambition seems to center in the social aspect of the situation. Flowers and wine and food, and slow pacing with a lady on his arm, and a quotation from Thackeray or Dickens, or an old Joe Miller . . . make up his book of life." Harriet Stanwood (Mrs. James G.) Blaine, 1882.

Grover Cleveland

724 "[Cleveland is] a man of force & stubbornness with no breadth of view, no training in our history & traditions & essentially coarse fibred & self sufficient." Henry Cabot Lodge, 1896.

725 "I feel myself strongly attracted to Mr. Cleveland as the best representative of the higher type of Americanism that we have seen since Lincoln was snatched from us." James Russell Lowell, 1887.

726 "When Judas betrayed Christ, his heart was not blacker than this scoundrel, Cleveland, in deceiving the Democracy. . . . He is an old bag of beef and I am going to Washington with a pitchfork and prod him in his old fat ribs." Benjamin Tillman, 1894 (see number 85).

Commemorative cards, Grover
Cleveland and Mrs. Cleveland.
CULVER PICTURES, INC.

Benjamin Harrison

727 "Outside the White House and at dinner [Harrison] could be a courtly gentleman. Inside the Executive Mansion, in his reception of those who solicited official appointments for themselves or their friends, he was as glacial as a Siberian stripped of his furs." Thomas Collier Platt, 1910.

MARSHALL & BALL,
CLOTHIERS,
807, 809, 811 & 813 BROAD STREET
NEWARK, N. J.

Trade card depicting Benjamin
Harrison. CULVER PICTURES, INC.

728 "[Harrison] was a plain little man, white as to hair and beard, who kept his elbows to himself at dinner and . . . who insisted always that public affairs should be conducted in a public manner and not after the informal fashion of the Forty Thieves." William Allen White, 1928.

729 "We have one of the smallest Presidents the U.S. has ever known. [Harrison] is narrow, unresponsive and, oh, so cold. . . . As one Senator says: 'It's like talking to a hitching post.'" Walter Wellman, 1889.

William McKinley

730 "McKinley has a chocolate-éclair backbone." Theodore Roosevelt, 1898. The line more frequently appears as "McKinley has about as much backbone as a chocolate éclair."

Lithograph of William McKinley and Mrs. McKinley.
CULVER PICTURES, INC.

731 "[McKinley] had such a good heart that the right thing to do always occurred to him." William Howard Taft, 1916.

732 "McKinley keeps his ear to the ground so close that he gets it full of grasshoppers much of the time." Joseph Cannon.

1900–45

Theodore Roosevelt

733 "I am afraid he is too pugnacious. . . . I want peace and I am told that your friend Theodore is always getting into rows with everybody." William McKinley, 1897.

Theodore Roosevelt.
CULVER PICTURES, INC.

734 "[Roosevelt] is still mentally in the Sturm and Drang period of early adolescence, [he] . . . gushes over war as the ideal condition of human society, for the manly strenuousness which it involves, and treats peace as a condition of blubber-like and swollen ignobility." William James, 1899.

735 "[Roosevelt] was very likeable, a big figure, a rather ordinary intellect, with extraordinary gifts, a shrewd and I think pretty unscrupulous politician. He played all his cards—if not more." Oliver Wendell Holmes, Jr., 1921.

William Howard Taft

736 "Taft is a large body, entirely surrounded by men who know exactly what they want." Jonathan P. Dolliver, 1909.

737 "[Taft] is evidently a man who takes color from his surroundings. He was an excellent man under me, and close to me. . . . He has not the slightest idea of what is necessary if this country is to make social and industrial progress." Theodore Roosevelt, 1910, 1911.

738 "As a man and as a real honest-to-God fellow, Mr. Taft will go to his grave with more real downright affection and less enemies than any. . . . We are parting with three hundred pounds of solid charity to everybody, and love and affection for all his countrymen." Will Rogers, 1930.

Photo of William Howard Taft.
CULVER PICTURES, INC.

Woodrow Wilson

739 "[Wilson] is a perfect jackrabbit of politics, perched upon his little hillock of expediency, with ears erect and nostrils distended, keenly alert to every scent or sound and ready to run and double in any direction." William Randolph Hearst, 1912.

740 "The spacious philanthropy which [Wilson] exhaled upon Europe stopped quite sharply at the coast of his own country. . . . Peace and goodwill among all nations abroad, but no truck with the Republican Party at home." Winston Churchill, 1929.

Woodrow Wilson.
CULVER PICTURES, INC.

741 "[Wilson] failed as Jesus Christ failed, and, like Christ, [he] sacrifices his life in pursuance of his noble ideal." David Lloyd George, 1924.

Warren G. Harding

742 "This is a hell of a job! I have no trouble with my enemies. I can take care of my enemies all right. But my damn friends, my God-damned friends . . . they're the ones who keep me walking the floor nights!" Warren G. Harding, 1923.

743 "[Harding] was a 'good fellow' in the ordinary locker-room, poker-game sense of that term; far too much of a 'good fellow,' in fact, to be entrusted with great authority. . . . His speeches left the impression of an army of pompous phrases moving over the landscape in search of an idea. Sometimes these meandering words would actually capture a straggling thought and bear it triumphantly, a prisoner in their midst, until it died of servitude and overwork." William Gibbs McAdoo, 1931.

744 "Harding was not a bad man. He was just a slob." Alice Roosevelt Longworth, 1933.

Warren G. Harding.
CULVER PICTURES, INC.

745 "Mr. Harding appears to me to be a kind gentleman, one whom I believe possesses humane impulses. We understand each other perfectly." Eugene V. Debs, 1921. In 1921 Harding ordered Debs released from federal prison where, as an opponent of the World War, he had been confined since 1918.

Calvin Coolidge

746 "I have noticed that nothing I never said ever did me any harm." Calvin Coolidge.

Calvin Coolidge throws the first ball for the 1924 World Series.
CULVER PICTURES, INC.

747 "Mr. Coolidge's genius for inactivity is developed to a very high point. It is far from being an indolent inactivity. It is a grim, determined, alert inactivity which keeps Mr. Coolidge occupied constantly." Walter Lippmann, 1928.

748 "[Coolidge] was wholly lacking in imagination. . . . The lighter side of life and its amusements meant little to him. He went through this part of his official routine with a sort of patient resignation but the expression of his face was about the same when he opened a baseball game as when he sat and listened to his favorite preacher at church on Sunday morning." Nicholas Murray Butler, 1939.

Herbert Hoover

749 "[Hoover] is certainly a wonder, and I wish we could make him President. There couldn't be a better one." Franklin D. Roosevelt, 1920.

Herbert Hoover, 1928.
CULVER PICTURES, INC.

750 "That man [Hoover] has offered me unsolicited advice for six years, all of it bad." Calvin Coolidge, 1928.

751 "Underneath his shyness, [Hoover] is so sensitive and really human that it is a tragedy that he cannot, apparently, make that side of his nature felt in his public contacts." Henry L. Stimson, 1930.

Franklin D. Roosevelt

Franklin Delano Roosevelt.
CULVER PICTURES, INC.

752 "[Roosevelt] is a pleasant man who, without any important qualifications for the job, would very much like to be President." Walter Lippmann, 1932.

753 "In speaking of the impossibility of realizing the principles of planned economy while preserving the economic basis of capitalism I do not in the least desire to belittle the outstanding personal qualities of Roosevelt, his initiative, courage and determination. Undoubtedly Roosevelt stands out as one of the strongest figures among all the captains of the contemporary capitalist world." Joseph Stalin, 1934.

754 "Make no mistake, [Roosevelt] is a

force—a man of superior but impenetrable mind, but perfectly ruthless, a highly versatile mind which you cannot foresee." Carl Jung, 1936.

755 "Roosevelt is a Jeffersonian democrat, projected into the industrial age. Deeply religious, profoundly American, an aristocrat with that magnanimity of spirit which loathes cruelty and special privileges, he is less concerned with inferences from a system than with adaptation of intuitions." Harold J. Laski, 1942.

1945–88

Harry S Truman

756 "I never gave them hell, I just tell the truth and they think it's hell." Harry S Truman, 1956.

757 "[Truman] is a man of immense determination. He takes no notice of delicate ground, he just plants his foot down firmly on it." Winston Churchill, 1945.

758 "[Truman] is a small opportunistic man, a man of good instincts but, therefore, probably all the more dangerous. As he moves out more in the pub-

lic eye, he will get caught in the webs of his own making." Henry A. Wallace, 1944.

759 "[Truman] is a man totally unfitted for the position. His principles are elastic, and he is careless with the truth. He has no special knowledge of any subject, and he is a malignant, scheming sort of an individual who is dangerous not only to the United Mine Workers, but dangerous to the United States of America." John L. Lewis, 1948.

Harry S Truman.
CULVER PICTURES, INC.

Dwight D. Eisenhower

760 "General Eisenhower is a very great man, not only because of his military accomplishments but because of his human, friendly, kind and frank nature. He is not a *grubi* [coarse, brusque] man like most military." Joseph Stalin, 1945.

Dwight D. Eisenhower, 1958.
CULVER PICTURES, INC.

761 "If Eisenhower should become president, his administration would make Grant's look like a model of perfection." Harry S Truman, 1950.

762 "President Eisenhower's whole life is proof of the stark but simple truth—that no one hates war more than one who has seen a lot of it." Richard M. Nixon, 1959.

John F. Kennedy

763 "There is something very eighteenth century about this young man. He is always on his toes during our discussion. But in the evening there will be music and wine and pretty women." Harold Macmillan, 1962.

764 "[Kennedy] leaves little doubt that his idea of the 'challenging new world' is one in which the Federal Government will grow bigger and do more and of course spend more. . . . Under the tousled boyish hair cut it is still old Karl Marx." Ronald Reagan, 1960.

765 "[Kennedy] was responsive, sensitive, humble before the people, and bold in their behalf." Martin Luther King, Jr.

John F. Kennedy greets his son John. CULVER PICTURES, INC.

Lyndon B. Johnson

766 "[Johnson] is a small man. He hasn't got the depth of mind nor the breadth of vision to carry great responsibility. . . . Johnson is superficial and opportunistic " Dwight D. Eisenhower, 1960.

767 "Johnson's instinct for power is as primordial as a salmon's going

Lyndon Baines Johnson.
CULVER PICTURES, INC.

upstream to spawn." Theodore H. White, 1965.

768 "Johnson knew how to woo people. He was a born political lover. Many people looked upon him as a heavy-handed man. That was not really true. He was sort of like a cowboy making love." Hubert H. Humphrey.

Richard M. Nixon

769 "[Nixon] is a filthy, lying son-of-a-bitch, and a very dangerous man." John F. Kennedy, 1960.

770 "[Nixon] is the kind of politician who

Richard M. Nixon and Spiro Agnew. CULVER PICTURES, INC.

would cut down a redwood tree and then mount the stump to make a speech for conservation." Adlai E. Stevenson, 1956.

771 "[Nixon] struck me as one of those frank and steady personalities on whom one feels one could rely in the great affairs of State if ever they were to reach the highest office." Charles de Gaulle, 1971.

772 "Most of all, [Nixon] produces the impression of a slightly fraudulent, petty storekeeper, capable of selling tainted herring or representing kerosene-soaked sugar as good merchandise." Nikita Khrushchev, 1962.

Gerald R. Ford

773 "I could think of no public figure better able to lead us in national renewal than this man so quintessentially American, of unquestioned integrity, at peace with himself, thoughtful and knowledgeable of national affairs and international responsibilities, calm and unafraid." Henry Kissinger, 1982.

774 "Jerry Ford is so dumb he can't walk and chew gum at the same time. . . . He is a nice fellow, but he spent too much

time playing football without a helmet." One of several versions of these remarks attributed to Lyndon Johnson.

775 "I like [Ford] as an individual, but cripes, he's an awful President. . . . Don't misunderstand. Jerry Ford is no dunce by any means. Jerry Ford's a smart fellow. But Jerry Ford doesn't want to learn new tricks." Thomas "Tip" O'Neill, 1976.

Gerald R. Ford signs Nixon's pardon, 1974.
CULVER PICTURES, INC.

James Earl Carter

776 "President Carter is true to himself and true to others. It is because he is so honest with others, that is why I have no difficulty in dealing with him. . . . [He is] a man impelled by the power of religious faith and lofty values—a farmer, like me." Anwar Sadat, 1978.

777 "Carter is a nice fellow, but he is the most poorly equipped man

ever to sit in the White House." Barry Goldwater, 1978.

James Earl Carter, 1977.
RICK SMOLAN

778 "No useful purpose is served by talking with Carter. During our next telephone conversation, I will read out to him the Cologne–Euskirchen railroad timetable. He does not listen anyhow." Helmut Schmidt, 1978.

Ronald Reagan

779 "[Reagan] has contributed a spirit of good will and grace to the Presidency and American life generally." Edward M. Kennedy, 1986.

780 "We showed his films on TV because we couldn't believe it was true that such a man was President of America. We rolled about laughing. . . . Reagan embodies nothing more than the peak of a capitalist rotten society in which everyone is ready to make any promise so long as he is elected." Muammar Qaddafi, 1981.

781 "[Reagan is] a person with whom you can't seriously discuss serious issues. . . . Many, many times . . . I have been with members of Congress in Mr. Reagan's presence, and I don't have the feeling that ever once, any of us have gotten through to him with any point of view other than the one he entered the meeting with." Jim Wright, 1987.

Ronald Reagan, 1986.
UPI/BETTMANN NEWSPHOTOS.

PART VI
Literature and Music

BOOKS EVERYONE OUGHT TO READ SOMETIME

782 William Bradford, *Of Plymouth Plantation*. This is the first account of American history, written by the governor of the Plymouth colony. It tells the story of the Pilgrims, from their departure for Holland through the voyage of the *Mayflower* and the founding of Plymouth, and on to 1646. The manuscript, which contains the oldest-known copy of the May-flower Compact, disappeared at the time of the Revolution. It was discovered many years later in England and was published in 1856. Massachusetts Senator George Frisbie Hoar's claim that with the possible exception of the Bible the manuscript was "the most precious on earth" is a fine example of political hyperbole, but *Plymouth Plantation* is a moving account of an American epic.

783 Thomas Paine, *Crisis Papers* (1776–83). The first of these essays begins with the famous lines "These are the times that try men's souls. The summer soldier and the sunshine patriot will, in this crisis, shrink from the service of their country; but he that stands it *now,* deserves the love and thanks of man and woman." Although less well known than *Common Sense, Crisis Papers* makes for more interesting reading today. They are both remarkable examples of wartime propaganda and are vivid recreations of the revolutionary spirit of the 1770s.

1808 cartoon lampooning a (personal) crisis for the author of *Crisis Papers*.
AMERICAN ANTIQUARIAN SOCIETY.

784 Thomas Jefferson, *Notes on Virginia* (1785). This work, Jefferson's only full-length publication, was written in response to a series of questions posed him in 1781 by a French diplomat. Working from notes that he had collected over the years, Jefferson produced a detailed account of the history, geography, natural resources, people, government, economy, churches, schools, and other institutions of Virginia. It is a mine of useful information about the region and a source of insights into the workings of Jefferson's mind. On Indians: "The women are submitted to unjust drudgery. This I believe is the case with every barbarous people." On blacks: "I advance it, therefore, as a suspicion only, that the blacks . . . are inferior to the whites in the endowments both of mind and body." On religious toleration: "It does me no injury for my neighbor to say there are twenty gods, or no God. It neither picks my pocket nor breaks my leg." On reason: "It is error alone that needs the support of government. Truth can stand by itself."

785 Richard Henry Dana, *Two Years Before the Mast* (1840). Dana, whose love affair with the sea began in boyhood, left Harvard after his sophomore year in 1834 to sail "round the Horn" to California on the brig *Pilgrim*. The book is based on a journal that he kept during the voyage and is full of nautical language and lore; it is both an incomparable picture of the life of ordinary seamen in the days of sail and a kind of poem about the sea. It was an enormous popular success in America and abroad. Two thousand British sailors were said to have purchased it in a single day when it was published in that country.

786 Henry David Thoreau, *Walden* (1854). This is an account of two years that Walden spent living on Walden Pond in Massachusetts. Thoreau did not depend entirely on his own devices—his average weekly expenditure came to twenty-seven cents. But he tried to show that he could, if necessary, do without the products of civilization. He used store-bought plaster in making his house, but also made a little out of clamshells to prove it could be done. But *Walden* is also his attempt "to live deep and suck out all the marrow of life" and an attack on middle-class values and the "lives of quiet desperation" that so many of his contemporaries seemed to him to be leading.

Manuscript page of *Walden*, "Life in the Woods." COURTESY OF THE NEW YORK PUBLIC LIBRARY, RARE BOOKS DIVISION.

787 Mark Twain, *Life on the Mississippi* (1883). From 1857 until the Civil War, Mark Twain was a pilot on Mississippi steamboats. This description of his experiences is part autobiography, part an account of the lore and technology of that profession, and part background for his great novels, *Tom Sawyer* and *Huckleberry Finn*.

Illustration from *Life on the Mississippi*. COURTESY OF THE NEW YORK PUBLIC LIBRARY.

788 Ulysses S. Grant, *Personal Memoirs* (1885). No doubt *General* Grant's place in history was secure from the moment Robert E. Lee surrendered to him at Appomattox Courthouse; but the reputation of Grant the man rests, to a very large extent, on this book. His political career after the war had been undistinguished at best; when that ended, his inadequacies as a businessman and judge of the character of most civilians led to disaster. He invested all his capital and a good deal of borrowed money in a partnership with an unscrupulous broker whose "rascality" (Grant's word) left him penniless. Even his wartime souvenirs were lost. Not long thereafter, he learned that he was dying of cancer. To provide for his family, he set out to complete his memoirs— "the only civil task he had learned how to do well," as a biographer noted. The result is a classic.

789 Henry George, *Progress and Poverty* (1879). Over the years Henry George, a San Francisco newspaperman, was increasingly disturbed by the extent to which land speculators were making enormous profits merely by holding on to land while the population increased, and by what seemed to him a continually widening gap between rich and poor. "Where population is densest, wealth greatest, and the machinery of production and exchange most highly developed," he wrote, "we find the deepest poverty, the sharpest struggle for existence, and the most of enforced idleness." George called for a property tax that would confiscate the "unearned income" earned by landowners, which, he claimed, would make all other forms of taxation unnecessary and provide enough money to build new and better schools, museums, and other valuable public institutions. *Progress and Poverty* attracted wide attention and "single tax" clubs sprang up all over the nation, though of course such a tax was never enacted.

790 Thorstein Veblen, *The Theory of the Leisure Class* (1899). This was an even more savage assault on the acquisitive character of American society than Henry George's. Veblen argued that Americans tended slavishly to ape the standards and values of the wealthy. He coined the term "conspicuous consumption" and heaped scorn on those who practiced it.

791 W. E. Burghardt Du Bois, *The Souls of Black Folk* (1903). This book of essays and stories, the most famous of which is "Of Mr. Booker T. Washington and Others" (see number 324), sought to change the way American blacks dealt with segregation and other aspects of their white-dominated world. Du Bois urged black people to be proud of their blackness and their African origins. Like Washington, he believed blacks should work hard, but not in order to prove them-

selves to whites. They must stop "measuring one's self through the eyes of others" and strive for political power and educational opportunities as well as economic security. Du Bois was a militant (to white Southerners at the time he seemed a dangerous radical) but not then a radical. He ended the book with the hope that "infinite reason [might] turn the tangle straight."

Writer W. E. B. DuBois in his office at N.A.A.C.P. headquarters. COURTESY OF THE N.A.A.C.P.

792 Henry Adams, *The Education of Henry Adams* (1918). Adams wrote this account of his own life in order (or so he claimed) to discourage future biographers from writing about him. He described autobiography as a "shield of protection in the grave," and advised the novelist Henry James "to take your own life in the same way, in order to prevent biographers from taking it in theirs." His use of the third person in telling his story may have been related to this purpose. Of course he failed to keep others from

writing about him; indeed, both what he said and what he did not say in his *Education* (for example, he made no mention of his wife) has proved a stimulus to his many biographers. But this is one of the great life stories of an American.

793 Frederick Lewis Allen, *Only Yesterday* (1931). Few "popular" histories have had either the influence on scholars or the continuing appeal to the general public that this "informal history" of the twenties has had. Allen was interested both in great events and in the odd and interesting events and people that gave the decade its particular character. He dealt with culture (high and low) as well as with more conventional political and economic events. Both in his insights and in his brilliant use of unexpected examples—and despite what one historian has called his "freewheeling, inventive style of historical argumentation"—Allen was indeed "the Herodotus of the Jazz Age."

794 Richard Wright, *Native Son* (1940). This story of one Bigger Thomas, an uneducated black man who is so furious at the way white society functions that he almost becomes his own worst enemy, was the first novel by a black

author to reach a large white audience. It was a Book-of-the-Month Club selection and was later made into a successful Broadway play. The novel is important both as a picture of what life was like for poor blacks and as an account of how black radicals (Wright at that time was a member of the Communist Party) and probably most ordinary black people experienced living in a white-dominated world.

Richard Wright, June 23, 1939. LIBRARY OF CONGRESS.

WORDS THAT CHANGED OUR MINDS

795 **Common Sense** (1776) by Thomas Paine. The famous pamphlet that, with its bold call for outright independence rather than reform of the British imperial system, and its harsh attack on both

George III (he called the king a "Royal Brute") and the very idea of monarchy, persuaded thousands to favor a complete break with Great Britain (see numbers 260, 783).

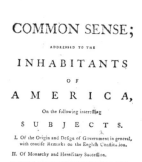

Frontispage, *Common Sense*. COURTESY OF THE NEW YORK PUBLIC LIBRARY.

796 **Uncle Tom's Cabin** (1852) by Harriet Beecher Stowe. Whether or not Abraham

1852 advertisement for *Uncle Tom's Cabin*. BELLA LANDAUER COLLECTION, COURTESY OF THE NEW-YORK HISTORICAL SOCIETY.

Lincoln actually said to Stowe, "So you're the little woman who wrote the book that made this great war," this book had an enormous impact on how Northerners felt about slavery. This was principally because of Stowe's ability to describe plantation slaves as individual people with deep feelings caught in an evil system, and to do so without treating every white character in the story as an unmitigated villain. Stowe avoided the self-righteous accusatory tone of most abolitionist writings; she sought to persuade rather than to condemn, and she succeeded brilliantly.

797 **The Impending Crisis of the South** (1857) by Hinton Rowan Helper. Although a Southerner, Helper argued with a mass of statistical evidence that slavery was weakening both the economy of the South and the structure of southern society. His book had little influence in the slave states; but since it was written by a Southerner, it impressed many Northerners. The Republicans made effective use of it in the 1860 election.

798 **The Influence of Sea Power Upon History, 1660–1783** (1890) by Alfred Thayer Mahan. Captain Mahan's ar-

gument was that throughout history, nations with powerful navies and the overseas bases necessary to support them were victorious in war and prosperous in peacetime. While not a widely read book, it had a wide influence among the American military and political leaders who devised and carried out the Large Policy (see number 77).

799 **Wealth Against Commonwealth** (1894) by Henry Demarest Lloyd. This powerful, if somewhat exaggerated, attack on the Standard Oil monopoly attracted wide attention. Besides denouncing Standard's business practices—Lloyd quipped that the trust did everything to the Pennsylvania legislature except refine it—he denounced *laissez-faire* economics and the application of Darwinian ideas about the survival of the fittest to social affairs.

800 **The School and Society** (1899) by John Dewey. In this book the philosopher John Dewey developed the basic ideas of what was later to be known as "progressive" education. Schools should build character and train children to be good citizens, not merely provide them with new knowledge. They should make use of the child's curiosity, imagination, and past experience, not rely on discipline and rote memory to teach.

801 **The Jungle** (1906) by Upton Sinclair. Few novels have had an impact on public policy even approaching that of this book. Sinclair's story of the life of a Chicago stockyard worker described both the filthy conditions under which cattle were slaughtered and the ways in which the meat packers exploited their workers. The novel was a bestseller. President Theodore Roosevelt reacted to it by setting in motion a government investigation that led to federal meat inspection and the passage of the Pure Food and Drugs Act of 1906.

Rachael Carson, 1952.
UPI/BETTMANN NEWSPHOTOS.

802 **Silent Spring** (1962) by Rachel Carson. This book brought environmentalism to the attention of masses of people. It showed how pesticides (such as the then widely used DDT) affected birds and other animals and, indirectly, humans. *Silent Spring* caused a public furor that led to the banning of many such substances and to the modern attack on all forms of pollution.

803 **The Other America** (1962) by Michael Harrington. This book was a major force behind the so-called War on Poverty of the Lyndon Johnson era. Harrington called attention to what he called "the invisible land." Forty or fifty million souls, "somewhere between 20 and 25 per cent of the American people," were living below the poverty line, he claimed. Most of them were crowded into inner-city slums, "invisible" to the prosperous middle-class residents of the rapidly expanding suburbs.

804 **Sexual Behavior of the Human Male** (1948) by Alfred Kinsey. This study, based on more than five thousand interviews with men of all ages and positions in life, and a similar volume on women, published in 1953, demonstrated scientifically that people of all kinds en-

145

gaged in a great variety of sexual practices. The books had an enormous liberating influence on public attitudes toward human sexuality.

805 **The Feminine Mystique** (1963) by Betty Friedan. If this work did not give birth to the modern feminist movement, it surely raised it to maturity. Friedan argued that most of the opinion-shaping forces of modern society were engaged in a witless effort to convince women of the virtues of domesticity. By so doing, they were wasting the talents of millions. Women should resist these pressures, said Friedan. "The only way for a woman . . . to know herself as a person," she wrote, "is by creative work."

Writer Betty Friedan at 1972 Democratic Convention with Bella Abzug and Gloria Steinem. © 1972, FRED W. MCDARRAH

POEMS ABOUT AMERICAN HISTORY

There are many poems and songs that deal with historical events and people of his-

"The Star Spangled Banner," 1814 songsheet.
PRIVATE COLLECTION

torical importance. The most famous, of course, is the poem, "The Star-Spangled Banner" (1814), by Francis Scott Key, written during the bombardment of Fort McHenry by a British squadron in the War of 1812 (see number 923). Here are some others:

806 **"The Vision of Columbus"** (1779–87) by Joel Barlow, an enormous epic in nine "books," containing more than five thousand lines. Columbus, imprisoned in Spain, has a vision in which he sees the marvelous future of the land he discovered.

807 **"The Embargo"** (1808) by William Cullen Bryant, an intemperate attack on Thomas Jefferson ("Go, wretch, resign the presidential chair"), composed to his later embar-

rassment, when Bryant was fourteen.

808 **"Old Ironsides"** (1830) by Oliver Wendell Holmes, Sr., written to protest news that the frigate *Constitution* (see number 898) was to be scrapped, an event which this poem helped to prevent.

809 **"Hymn Sung at the Completion of the Battle Monument, Concord"** (1837) by Ralph Waldo Emerson, written to celebrate the victory of the Minutemen over the British at "the rude bridge that arched the flood" at Concord, Massachusetts, in 1775.

810 **"Paul Revere's Ride"** (1860) by Henry Wadsworth Longfellow, about Revere's famous "midnight ride" to alert the countryside to the approach of the Redcoats.

G. P. A. Healy photo of Henry Wadsworth Longfellow and companion, with a grid superimposed for painting.
THE SMITHSONIAN INSTITUTION.

811 "Shiloh, A Requiem" (1962) by Herman Melville, written after the bloody battle at that site (see number 865).

Tintype of Herman Melville around 1870. THE BERKSHIRE ATHENAEUM, PITTSFIELD, MASSACHUSETTS.

812 "Barbara Frietchie" (1863) by John Greenleaf Whittier describes an incident that was said to have taken place the previous year in Frederick, Maryland, when a Confederate column led by Stonewall Jackson (see number 878) passed through the town.

813 "O Captain! My Captain!" (1865)

Photo of Walt Whitman. CULVER PICTURES, INC.

by Walt Whitman, written after Lincoln's assassination.

814 "The New Colossus" (1883) by Emma Lazarus, a sonnet written to celebrate the erection of the Statue of Liberty. Lazarus had been roused by the persecution of Russian Jews and was involved in relief efforts on behalf of refugees arriving in America.

815 "Bryan, Bryan, Bryan, Bryan" (1919) by Vachel Lindsay, written about the 1896 presidential campaign. Lindsay wrote many poems dealing with American history, including "Our Mother, Pocahontas," "The Statue of Old Andrew Jackson," and "Abraham Lincoln Walks at Midnight."

816 "The Lincoln and Douglas Debates" (1916) by Edgar Lee Masters provides a wonderful picture of the classic confrontation between "Linkern" and "the Little Giant."

817 "the first president to be loved by his . . ." (1923) by e. e. cummings, written about the death of Warren G. Harding. Cummings was under

the impression that Harding died of food poisoning resulting from his having eaten tainted crabmeat ('Yapanese Craps"). The truth seems to have been that the President had suffered a heart attack. At about the same time, but in a different mood, cummings wrote a powerful antiwar poem, "next to of course god."

e. e. cummings. CULVER PICTURES, INC.

818 "Nightmare at Noon" (1940) by Stephen Vincent Benét is less well known than Benét's "John Brown's Body" (1928). It is a scornful attack on the isolationism of the thirties.

819 "For the Union Dead" (1964) by Robert Lowell, an attack on modern commercialism, focuses on sculptor Augustus Saint-Gauden's Civil War memorial in the Boston Common.

SONGS

Parlor entertainment.
CULVER PICTURES, INC.

820 "Yankee Doodle" by an unknown (probably British) composer, popular in America by the time of the Revolution.

821 "Chester," written during the Revolution by William Billings, begins:

Let tyrants shake their iron rod,
The foe come on with mighty stride,
And slavery clank her galling chains,
Our troops advance with martial noise.

We fear them not. We trust in God.
Their veterans flee before our youth. . . .

822 "Dixie" (1859) by Daniel D. Emmett, a minstrel and former army musician, was an instant hit. It became the unofficial war song of the Confederacy. Though he traveled widely in the South with his troupe, Emmett was a Northerner, born in Ohio and a longtime resident of Chicago. "Dixie" was first performed in January 1861.

Daniel Decatur Emmett, 1895.
CULVER PICTURES, INC.

823 "John Brown's Body" (1852), by William Steffe. The popularity of this abolitionist song inspired the writing of

Julia Ward Howe.
LIBRARY OF CONGRESS.

824 "The Battle Hymn of the Republic" (1861), with lyrics by Julia Ward Howe and music attributed to Steffe, which begins:

Mine eyes have seen the glory of the coming of the Lord,
He is trampling out the vintage where the grapes of wrath are stored . . .

825 "When Johnny Comes Marching Home" (1863) by Union Army bandmaster Patrick S. Gilmore.

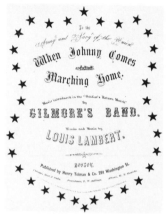

Songsheet cover, "When Johnny Comes Marching Home."
COURTESY OF THE MUSIC DIVISION, THE NEW YORK PUBLIC LIBRARY.

826 "The Union Forever, Hurrah, Boys, Hurrah," author unknown.

"The Union Forever."
CULVER PICTURES, INC.

827 "Over There" (1917), by George M. Cohan.

828 "Oh, How I Hate to Get Up in the Morning" (1917), by Irving Berlin, written for an army show, *Yip, Yip. Yaphank,* after he was drafted.

829 "I Didn't Raise My Boy to Be a Soldier" was an anti–World War I song, written by Alfred Bryan and Al Pianpadosi.

830 "Brother, Can You Spare a Dime?"—a song about unemployment in the Great Depression, written by Gorney and Harberg. It was the hit of the 1933 musical *Americana* by Corey Ford and Russell Crouse.

831 "Praise the Lord, and Pass the Ammunition," a World War II song about a fighting chaplain, was written by Frank Loesser.

832 "Rosie the Riveter," a "home front" ballad popular during World War II, written by Jay Loeb and R. Evans.

PART VII
Military Matters

QUOTES

833 "I heard the bullets whistle, and, believe me, there is something charming in the sound." George Washington, writing to his brother after his first experience in battle in 1754. When the letter was published in Great Britain, King George II is said to have remarked that the young soldier would not have found the sound of bullets so charming "if he had been used to hearing it more."

John Paul Jones, 1906 painting by Cecelia Beaux. U.S. NAVAL ACADEMY MUSEUM

834 "I have not yet begun to fight!" Captain John Paul Jones (see number 492) commanding *Bon Homme Richard* during its epic battle with HMS *Serapis,* 1779. Captain Richard Pearson, commander of *Serapis,* had hailed Jones and asked if he was ready to surrender after his attempt to board the Britisher had been repulsed.

835 "Don't give up the ship!" Captain James Lawrence, after being mortally wounded in the battle between the USS *Chesapeake* and HMS *Shannon,* 1813. A somewhat fuller version of the line runs, "Tell the men to fire faster and not to give up the ship; fight her till she sinks."

836 "We have met the enemy and they are ours." Captain Oliver Hazard Perry after defeating a British squadron at the Battle of Put-in-Bay on Lake Erie, 1813.

837 "It is well that war is so terrible—we should grow too fond of it." General Robert E. Lee, speaking to General James Longstreet while watching Union troops charging entrenched Confederate forces during the Battle of Fredericksburg, 1863.

Battle of Fredericksburg, December 13, 1862, Currier & Ives print. LIBRARY OF CONGRESS.

838 "I am heartily tired of hearing about what Lee is going to do. Some of you always think he is suddenly going to turn a double somersault, and land in our rear and on both flanks at the same time. Go back to your command, and try to think about what we are going to do ourselves." General Ulysses S. Grant, speaking to a subordinate during the Battle of the Wilderness, 1864.

839 "There is many a boy here today who looks on war as all glory, but, boys, it is all hell." General William Tecumseh Sherman speaking extemporaneously to a group of Civil War veterans, 1880.

840 "You may fire when you are ready, Gridley." Order given by Commodore George Dewey to Captain Charles Gridley, commander of the USS *Olympia.* The resulting salvo began the Battle of Manila Bay in May 1898, the first action in the Spanish-American War.

841 "Are you afraid to stand up when I am on horseback?" Theodore Roosevelt, ordering a soldier discovered lying behind a bush to get up and join the famous Rough Rider charge during the Spanish-American War, 1898. The source is Roosevelt himself, in his *Autobiography* and in *The Rough Riders.* Roosevelt added, "As I spoke, he suddenly fell forward on his face, a bullet having struck him and gone through him lengthwise. I suppose the bullet had been aimed at me." The humorist Finley Peter Dunne suggested that Roosevelt should have titled *The Rough Riders,* "Alone in Cubia."

842 "Nuts!" General Anthony C. McAuliffe's written response to a German demand that he surrender his troops at Bastogne during the Battle of the Bulge, 1944. What General McAuliffe *said* is thought to have been unprintable, even in a response to an enemy.

843 "It became necessary to destroy the town to save it." An unidentified Army major explaining the shelling and bombing of the city of Ben Tre, South Vietnam, during the Tet Offensive, 1968.

Film version of South Vietnamese refugees in 1967. CULVER PICTURES, INC.

REBELLIONS

Americans have waged only one real Civil War and they have been adept (see numbers 174–80) at solving conflicts by compromising. But in the colonial period and in the early decades of the Republic there were a substantial number of internal conflicts that led Americans to take up arms against one another. Here are some of them.

Engraving of Sir Nathaniel Bacon. LIBRARY OF CONGRESS.

844 **Bacon's Rebellion,** 1676. An uprising of western Virginia planters against the eastern establishment headed by Sir William Berkeley, the royal governor. The Westerners, led by Nathaniel Bacon, resented the social pretensions of the Berkeley group —which in turn considered the Baconites "a giddy and unthinking multitude"— and also Berkeley's unwill-

ingness to support their attacks on local Indians. Bacon raised a small army, murdered some peaceful Indians, burned Jamestown, and forced the governor to flee. But Bacon then came down with a "violent flux" and died. Soon thereafter, order was restored by the arrival of British troops.

845 **Leisler's Rebellion,** 1689–91. In 1689, after news of the abdication of King James II reached New York, Jacob Leisler, a local militia captain, proclaimed himself governor of the colony. He claimed to rule in the name of the new monarchs, William and Mary, and attempted without success to organize an expedition against French Canada during King William's War (see number 956). In 1691, after a governor appointed by King William arrived in New York, Leisler resisted turning over power. He was arrested, tried for treason, and executed.

846 **Paxton Boys Uprising,** 1763–64. Pennsylvania frontiersmen —many from the town of Paxton—were angered by the eastern-dominated colonial assembly's unwillingness to help in the defense against Indian attacks. These frontiersmen mur-

dered some peaceful Indians (always easier than taking on warlike tribes) and marched on Philadelphia. They were persuaded to return to their homes by a group headed by Benjamin Franklin, who promised that the assembly would authorize paying bounties for Indian scalps.

847 Pontiac's Rebellion, 1763–64.
This was a war, not a rebellion or a "conspiracy," as the historian Francis Parkman (see number 529) called it. The Indians of the Ohio Valley, led by Pontiac (see number 537), attempted unsuccessfully to drive the British out of their territory and check the influx of white settlers who invaded the region after the end of the French and Indian War.

Major Robert Rogers smokes a peace pipe with the Ottawas' Chief Pontiac.

848 Regulator War, 1769–71. Another east-west conflict, this one in North Carolina, triggered by the domination of the colonial assembly by eastern counties. This one culminated in the Battle of Almance (May 1771) in which one thousand government troops overwhelmed a (western) Regulator force twice that size.

849 Shays's Rebellion, 1786–87. This Massachusetts uprising was both a result of unstable economic conditions following the Revolution and an important cause of the movement to strengthen the central government (which resulted in the drafting of the Constitution). Debt-ridden western Massachusetts farmers, led by Daniel Shays, sought to stop foreclosures and obtain the printing of new issues of paper money by the state. They marched on Springfield, where they hoped to seize a government arsenal, but militia units easily defeated them. Shays fled the state and the "rebellion" then collapsed.

850 Whiskey Rebellion, 1794. When Congress enacted a stiff excise tax on whiskey in 1791, farmers in western Pennsylvania were hit especially hard. They were accustomed to turning their surplus grain into whiskey, which was much easier to store and ship to market than grain itself. When the farmers organized protest meetings and threatened to prevent the collection of the tax, President Washington announced that their actions "amount to treason," and ordered them "to disperse and retire peaceably to their respective abodes." When they did not, he called up thirteen thousand militiamen (a larger army than he had ever commanded during the Revolution) and marched against them. Faced with this overwhelming force, the protesters did what the President had asked. Thomas Jefferson, who was popular throughout the West, saw to it that the tax was repealed after he became President in 1801.

851 Dorr Rebellion, 1841–42. After the Revolution, Rhode Island continued to function under a charter dating from the seventeenth century, which restricted suffrage to substantial landowners and their oldest sons. Roughly half the adult male population (and of course all the women) did not have the right to vote. When the legislature refused to remedy this situation, a People's Party, led by well-to-do lawyer Thomas W. Dorr, drafted a constitution and submitted it to a popular vote. It was overwhelmingly approved, and the People's Party then elected Dorr governor. Of course, the existing government did not recognize these actions. The legal governor proclaimed martial law and sent militia units against the Dorrites. Dorr surrendered and was convicted of treason. He was sentenced to life imprisonment, but was soon released.

852 **Antirent War,** 1839–46. A protest movement occasioned by the attempt of Hudson Valley landlords to collect what amounted to feudal dues based on "leases" dating from the colonial period. In 1839, after the death of Stephen Van Rensselaer (see number 628), who owned roughly three thousand farms and was "owed" some $400,000 in back rents, his heirs attempted to collect these debts. Van Rensselaer had been lax about these obligations and the tenants resorted to violence to prevent foreclosures. The New York State militia was called out and order was restored. In 1844, a legislative committee decided that the Van Rensselaer titles were legal. This caused farmers, disguised as Indians, to riot again. After a sheriff had been killed by the antirenters, martial law was again declared, and order restored. Finally in 1846, a new state constitution put an end to the old tenures, and the tenants obtained title to their farms.

CIVIL WAR BATTLES

The key battles of the Civil War, and their relationship to the overall course of the conflict, can best be kept straight by separating the fighting east of the Appalachians from that in the Mississippi Valley. In some cases the Confederates named the battles after towns, the Northerners after rivers.

Eastern Theater

Photo by Barnard and Gibson showing the ruins of Manassas Junction in March 1862.
LIBRARY OF CONGRESS.

853 **First Bull Run (First Manassas),** fought in Virginia, twenty miles south of Washington, D.C., July 21, 1861. This was a seesaw struggle. Early Union gains were erased by a Confederate counterattack that led to a Union rout. But the inexperienced Confederates were unable to follow up their victory by capturing Washington.

854 **Seven Days Before Richmond,** June 25–July 1, 1862. Slow Union advances from bases at Fortress Monroe (see number 929) on Chesapeake Bay were checked by a ferocious Confederate attack that forced Union troops back to the protection of the guns of the Navy. There were heavy losses on both sides.

855 **Second Bull Run (Second Manassas),** August 29–30, 1862. This was another rout of Union forces, and on the same field as the First Bull Run.

856 **Antietam,** September 17, 1862 (also known as Sharpsburg). A Confederate advance into Pennsylvania was checked, both sides suffering heavy losses. The battle was a draw, but the Confederates were forced to withdraw south of the Potomac.

The Hagerstown Turnpike on September 17, 1862.
LIBRARY OF CONGRESS.

857 Fredericksburg. On December 13, 1862, a Union assault on entrenched Confederates was repulsed with heavy losses (see number 837).

858 Chancellorsville, May 1–4, 1863. A Union assault was crushed by a flank attack, but Union lines held and the battle stabilized. The Union troops then withdrew.

859 Gettysburg, July 1–3, 1863. A Confederate invasion of Pennsylvania was checked when a small skirmish at Gettysburg expanded into an all-out battle. There were heavy losses on both sides, but the battle was an important Union victory, since the Confederates were incapable of continuing the fight and retreated to Virginia.

860 The Wilderness, May 5–6, 1864. This was a bloody struggle in tangled country south of the Rappahannock River in northern Virginia. It ended when a Union flanking movement forced the Confederates to retreat.

861 Spotsylvania Courthouse, May 8–9, 1864. A continuation of the above, marked by much hand-to-hand fighting. Union losses were twice as heavy as Confederate, but renewed flanking moves again forced the Confederates to retreat further south.

862 Cold Harbor, June 3, 1864. A foolish Union attack on entrenched Confederates was repulsed with heavy losses.

Union troops during the siege of Petersburg. THE NATIONAL ARCHIVES.

863 Siege of Petersburg, June 1864– April 1865. This protracted engagement was marked by continual Union pressure on the defenses of the city as the battle lines were steadily extended to the south and west. The Confederates were unable to retreat without abandoning Richmond.

864 Appomattox Courthouse, April

SURRENDER OF GEN. LEE!

"The Year of Jubilee has come! Let all the People Rejoice!"

200 GUNS WILL BE FIRED

On the Campus Martius,
AT 3 O'CLOCK TO-DAY, APRIL 10,
To Celebrate the Victories of our Armies. *1865*

Every Man, Woman and Child is hereby ordered to be on hand prepared to Sing and Rejoice. The crowd are expected to join in singing Patriotic Songs. ALL PLACES OF BUSINESS MUST BE CLOSED AT 2 O'CLOCK. Hurrah for Grant and his noble Army.

By Order of the Peop.

Broadside announces the surrender of General Lee, 1865. COURTESY OF THE DETROIT PUBLIC LIBRARY.

9, 1865. The Confederates, finally retreating from Petersburg, were overwhelmed by much superior Union forces and surrendered.

Western Theater

865 Shiloh, April 6–7, 1862. A Union army advancing in the direction of Corinth, Mississippi, an important railroad junction, was surprised by a large Confederate army at Shiloh, Tennessee, twenty miles north of Corinth. It was saved from defeat by the arrival of reinforcements, and on the second day of fighting the Confederates were forced to retreat. Union troops then occupied Corinth.

Diary watercolor by soldier Fred E. Ransom shows the fight at Shiloh for Wallace's 11th Regiment. ILLINOIS STATE HISTORICAL LIBRARY.

866 Corinth, October 3–4, 1862. Confederate troops, seeking to dislodge the Union army in Corinth, were thrown back with heavy losses.

867 New Orleans, April 26, 1862. At night, a Union naval squadron in the Gulf of Mexico bypassed forts guarding the city and landed troops easily driving off the outnumbered Confederate defenders.

868 Siege of Vicksburg, May 22–July 4, 1863. After defeating one Confederate army in the vicinity of Jackson, Mississippi, Union troops drove another behind the defenses of Vicksburg. After a long siege, the city surrendered. The fall of Vicksburg allowed Union gunboats to control the entire length of the Mississippi River and thus to cut the Confederacy in two.

The 8th Wisconsin Regiment display their battle eagle "Old Abe" during the siege of Vicksburg, 1863.
LIBRARY OF CONGRESS.

869 Chickamauga, September 19–20, 1863. An indecisive, ineptly managed engagement. Union forces were driven off temporarily, but regained control of the city.

870 Chattanooga, November 25, 1863. Confederate troops seeking to capture Union-held Chattanooga were badly defeated after the arrival of strong Union reinforcements.

Lithograph, "After Destroying Missionary Ridge." COURTESY OF THE CHICAGO HISTORICAL SOCIETY.

871 Atlanta, September 2, 1864. After a slow advance from Chattanooga, a large Union army pounded its way into Atlanta. Then, when the retreating Confederate army headed north in the direction of Nashville, one Union force pursued it, while the rest of the Army "marched through Georgia" unopposed to

Rebel works in front of Atlanta, Georgia, photographed by George N. Barnard.
THE MUSEUM OF MODERN ART.

872 Savannah, December 21, 1864. After a skillful but essentially fu-

tile defense of the city, the greatly outnumbered Confederate defenders retreated northward.

873 Columbia, February 17, 1865. Driving north from Savannah to join the troops besieging Petersburg, Virginia, the Union army captured Columbia, South Carolina, and burned the city to the ground.

CIVIL WAR GENERALS

The Confederate Generals

874 Pierre G. T. Beauregard graduated from West Point in 1838, second in his class. He was known as "the Napoleon in Gray" because of his skill as a tactician. (He was not much of a strategist, but as one historian says, he was "a valuable man to have in command in a tight spot.") In the Mexican War, he was cited for gallantry and was twice wounded. In 1860, he was named superintendent of West Point, but he resigned to become a Confederate brigadier. He commanded the forces that began the war by attacking Fort Sumter (see number 926) and was second in command under General Joseph E. Johnston at First

Bull Run. Next he took part in the battles of Shiloh and Corinth. In 1864, back in the eastern theater, he protected Lee's flank during the Wilderness Campaign by outmaneuvering an army commanded by Benjamin Franklin Butler, and he performed brilliantly in the defense of Petersburg. Beauregard was a small, dapper man, full of grandiose schemes that never quite came off. He had trouble getting along with President Jefferson Davis and many Confederate generals. After the war, he was president of a railroad, head of the Louisiana lottery, and commissioner of public works in New Orleans.

Pierre C. T. Beauregard. COOK COLLECTION, VALENTINE MUSEUM.

875 Braxton Bragg graduated from West Point in 1837. He fought in the Seminole War and the Mexican War, but resigned his commission in 1856. He was commissioned a Confederate brigadier in 1861. He did well at the Battle of Shiloh, but thereafter performed indifferently in various engagements in Kentucky and Tennessee. He commanded the Army of Tennessee in the Battle of Chickamauga and won an early victory, but did not pursue his advantage effectively. (In general, he lacked decisiveness and was not persistent enough.) When he finally attacked at Chattanooga, Union reinforcements had arrived and he was badly defeated. After Chattanooga, a subordinate wrote, "I am convinced that nothing but the hand of God can save us or help us as long as we have our present commander." After the war he worked as a civil engineer in Alabama and Texas.

876 A. P. (Ambrose Powell) Hill graduated from West Point in 1847. After serving in the Mexican War, he was on garrison duty for a time, then spent five years with the Coast Survey in Washington, D.C. He distinguished himself during the Seven Days Before Richmond and fought well at Second Bull Run, Antietam, and at Chancellorsville, where he was wounded. During this period, however, he repeatedly

Ambrose Powell Hill. COOK COLLECTION, VALENTINE MUSEUM.

clashed with his superior, Stonewall Jackson. He did not do well at Gettysburg and saw action only infrequently in the Wilderness battles, being frequently away from the field on sick leave. On April 2, 1865, he was killed while trying to rally his men during final Confederate retreat. As the historian Douglas Southall Freeman put it, Hill "received more than his share of the Army's adversity." He was well liked by his foot soldiers, though he tended at times to be reckless, and this cost many of them their lives. But he was both overly sensitive and punctilious and often ill-tempered. His relations with other generals, and especially with his superiors—first Jackson and then Longstreet—were frequently strained.

877 John B. Hood graduated from

West Point near the bottom of his class in 1853. He served in California and Texas before resigning to join the Confederate Army. In action he quickly displayed both gallantry and military skill, rising from lieutenant to lieutenant general. He fought at Second Bull Run, Antietam, and Gettysburg (where he was wounded). Later, at Chickamauga, he lost a leg. He commanded a corps in the Army, resisting Sherman's advance into Georgia (1864), and in July took over supreme command of that force. After the fall of Atlanta, however, he retreated into Tennessee, where he suffered a final defeat at Nashville in December 1864. He became a merchant in New Orleans after the war. As a soldier he was a first-rate combat officer, "a true captain of men." "The number of colors and guns captured, and prisoners taken," he once said, was "the true test of the work done by any command." But he was a lax administrator, easily bored by camp routine.

878 **Thomas J. Jackson** graduated from West Point in 1846. He served in the artillery in the Mexican War, rising to the rank of major in less than two years. In 1851, he be-

came a teacher at Virginia Military Institute, but proved to be so indifferent a pedagogue that his students called him "Tom Fool Jackson." He won his better-known nickname, "Stonewall," at First Bull Run, and soon thereafter developed a reputation as a daring tactician, capable of moving large masses of men so swiftly from place to place that they were known as foot cavalry. He fought in the battles of the Seven Days Before Richmond and conducted a remarkable flanking maneuver that led to the Confederate victory at Second Bull Run. He played important parts in the battles of Antietam and Fredericksburg. At the Battle of Chancellorsville, he led a flanking maneuver similar to the one at Second Bull Run, but he was mortally wounded in the confusion by the fire of his own men. Jackson was a profoundly religious man (as the historian Freeman wrote, "He lives by the New Testament and fights by the Old"), but he quarreled fiercely with many of his subordinates. Some of those who knew him well believed he was insane.

879 **Joseph E. Johnston** graduated from West Point in 1829. During the Mexican War, he rose from captain to lieutenant

colonel. He was wounded several times during the campaign against Mexico City. By 1860, he had risen to brigadier, but he resigned to join the Confederate Army. He distinguished himself at First Bull Run and was put in command of the Army of Northern Virginia. He was seriously wounded during the battles around Richmond in July 1862 and was replaced by Robert E. Lee. After his recovery he was put in charge of Confederate armies in the West, where he was criticized, probably unfairly, for failing to concentrate enough troops to prevent the fall of Vicksburg. He commanded the army resisting Sherman's advance toward Atlanta in 1864, but was relieved by Hood before the city fell. He surrendered the last Confederate forces on April 26, 1865. Although Johnston tended to stress defense, which in the long run was unlikely to win the war, he was an excellent strategist. But he was not a very good administrator. His main problem, however, was his inability to get along with President Jefferson Davis, with whom he bickered constantly over policy.

880 **Albert Sidney Johnston** graduated from West Point in 1826. He took part in the

Black Hawk War, but resigned in 1834 and moved to Texas. He served in the Texas Army from 1836 to 1838 and was Secretary of War of the Republic of Texas from 1838 to 1840. In 1849 he rejoined the U.S. Army, but resigned in 1861 to become commander of Confederate forces in the West. After retreating before superior Union forces, he concentrated his troops at Corinth, Tennessee. On April 6, 1862, he surprised Grant's approaching army at Shiloh, but at the height of the battle, when victory seemed at hand, he was killed.

881 Robert E. Lee

graduated second in the class of 1829 at West Point. During the Mexican War he fought in the battles of Veracruz, Cerro Gordo, and the other clashes that occurred during the Mexico City campaign. He received a slight wound at Chapultepec. In 1852–53, he served as superintendent of West Point; later he commanded the troops that captured John Brown at Harpers Ferry. Although opposed to secession, he sided with his native state, Virginia, when it left the Union, and became President Jefferson Davis's military adviser. After the death of Albert Sidney Johnston, Davis made

1885 lithograph of the "Southern Commanders." Robert E. Lee stands at center, next to Stonewall Jackson. Davis is seated. LIBRARY OF CONGRESS.

Lee commander of the Army of Northern Virginia, which he led in every battle in the eastern theater during the remainder of the war. Lee "looked like a perfect soldier, and was." He was a brilliant tactician. As a strategist, he made the difficult but essential decision that the South must take the offensive against the North's superior numbers or face slow strangulation. He had an uncanny knack for anticipating the moves of his opponents; consequently he was daring, but not reckless. Deeply concerned with the welfare of his troops, he was revered by them and by his officers. "I would follow him blindfold," Stonewall Jackson once said. After Appomattox, Lee was indicted for treason, but never brought to trial. From 1865 until his death in 1870 he served as president of Washington College in Lexington, Virginia, the name of which was changed to Washington and Lee in 1871.

882 James Longstreet

graduated from West Point in 1842 near the bottom of his class. He was wounded in the Mexican War during the campaign against Mexico City. As a Confederate he fought extremely well at First Bull Run, less successfully during the Seven Days Before Richmond. Then he played a large part in the battles of Second Bull Run and Antietam. He bore the main force to the Union attack at Fredericksburg, the victory there convincing him that the Confederates—being, in his opinion, capable of throwing back any Union assault—should concentrate on defense. This attitude caused him to oppose Lee's decision to attack at Gettysburg, and his reluctance was partly responsible for the loss of that battle. Thereafter, he played a smaller but thoroughly competent part in the fighting. His main strength was as a battlefield commander; cool, efficient, and capable of adjusting to rapid change, he had a well-deserved reputation as a first-class poker player. But he could be sulky and was capable of fits of rage. At one point he almost fought a duel with another touchy character, A. P. Hill. After the war, he went into the insurance business but then joined the Republican Party and held a number of federal offices, much to the disgust of his friends and neighbors.

James Longstreet. COOK COLLECTION, VALENTINE MUSEUM.

883 **George E. Pickett** graduated from West Point in 1846, dead last in his class. But he performed well in the Mexican War, and then in Indian fighting in the Northwest. He fought in the Seven Days Before Richmond, where he was wounded, and at Fredericksburg. His claim to fame, of course, came at Gettysburg, where he led the famous, futile charge on Union positions on Cemetery Ridge. He worked for a life insurance company after the war.

884 **James E. B. "Jeb" Stuart** graduated from West Point in 1854. He became a cavalry officer and spent several years on duty in Kansas. He participated in the capture of John Brown after Brown's raid at Harpers Ferry. After joining the Confederate Army, he fought at First Bull Run and thereafter organized the Confederate cavalry in a most efficient manner. During the Seven Days Before Richmond, and again at Second Bull Run and Antietam, he made a number of brilliant cavalry raids, capturing many horses and prisoners and bringing back valuable information about Union troop movements. Joseph E. Johnston described him as "wonderfully endowed by nature for the direction of light cavalry," and Lee called him "the eyes of the army." His achievements, his youthful good looks, and his romantic style made him the idol of his subordinates and a great hero throughout the South. He also performed admirably at Fredericksburg and Chancellorsville, but his absence from the army on a cavalry raid contributed to the Confederate defeat at Gettysburg. He was killed in a cavalry skirmish during the Wilderness fighting.

The Union Generals

885 **Don Carlos Buell** graduated from West Point in 1841. He fought in the Seminole War and in the Mexican War, then served in the adjutant general's department. He was given command of the Army of the Ohio in 1861. After advancing as far as Nashville, Tennessee, he was ordered to move on Corinth. By chance, he reached Shiloh just in time to turn the tide in the fighting there. After various maneuvers in Tennessee and Kentucky, in which he showed a certain indecisiveness, he defeated the army of Braxton Bragg. But he failed to follow up his advantage (a court of inquiry charged that he "lost two days before taking any decisive action"), and this vexed Lincoln, who ordered him relieved of his command in October 1862. He resigned his commission in 1864. He lived in Kentucky after the war.

886 **Ambrose E. Burnside** graduated from West Point in 1847. After brief service in the Mexican War, he resigned in order to manufacture a rifle he had designed, but returned to the army when the war broke out. His troops fought with distinction at First Bull Run and at Antietam. Lincoln put him in command of the Army of the Potomac in October 1862, but he suffered a bloody defeat at

Fredericksburg. He offered to resign, but was merely relieved of command and put in charge of the Department of the Ohio, where he took stern action against Copperheads, most importantly by arresting Clement Vallandigham (see number 72). Back in the East, he took part in the Wilderness campaign, but he was judged responsible for heavy Union losses during the siege of Petersburg and resigned from the Army. Despite his failures, Burnside was a competent officer in most situations. After the war he entered Rhode Island politics, serving as governor and U.S. senator.

887 Ulysses S. Grant graduated from West Point in 1843 in the middle of his class. During the Mexican War, to which he was unsympathetic (saying, "If we have to fight, I would like to do it all at once and then make friends"), he nonetheless served with distinction. But peacetime service in the West proved discouraging. He took to drink and in 1854 resigned his commission. A number of unsuccessful business ventures followed. When the war broke out, Grant received a colonelcy and was soon promoted to brigadier. In 1862, after capturing forts Henry and Donelson

(see numbers 927, 928), he advanced toward Corinth, Mississippi, a Confederate strong point. At Shiloh he fought and won a confused, bitterly contested battle despite heavy losses. In 1863, however, he carried out a brilliant campaign against the key city of Vicksburg and won another important battle at Chattanooga. Then, after Lincoln had given him command of all Union forces, he began a relentless advance toward Richmond, fighting major battles in the Wilderness and at Spotsylvania Courthouse, Cold Harbor, and Petersburg. He finally overwhelmed the Confederate Army and forced Lee to surrender at Appomattox. After the war, he was Andrew Johnson's Secretary of War and, for two terms, President of the United States (1869–76). (See number 788.)

Ulysses S. Grant at Cold Harbor.
CULVER PICTURES, INC.

888 Henry W. Halleck graduated third in his class from West Point in 1839. He was of an intellectual bent, as his nickname "Old Brains" indicates, and published important works on strategy. He served in California during the Mexican War, and in 1854 he resigned to head a California law firm. He rejoined the Army in 1861 and was soon given command of the western theater. From 1862 to 1864, he served in Washington as general-in-chief. He then became chief of staff under Grant. Besides his scholarly achievements, Halleck was an excellent organizer, but he was not always tactful in dealing with the civilian authorities. As a battlefield commander, he tended to be indecisive and was not particularly good at dealing with other generals. He quarreled frequently with McClellan (who was even more indecisive). On the other hand, he served Grant loyally when subordinate to him in 1864–65. He remained in the Army for the rest of his life.

889 Joseph Hooker graduated from West Point in 1837. He was a staff officer during the Mexican War, but clashed with General Winfield Scott and resigned his commission in 1853. He then farmed for some years in California. After watching the First Battle of Bull Run, he wrote to Lincoln, "I am a damned sight better general than any you, Sir, had on that field" and was soon a general himself. He fought at Second Bull Run and at Antietam, where he was wounded in the foot. He proved to be a fine battlefield commander, but (in Lincoln's words) he was frequently "guilty of unjust and unnecessary criticisms of the actions of his superiors, and of the authorities." Nevertheless, after Burnside's failure at Fredericksburg, Lincoln made Hooker commander of the Army of the Potomac. Hooker promptly announced, "My plans are perfect . . . may God have mercy on General Lee, for I will have none," but he was wrong about his plans and was badly defeated at Chancellorsville. Soon

1884 lithograph of Union commanders. Joseph Hooker is to the right of Grant; Sherman has his back to Lincoln. ARCHIVES OF THE UNIVERSITY OF NOTRE DAME.

thereafter, he asked to be relieved of his command on the ground that the Administration was not giving him enough support. He was assigned to the western theater for the rest of the war.

890 **George B. McClellan** graduated from West Point in 1846, second in his class. He was sent immediately to Mexico, where he served with distinction in General Scott's command. After the war, he taught engineering at West Point for three years, and had several engineering assignments in the West and one in Europe before resigning from the Army in 1857 to work for the Illinois Central Railroad. He returned to the Army when the war broke out and was put in command of the Army of the Potomac in July 1862. Although an excellent trainer of troops, he was an incurable romantic and a most egotistical person. He also had political ambitions and was extremely critical of Lincoln, whom he considered unfit "to have any general direction over military men." As a field commander, he was inordinately slow to take the offensive, tending to overestimate enemy numbers. His advance on Richmond was a failure, and Lincoln removed him from command, but put

him in charge again after the Union defeat at Second Bull Run. He won a victory at Antietam, but when he failed to follow it up aggressively, he was replaced by Burnside. In 1864, he was the Democratic candidate for President of the United States. The military historian Kenneth P. Williams said that McClellan "was not a real general" but "merely an attractive but vain and unstable man, with considerable military knowledge, who sat a horse well and wanted to be President." In later years, he held administrative posts in New York City and was governor of New Jersey from 1878 to 1881.

George B. McClellan. COURTESY OF THE NEW-YORK HISTORICAL SOCIETY.

891 **Irvin McDowell** graduated from West Point in 1838. Between that date and the outbreak of the Civil War, he mainly held staff positions, and this experience (together with his having spent a year abroad studying the French military system) led to his appointment as commander of the army being gathered in Washington. However, he lost control of his inexperienced troops during the First Battle of Bull Run. A rout resulted, and he was soon replaced as commander by McClellan. After the Second Battle of Bull Run, he was relieved of command and charged with drunkenness, but he demanded a court of inquiry and was cleared. (He was actually a teetotaler; his weakness was for food rather than drink—he was known to have consumed an entire watermelon for dessert.) He did not again command troops in battle, however. For the rest of the war he was territorial commander in San Francisco. His later army career was spent at various posts. Late in life, he was park commissioner of San Francisco.

892 **George G. Meade** graduated from West Point in 1835, but resigned in 1836. After working as a surveyor for some years, he rejoined the Army as a topographical engineer and served under General Zachary Taylor in the Mexican War. He fought in the First Battle of Bull Run and was severely wounded during the Seven Days Before Richmond. During the Second Battle of Bull Run, and at Antietam, Fredericksburg, and Chancellorsville, he earned a reputation as an efficient and aggressive commander. Meade was Lincoln's choice to command the Army of the Potomac when Hooker resigned the post. His management of the Battle of Gettysburg was excellent, but he failed to strike Lee's exhausted forces after it ended, causing Lincoln to write (but not send) a letter to him accusing him of letting "the enemy move away at his leisure without attacking." Meade was a master of tactical warfare, but without imagination as a strategist. One historian refers to his "cautious irresolution." During the Battle of the Wilderness and the fighting that followed, he was subordinate to Grant but retained his title as commander of the Army of the Potomac. After the war, he commanded occupation forces in the Deep South.

893 **Philip H. Sheridan** graduated from West Point in 1853, after being suspended for a year for fighting with another cadet. He took part in Indian warfare in the Northwest and became a staff officer in the western theater after the outbreak of the Civil War. He was transferred to the cavalry in 1862. After participating in various campaigns in the West, he was brought east by Grant to reorganize the cavalry in that theater. He played an important role in all the battles from the Wilderness to Appomattox, cutting communications and destroying Confederate supplies in the Shenandoah Valley. After the war he commanded occupation forces in Louisiana and Texas, and then took part in the fighting against the Plains Indians (see number 361). He was named commander-in-chief of the Army in 1884. Unlike most generals of his day, Sheridan believed in total war, the object being not merely to defeat the enemy army but to destroy the enemy's ability to fight.

894 **William Tecumseh Sherman** graduated from West Point in 1840. He saw no action in the Mexican War and in 1853 resigned to work for a bank in San Francisco. Later he engaged in various business ventures, all with disappointing results. He became superintendent of a Louisiana military school in 1859, but he resigned when Louisiana seceded in 1861. Back in the Army, he fought at First Bull Run, but thereafter fought in the western theater. He served under

165

William Tecumseh Sherman.
LIBRARY OF CONGRESS.

Grant at Shiloh, Vicksburg, and Chattanooga. He commanded the army that captured Atlanta, then marched through Georgia to Savannah and north through the Carolinas. The last Confederate units surrendered to him on April 26, 1865. Although Sherman is famous for his belief in all-out war, typified by his relentless "march through Georgia," he opposed harsh reconstruction policies. He succeeded Grant as commander of the Army when Grant became President, serving until his retirement in 1883. Thereafter he sternly resisted efforts to entice him into politics (see number 317).

895 **George H. Thomas** graduated from West Point in 1840. He fought against the Seminole Indians in Florida and under Zachary Taylor in the Mexican War. He taught at West Point from 1851 to 1854. Although a Southerner, he sided with the Union in the Civil War. He fought at Corinth and, under Buell and William S. Rosecrans, in later battles in the West, serving with distinction most particularly at Chickamauga and Chattanooga. His troops were part of the army that captured Atlanta, but while Sherman marched unopposed from there to Savannah, Thomas pursued the Confederates northward and defeated them at Nashville. He was stationed in California after the war. Thomas's deliberateness in preparing for battle earned him a reputation for indecisiveness that was disproved every time he actually engaged in combat. He was probably the most underappreciated of all Union commanders.

FAMOUS WARSHIPS

Bonhomme Richard,
commemorative coin, 1779.
PRIVATE COLLECTION

896 **Bonhomme Richard.** The forty-two-gun flagship of Captain John Paul Jones (see number 492) during the Revolution. In a bloody battle off the east coast of England in 1779, *Bonhomme Richard* defeated HMS *Serapis* (see number 834).

897 **Philadelphia.** This American frigate that ran aground off the North African city of Tripoli in 1803 while pursuing enemy vessels during the War with the Barbary Pirates. It was taken over by the Tripolitanians and refitted, but a daring American naval raiding party, led by Lieutenant Stephen Decatur, entered the harbor of the city, boarded the ship, and burned it to the water's edge.

898 **Constitution.** A forty-four-gun frigate. During the War of 1812, while under the command of Captain Isaac Hull, *Constitution* defeated HMS *Guerrière*. Later in the war, while commanded by William Bainbridge, *Constitution* destroyed HMS *Java*. The vessel got its nickname, "Old Ironsides," from the poem of that name by Oliver Wendell Holmes, written in 1830 to protest plans to scrap it (see number 808). Much rebuilt, *Constitution* can be visited today at the Boston Navy Yard.

899 **Monitor** and **Merrimack.** Contestants in the first battle of "ironclad" warships off Hampton Roads, Virginia, in March 1862. When the Norfolk naval base was about to fall into Confederate hands after the outbreak of the Civil War, the steam-powered USS *Merrimack* was scuttled. However, the Confederates refloated the vessel, renamed it *Virginia,* and covered the hull with

Detail of plan for the *Merrimack.*
COURTESY OF THE NEW-YORK
HISTORICAL SOCIETY.

The ironclad *Monitor* at sea.
LIBRARY OF CONGRESS.

armor. News of this led to the hasty design and construction, by John Ericcson, of USS *Monitor,* the famous "cheesebox on a raft." After *Virginia* had made short work of several Union vessels, it and *Monitor* fought their three-hour battle. As a fight it was inconclusive, but it marked the beginning of the end of wooden warships.

900 **Alabama.** A 220-foot Confederate warship, powered by steam and sail, that was built during the Civil War in England (in violation of the British Foreign Enlistment Act, which prohibited the construction of warships for belligerents). Between July 1862, when it put to sea, and its destruction in a battle with USS *Kearsarge* in June 1864, in the English Channel off Cherbourg, France, *Alabama* captured or destroyed sixty-two Union ships. In 1872, arbitrators awarded the United States $15.5 million in compensation for damage to its shipping done by *Alabama* and two other Confederate raiders built in England during the war.

901 **Maine.** The first modern American warship, completed in the early 1890s. During the crisis preceding the outbreak of the Spanish-American War, it was sent from its base at Key West to Havana Harbor—presumably as a gesture of goodwill, but actually to be on hand to protect American citizens in Cuba in case of trouble. On February 15, 1898, the ship was rocked by an explosion and sank in the harbor. A naval court of inquiry determined that it "was destroyed by the explosion of a submarine mine," but the exact cause has never been determined. The sinking was a major cause of the declaration of war by the United States (see number 103).

902 **Oregon.** This "seagoing, coast-line" battleship, completed in 1896, is best known for its forced-draft fifteen-thousand-mile voyage from its base on the Pacific Coast around South America to the West Indies in order to be available in case of war with Spain over Cuba. The vessel accomplished its object, playing a major role in the destruction of the Spanish fleet after the war started. But the time the trip took—well over two months—was one of the reasons the United States undertook the construction of the Panama Canal.

USS *Oregon,* 1893 stereoscopic card. COURTESY OF COMMANDER DONALD J. ROBINSON, U.S. NAVAL HISTORICAL CENTER.

903 **Greer.** This old "four-stacker" destroyer fired the first American shots of World War II in September 1941. While carrying mail to Iceland, the *Greer* received a message from a patrolling British plane that it had sighted a German submarine nearby. The *Greer* made sonar contact with the U-boat and began to trail it relentlessly. After the British plane had dropped four depth charges in the area, and the *Greer* continued to follow its maneuvers closely, the U-boat fired two torpedoes at the destroyer. The *Greer* then dropped a total of nineteen depth charges in an unsuccessful effort to sink the sub. In announcing the engagement, President Roosevelt ordered the Navy to attack German vessels in the North Atlantic on sight. "When you see a rattlesnake poised to strike," he said, "you do not wait until he has struck before you crush him." Roosevelt neglected to inform the public, however, that the *Greer* had been cooperating with British forces when the submarine launched its torpedoes.

904 **Arizona.** One of the many battleships and lesser vessels destroyed by the Japanese surprise attack on Pearl Harbor, the *Arizona* was struck by "Kate" torpedo bombers and "Val" dive bombers in the first minute of the attack. A direct hit on the forward magazine caused enormous damage and sent the ship to the bottom before hundreds of crewmen could reach the deck. More than 1,100 of the 2,000-odd servicemen who died at Pearl Harbor were members of the *Arizona*'s crew. The ship, a symbol of the Pearl Harbor tragedy, was never decommissioned and is today a memorial.

Arizona, **sustaining an attack at Pearl Harbor, 1941.**
THE NATIONAL ARCHIVES.

905 **PT-109.** Famous only because when the Japanese destroyer *Amagiri* cut it in two in the black of an August night in 1943, it was commanded by Lieutenant (j.g.) John F. Kennedy.

906 **Missouri.** Flagship of the U.S. Third Fleet during the last stages of the Pacific War. The *Missouri* was slightly damaged by a kamikaze attack off Okinawa, but, like most battleships, it did not play a major role in the fighting at sea. It was, however, the site of the formal Japanese surrender in Tokyo Harbor on September 2, 1945.

OTHER FAMOUS SHIPS

907 **Susan Constant.** The caravel *Susan Constant* was the flagship of the fleet that carried the first settlers to Jamestown in 1607. (The other vessels were named *Godspeed* and *Discovery*.) *Susan Constant* was a vessel of one hundred tons; the others were much smaller.

908 **Halve Maen (Half Moon).** This tiny Dutch boat (it was less than half the size of the *Mayflower*) carried Henry Hudson and his crew on the voy-

Engraving of the *Half Moon*.
CULVER PICTURES, INC.

age when he discovered the Hudson River in 1609. Hudson sailed the *Half Moon* as far as present-day Albany. The voyage laid the basis for the Dutch claim to New Amsterdam.

909 Mayflower. Little is known about the Pilgrims' *Mayflower,* despite its fame. It apparently had 3 masts, was about 90 feet from bow to stern, and weighed about 180 tons.

910 Arbella. This was the flagship of the fleet that carried the first Puritans to Massachusetts. It is said to have been a vessel of some 350 tons, built originally for the wine trade with Portugal.

911 Gaspée. The *Gaspée* was a British revenue cutter assigned to chase smugglers in the Narragansett Bay area of the colony of Rhode Island in 1772. After it ran aground while pursuing a smuggler, local people burned it to the water's edge. Though the culprits were well known, sentiment against the prosecution of smugglers was so intense that no one could be persuaded to testify against them. The incident increased tensions between the colonists and the British authorities and thus was a step, small but significant, in the march of events leading to the Revolution.

912 Clermont. This paddle wheeler, the world's first commercially successful steamboat, was named after the country home of Robert R. Livingston, the person who financed its design and construction. Its full name was *The North River Steamboat of Clermont.* Before it proved itself by steaming up the Hudson from New York to Albany at a speed of about five knots, it was called by skeptics "Fulton's Folly," after its designer, Robert Fulton.

913 Amistad (Friendship). In 1839 this ironically named Cuban coastal schooner was carrying about fifty Africans when the blacks, led by one Cinqué, succeeded in breaking their chains and seizing the ship. They hoped to sail back to Africa, but ended in Long Island waters, where they were captured and charged with piracy. When the Spanish minister to Washington sought to reclaim them, the Supreme Court declared (*U.S.* v. *Schooner Amistad,* 1841) that they were free on the ground that since all the powers had declared the slave trade illegal, they had been kidnapped in Africa, not legally purchased. The case is notable in that ex-President John Quincy Adams, was one of the lawyers defending the blacks, although his role was more sentimental than legally significant.

914 Creole. In the same year that the *Amistad* case was decided, another slave ship, the *Creole,* was taken over by slaves while en route from Virginia to New Orleans. One member of the crew was killed in the action. The blacks took the vessel to Nassau in the Bahamas, a British possession, where all except those involved in the killing were freed. Two years later, however, a joint commission awarded an indemnity of more than $100,000 to the United States.

915 Lusitania. This 32,000-ton British liner was known as the "floating hotel." In May 1915, the *Lusitania* became important in American history when it was sunk by the German submarine *U-20* off the Irish coast (actually in sight of land). Nearly 1,200 people went down with the ship, 128 of them Americans. The incident roused enormous anti-German feeling in the United States, and while it did not lead directly to American entry into

World War I, it was an important reason why the Germans' resumption of unrestricted attacks on merchant vessels in 1917 did result in American entry.

Advertisement for a cruise
aboard the *Lusitania,* 1915.
CULVER PICTURES, INC.

916 Oskar II. This was Henry Ford's "Peace Ship," a Scandinavian Lines vessel chartered by the automobile manufacturer in 1915 to carry delegates to a planned Conference of Neutrals in Europe. The purpose of the conference was "to get the boys out of the trenches by Christmas." Ford was a pacifist, but a monumentally confused one. He believed that "Jews" and "capitalism, greed, [and] the dirty hunger for dollars" had caused the war. His plan was scorned by sophisticates, and Ford was subjected to much ridicule. Nevertheless in December 1915, *Oskar II* carried Ford, eighty-three "delegates," assorted hangers-on, and a horde of reporters from New York to Christiania (now Oslo), Norway—all at Ford's expense.

Henry Ford sails on the *Oskar II* for a peace mission to Europe, 1916. THE NATIONAL ARCHIVES.

917 Leviathan. When the United States entered World War I in 1917, it seized the German liner *Vaterland* and converted it into a troopship. Since it was the largest ship afloat (nearly a thousand feet in length and almost sixty thousand tons), it was renamed *Leviathan* at the suggestion of President Woodrow Wilson. It remained in American hands after the war and was used as a transatlantic passenger liner by the United States Lines.

918 United States. On its maiden voyage in 1952, *United States* crossed the Atlantic in three days, ten hours, and forty minutes, a record. It was, however, smaller than some of the earlier superliners, being only fifty-three thousand tons.

FAMOUS FORTS

919 Fort Necessity. A defensive position taken by George Washington after he had surprised and defeated a small French reconnaissance unit in western Pennsylvania, in May 1754. The site was poorly chosen, and a few weeks later a much larger force of French and Indians surrounded the position and forced Washington to surrender. Before being allowed to return to Virginia, the young officer was tricked into signing an admission (written in French, which he could not read) that he had "assassinated" the leader of the reconnaissance party. These engagements marked the beginning of the French and Indian War.

920 **Fort Duquesne.** A position (site of the city of Pittsburgh) established by the French in 1753 as part of their effort to cement their control of the Ohio River Valley. The troops that defeated Washington at Fort Necessity were based at Fort Duquesne. The French held the fort until 1758, when the position was overrun by British forces and renamed Fort Pitt, after William Pitt, the British Prime Minister.

921 **Fort Stanwix.** A fort in the Mohawk Valley, built by the British during the French and Indian War. It was later used as a trading post. In 1768, Sir William Johnson (see number 481) organized a conference of colonial leaders and representatives of the Iroquois, Delaware, Shawnee, and other Indian tribes there. In the resulting Treaty of Fort Stanwix, the Indians ceded vast tracts in the Ohio Valley for some £13 million.

922 **Fort Ticonderoga.** Another French-built fort, this one in northern New York, between lakes Champlain and George,

that was captured by the British during the French and Indian War. Massachusetts troops captured it from the British after the outbreak of the American Revolution, but it was retaken by General Burgoyne at an early stage of his ill-fated invasion of New York in 1777 (see number 12).

923 **Fort McHenry.** A fort on the Patapsco River in Maryland, defending the city of Baltimore. The sight of Old Glory, still flying over this fort after an all-night bombardment by a British fleet during the War of 1812, inspired Francis Scott Key to write "The Star-Spangled Banner."

924 **Fort Laramie.** A post in what is now Wyoming, built originally by fur traders, it became an important supply depot for pioneers on the Oregon Trail in the 1840s and 1850s. It later served as a military base during the post–Civil War Indian fighting.

Fort Laramie, 1866 painting by G. Moellman, Bugler Company G, 11th Ohio Cavalry. UNIVERSITY OF WYOMING LIBRARY.

925 **Sutter's Fort.** A post near Sacramento, famous because gold was discovered near it in 1848. The California Gold Rush resulted.

926 **Fort Sumter.** Famous as the site of the spark that ignited the Civil War. The fort, on an island in the harbor of Charleston, South Carolina, was held by a force commanded by Major Robert Anderson. After the Confederates bombarded it and forced Anderson to surrender (April 13, 1861), Lincoln issued a call for seventy-five thousand volunteers to suppress the rebellion, thus precipitating the Civil War.

"The Flag at Sumter, October 20, 1863," painting by Conrad Wise Chapman. CONFEDERATE MUSEUM.

927 **Fort Henry.** A Confederate strong point on the Tennessee River that was captured by Union gunboats commanded by General Grant in February 1862.

928 **Fort Donelson.** Another Confederate position, this one on the Cumberland River, captured after hard fighting by Grant about two weeks later. When the Confederate commander, General Simon H. Buckner, asked for an armistice, Grant responded, "No terms except unconditional and immediate surrender can be accepted. I propose to move immediately upon your works."

929 **Fortress Monroe.** A fortification on the Chesapeake Bay used as a base by General George B. McClellan during his unsuccessful attempt to capture Richmond in 1862.

930 **Fort Corregidor.** A fort on an island in Manila Bay, off the Bataan Peninsula in the Philippines. The last post held by the American Army during the invasion of the Philippines by the Japanese in 1941–42. It was the headquarters of General Douglas MacArthur (see number 150) until his departure from the Philippines by submarine.

MILITARY DISASTERS

931 **Deerfield Massacre,** February 29, 1704. During Queen Anne's War (see number 957), a French and Abnaki Indian force led by Hertel de Rouville surprised the village of Deerfield, Massachusetts, before dawn, killing about fifty of the three hundred inhabitants and carrying off another hundred-odd to Canada as prisoners.

Print depicting the Deerfield Massacre, 1704. *REDEEMED CAPTIVE RETURNED TO ZION,* JOHN WILLIAMS, 1833, COURTESY OF RARE BOOKS DIVISION, THE NEW YORK PUBLIC LIBRARY.

932 **Ambush of Braddock,** July 9, 1755. While leading an expedition of 1,200 British and colonial troops against Fort Duquesne in the French and Indian War, British Major General Edward Braddock marched into an ambush. Braddock and half his force were killed, the rest routed. George Washington, who was serving as Braddock's *aide de camp,* had two horses shot from under him but emerged from the fight unscathed.

933 **Burning of Washington,** August 24, 1814. An amphibious British force, commanded by General Robert Ross and Admiral Sir George Cockburn, routed American troops under General William H. Winder at Bladensburg, Maryland, swept into the capital, and put it to the torch. The Capitol, the White House, and many other public buildings were destroyed, and President Madison and other government officials had to flee the city. However, when the British moved on to attack Baltimore, they were checked and forced to withdraw.

"The Taking of the City of Washington in America," 1814 print by British artist Lee Madones. LIBRARY OF CONGRESS.

934 **Fall of the Alamo,** March 6, 1836. After Texas had declared its independence, Mexican President Antonio López de Santa Anna sought to regain control of the province. He lay siege to a force of 187 Texans commanded by Colonel William B. Travis in the Alamo, a mission in San Antonio. When the Mexicans finally broke into the mission, they killed all the defenders, the most famous being Davy Crockett and Jim

Bowie, inventor of the Bowie knife. This disaster gave rise to the cry "Remember the Alamo!" which inspired the Texans who later defeated Santa Anna and drove the Mexican forces from Texas.

1885 lithograph, "Fall of the Alamo," from a painting by T. Gentile. LIBRARY OF CONGRESS.

935 **Battle of First Bull Run,** July 21, 1861. This was the first major engagement of the Civil War, fought on a field south of Washington. A Confederate counterattack resulted in a rout in which the Union forces, commanded by General Irwin McDowell, fled helter-skelter back to the defenses of the capital.

936 **Battle of Second Bull Run,** August 30, 1862. On the same ground, General Robert E. Lee routed a northern army commanded by General John Pope. After thirteen months of fighting, the Union forces were no closer to defeating the South than at the start—a fact more damaging to morale than the defeat itself.

937 **Battle of Fredericksburg,** December 13, 1862. In this battle General Ambrose E. Burnside (after whom the whiskers called burnsides was named) foolishly ordered his troops to attack an entrenched Confederate army across an open field. In the resulting carnage, his men suffered more than ten thousand casualties (see number 837).

938 **Battle of Cold Harbor,** June 3, 1864. This was part of General Grant's ultimately successful campaign to capture Richmond, the Confederate capital. At Cold Harbor, nine miles northeast of Richmond, he threw 60,000 men against entrenched Confederate positions and lost 5,600 of them in a few hours without gaining an inch of territory.

939 **Battle of the Little Big Horn,** June 25, 1876. This was "Custer's Last Stand," in which General George Armstrong Custer and his entire force of over 250 cavalrymen lost their lives when attacked by a large force of Sioux Indians in southern Montana. One of the Sioux leaders, Crazy Horse, was later described by an army officer as "one of the great soldiers of his day and gen-

eration." Crazy Horse is reported to have said as he led the charge, "Today is a good day to fight, today is a good day to die." Coming almost on the eve of the nation's celebration of its hundredth birthday, this defeat was especially shocking.

Sioux view of the Battle of Little Big Horn. SMITHSONIAN NATIONAL ANTHROPOLOGICAL ARCHIVES.

940 **Pearl Harbor,** December 7, 1941. Franklin Roosevelt's "date which will live in infamy," when 181 Japanese planes struck the American Pacific fleet at Pearl Harbor Naval Base in Hawaii. In addition to the destruction of a large proportion of the 70 warships at the base and 180 planes, 2,300 soldiers and sailors were killed and more than 1,000 wounded.

941 **Battle of Bataan,** January–May 1942. After the Japanese assault on Manila in the Philippines, American troops under General MacArthur dug in on Bataan Peninsula (see number 150). However, they were soon short of food

and ammunition and unable to hold off the far more numerous Japanese. After MacArthur was ordered to Australia by President Roosevelt, the sixteen thousand survivors were forced to surrender. There followed the "Bataan death march," on which thousands of these weak and weary prisoners of war died. After the war, the Japanese commander responsible for this, General Masaharu Homma, was convicted of war crimes and executed.

942 **Battle of the Yalu,** November 1950–January 1951. This was a crucial turning point in the Korean War, which had many crucial turning points. When U.N. forces under General MacArthur advanced through North Korea toward the border of Red China, the Chinese suddenly sent thirty-three divisions across the border to attack them. MacArthur's troops suffered heavy casualties

United States Marines pass through South Korean villages en route to an engagement with North Korean forces.
CULVER PICTURES, INC.

and were driven all the way back into South Korea before the front was stabilized.

943 **Tet,** January 1968. This general attack on South Vietnamese cities by North Vietnamese and Viet Cong troops was not, strictly speaking, a military disaster for the United States, because the Communists suffered enormous losses and failed to hold any of the cities. However, it gravely undermined the willingness of many Americans to continue to support the Vietnam War.

MILITARY VICTORIES

944 **Trenton,** December 26, 1776. After his famous crossing of the Delaware River in a snowstorm on Christmas night, Washington launched a surprise dawn attack on hated Hessian mercenary troops encamped at Trenton, New Jersey. The resulting rout was of more psychological than strategic importance, but it was the first real victory for American troops in the Revolution.

945 **Saratoga,** October 17, 1777. In 1777, the British attempted to cut their rebelling colonies in two by launching a three-

pronged attack from Canada, Lake Ontario, and New York City. The campaign was a fiasco. The main force, commanded by General John Burgoyne (see number 12), made the most progress; but it was heavily burdened by unnecessary equipment (including thirty carts laden with Burgoyne's personal effects), constantly harassed by militia units, and stopped cold by Patriot defenses south of Saratoga. Soon Burgoyne was under siege, and when the other British forces failed to materialize, he had to surrender his entire army of 5,700 men. Still more significant, this victory resulted in recognition of the United States by France and an open alliance with that nation which greatly increased the likelihood that independence could be won.

British caricature critical of "the generals in America," 1779.
COURTESY OF THE NEW-YORK HISTORICAL SOCIETY.

946 **Yorktown,** October 17, 1781. This was the most complicated, the best-managed, and unquestionably the most decisive campaign of the Revolution. It ended British efforts to

regain control of the colonies. After a French fleet had defeated British naval units off the American coast, Washington marched a French and American army from New England around New York City and south to Virginia—where seventeen thousand British troops, commanded by Lord Cornwallis, were based at Yorktown, on the lower Chesapeake Bay. With Cornwallis unable to escape by water, he was soon pinned down; after a siege of a little more than a month, he surrendered.

1782 broadside celebrates the surrender of Cornwallis. COURTESY OF THE HENRY FRANCIS DU PONT WINTERTHUR MUSEUM.

947 **New Orleans,** January 8, 1815. In this battle, well-entrenched American troops under Andrew Jackson crushed an assault by a British army, inflicting enormous losses on the enemy. Since the Treaty of Ghent ending the War of 1812 had already been signed (see number 214), the battle was of no military significance, but it was the only real American victory in the war, and thus was a great boost to morale. It enhanced Jackson's already formidable reputation—he became known as "the hero of New Orleans"—and convinced the last of the European doubters that the United States was here to stay.

948 **Mexico City,** September 14, 1847. The Mexican War was a procession of victories for the United States, for the Mexicans were poorly equipped and short of well-trained officers. But General Winfield Scott's campaign against Mexico City was exceptional, being brilliantly conceived and carried out with dispatch. After landing his army of ten thousand at Veracruz on the east coast of

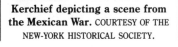

Kerchief depicting a scene from the Mexican War. COURTESY OF THE NEW-YORK HISTORICAL SOCIETY.

Mexico in March, Scott laid siege to that city. After it surrendered, he marched his troops across difficult terrain, won a series of battles against superior numbers, and, after waiting outside the capital for reinforcements, took it by storm.

949 **Gettysburg,** July 1–4, 1863. This was the first real Union victory of the Civil War, and thus had psychological, as well as purely military, significance. It began by chance when a small unit of Lee's invading army went looking for shoes and clashed with Union troops in the town of Gettysburg, Pennsylvania. Each side sent out calls for reinforcements, the armies concentrated, and a major battle resulted. The Union army occupied Cemetery Ridge, the Confederate Army Seminary Ridge, which faced it. The battle consisted of Confederate efforts to bombard the Union position and take Cemetery Ridge by storm. In itself the battle was a standoff; after three days of bloodshed, the positions were unchanged. But Lee's army was so weakened that he had to abandon the campaign and retreat to Virginia.

950 **Vicksburg,** July 4, 1863. The siege of Vicksburg was General

Grant's most brilliant campaign, and it probably decided the war. The city sits on a bluff overlooking a bend in the Mississippi River. Grant approached it from the north; after appearing to plan a direct attack against the city, he struck east to capture Jackson, the capital of Mississippi—cutting off the defender of Vicksburg, General John C. Pemberton, from other Confederate armies. Grant then drove Pemberton into Vicksburg and placed the city under siege. After enduring weeks of constant shelling, the Confederates surrendered. Grant took more than thirty thousand prisoners, but far more important was the fact that Texas, Arkansas, and Louisiana were thereafter cut off from the rest of the Confederacy.

951 **Argonne-Meuse Campaign,** September 26–November 1, 1918. In this climactic battle of World War I, as part of a general Allied offensive, the American First Army (1.2 million men) drove slowly through the Argonne Forest, which one historian has called "the most bitter terrain fighting men had yet known," from a point near Verdun toward Sedan, on the Meuse River. The carnage was terrifying— American casualties topped 120,000—but by November 1, the Germans were in full retreat and the end of the war was in sight.

952 **Midway,** June 4, 1942. This was the decisive naval battle of World War II. An enormous Japanese fleet consisting of nine battleships, four aircraft carriers, and more than 150 other vessels commanded by Admiral Isoroku Yamamoto advanced on the American base at Midway Island, a thousand-odd miles northwest of Hawaii. While planes from this fleet were bombing Midway, planes from three American carriers—*Enterprise, Hornet,* and *Yorktown*—sank the four Japanese carriers. By destroying them and their planes, the Americans, in the words of Samuel Eliot Morison, "had extracted the sting" from Admiral Yamamoto's huge fleet. He had to abandon the attack on Midway. The only significant American loss was *Yorktown,* which had already been badly damaged. This battle changed both the course of the war and the character of naval warfare. No warship fired a shell at an enemy vessel, or even came in sight of one. All the damage was done by airplanes and submarines.

953 **Normandy Beaches,** June 6–27, 1944. The crucial Allied cross-Channel landing on D Day involved more than five thousand vessels—ranging in size from battleships to landing craft—and wave after wave of bombers, all under the command of General Dwight D. Eisenhower. The Germans resisted stubbornly, and losses were heavy, but by the end of the month a beachhead containing more than a million Allied soldiers was firmly established.

Yanks go ashore in invasion of France, June 6, 1944.
WIDE WORLD PHOTOS.

954 **Inchon,** September 15, 1950. General MacArthur checked the North Korean attack on South Korea at the outskirts of the southern port of Pusan; he then carried out a daring amphibious attack on Inchon, on the west coast of Korea near the border between North and South Korea. Two days later, his troops retook the capital, Seoul. Outflanked, the North Koreans retreated in disarray. However, this encour-

aged MacArthur to invade the North, precipitating the Battle of the Yalu (see number 942).

OTHER PEOPLE'S AMERICAN WARS

The so-called Colonial Wars in which Americans took part were really minor aspects of European conflicts. Few settlers were deeply concerned with them. This is clearly indicated by the names the Americans gave these wars—they were someone else's wars, not their own. The exception was the one the colonists called the French and Indian War (the Seven Years' War in Europe) which richly deserved the name given it by historian Lawrence Henry Gipson (see number 7). If it had turned out differently, you might be reading this book in French.

Count Frontenac burning an Indian chief in 1696, from an 1863 painting by Leighton Lawson. ONONDAGO HISTORICAL ASSOCIATION.

955 **King Philip's War** (1675–76). Philip (his Indian name was Met-

acom), sachem of the Wampanoag Indians, joined with Narragansett and Nipmuck allies to wage a brutal guerrilla war against Puritan and Pilgrim settlements. More than a thousand colonists were killed before the Indians were defeated. Philip was killed in an ambush, then beheaded and drawn and quartered.

956 **King William's War** (1689–97), was the first of a series of conflicts between England and France in which the fighting in North America was of only tangential importance, at least to the Europeans. Aided by Indian allies, French raiders attacked Schenectady in New York and a number of communities on the New England frontier. The efforts of American colonists to mount attacks on Montreal and Quebec came to nothing, but a fleet of Massachusetts vessels captured Port Royal in Nova Scotia. When peace was restored in Europe, all captured positions in America were returned to the original owners.

957 **Queen Anne's War** (1702–13) was part of the European War of the Spanish Succession, which pitted England, Austria, and Holland against France and Spain. English

colonists again captured Port Royal, but French-backed Indians razed the town of Deerfield, Massachusetts (see number 931). A South Carolina force burned the Spanish city of St. Augustine, in Florida. In the Peace of Utrecht, France ceded Nova Scotia, Newfoundland, and land around the Hudson Bay to Britain.

958 **War of Jenkins's Ear** (1739–43). This war began with a naval skirmish between British and Spanish ships in which a British sailor, Robert Jenkins, lost an ear. Most of the fighting was in the Caribbean region, but a Georgia force, commanded by James Oglethorpe, conducted raids into northern Florida. On the larger world stage, this war became

959 **King George's War** (1744–48), called the War of the Austrian Succession in Europe. Like the others, it was marked in America mostly

Flag carried at the siege of Fort Louisbourg in 1745. COURTESY OF THE NEW-YORK HISTORICAL SOCIETY.

by frontier raids. New Englanders captured Fort Louisbourg, which guarded the mouth of the St. Lawrence River, but again the treaty ending the war in Europe required the return of all captured positions in America.

960 **The French and Indian War,** of 1754–63, was a part of the Great War for the Empire, involved the conflict between the French in Canada and the English colonists—principally the Virginians—for control of the Ohio Valley. The French had the advantage at the start, but after the war spread to Europe the British sent large numbers of troops to America, and eventually the French were thoroughly defeated.

PART VIII
Matters Economic and Otherwise

MODERN "ANONYMOUS" INVENTIONS

One of the ironies of modern times is the fact that while life is constantly being changed in profound ways by technological advances, the inventors who create the new technology are often unknown to most people. In the nineteenth and early twentieth centuries, great inventors were celebrities, almost national heroes. Everyone associates the telephone with Alexander Graham Bell, the electric light and the phonograph with Thomas A. Edison. Many people would assert, incorrectly, that the automobile was invented by Henry Ford. Here are some examples of modern inventions that everyone is familiar with. *Who* invented them is another matter.

961 **Cellophane,** invented by chemists at E. I. Du Pont de Nemours and Company in 1924.

962 **Penicillin,** discovered by Alexander Fleming, a Scottish bacteriologist, in 1928, and made available for general use during World War II.

963 **Nylon,** invented by Wallace Hume Ca-rothers, head of the Du Pont Experimental Station, in 1937. Nylon stockings came on the market in 1940 and took the country by storm. But they were in short supply during World War II, as seen in the lines of a song popularized by Nat "King" Cole to the effect that men were as "scarce as nylons." Carothers and his associates at Du Pont also invented the synthetic rubber neoprene.

Dr. Wallace Hume Carothers demonstrating the properties of neoprene. COURTESY OF THE HAGLEY MUSEUM AND LIBRARY.

964 **Junction transistor,** source of the electronic revolution, invented at the Bell Laboratories by William B. Shockley, John Bardeen, and Walter H. Brattain in 1949.

965 **Frequency Modulation (FM),** the system of transmitting sound patterns by varying the frequency of the carrier wave rather than its amplitude (as in AM), invented by Edwin H. Armstrong in 1933, but not developed commercially until after World War II.

Edwin Armstrong, the inventor of FM, in the early 1940s. EDWIN ARMSTRONG COLLECTION, RARE BOOKS AND MANUSCRIPT LIBRARY, COLUMBIA UNIVERSITY.

966 **Aerosol valve,** invented in 1949 by Robert H. Abplanalp (better known later for his friendship with Richard Nixon).

967 **Permanent wave,** invented by Karl

Parading for permanent wave, New York City, 1934. CULVER PICTURES, INC.

Ludwig Nessler, a German-born hairdresser. Over a period of years, ending in the mid-1920s, he perfected machines for making hair more porous so that it would absorb moisture. Moist hair holds a curl longer than dry hair, but not, of course, permanently.

968 **Oral contraceptives,** invented in 1960 by Gregory Pincus, who produced Enovid, the first "pill," by combining synthetic progesterone and estrogen.

An exception to the rule of anonymity of modern inventors is

969 **Quick-frozen foods,** invented by Clarence Birdseye, who first experimented with the concept while he was a fur trader in Labrador before World War I. Birdseye coined the term "quick-freeze" and sold his patents to the Postum Company (General Foods) in 1929. Under its management, "Birdseye's name became a famous trademark."

970 Then there is the invention that never was: George B. Selden's patent for a *road engine,* issued in 1895. In the 1870s, Selden had developed detailed designs for a

"horseless carriage," powered by a gasoline engine and complete with an ignition system, clutch, brakes, and other details. He never built even a prototype for such a machine, apparently because he was unable to obtain financing. In 1899, he assigned his patent to what became the Association of Licensed Automobile Manufacturers, and for many years this group licensed the actual manufacturers of cars, charging a small royalty. Henry Ford, however, refused to recognize the Selden patent, and in 1911, after a complicated legal battle, a U.S. circuit court held that while the patent was valid, the auto manufacturers were not violating it.

PANICS (DEPRESSIONS)

Business cycles are products of the Industrial Revolution, and despite what the economists say about controlling the ebb and flow of economic activity by "fine-tuning" monetary and fiscal policy, the economy continues to fluctuate in irregular rhythmic patterns. There have only been two Great Depressions in American history: *the* Great Depression of the 1930s and the Great Depression of the late nine-

teenth century, which was not really a depression at all (see numbers 647, 650). Nowadays we call "ordinary" economic downturns "recessions." In early times they were called "panics" because some sudden and unexpected collapse heralded the arrival of bad times. The steep decline of prices on the New York Stock Exchange in October 1929 was the panic that marked the start of the Great Depression. There have been a lot of panics in American history, to wit:

971 **Panic of 1819.** That year, the boom that had followed the War of 1812 ended. The subsequent downturn was triggered by the revival of European agriculture after the ending of the Napoleonic Wars and by the contraction of credit instituted by the Second Bank of the United States, which was paying off loans that had been made to finance the Louisiana Purchase (see number 213). Sales of undeveloped land on the frontier then slowed to a trickle, and the price of cotton and other crops dropped sharply. Many farmers were unable to pay their debts, and this led to foreclosures and to numerous bank failures. The bad times lasted until about 1822. Many Westerners blamed the

Bank of the United States for the troubles, even though it was not responsible for them. Among the accusers was Andrew Jackson, who took his revenge, so to speak, by vetoing a bill to extend the charter of the bank in 1832. Ironically, this set in motion events which led to the

972 Panic of 1837 and the following period of hard times. The transfer of federal monies from the conservative Bank of the United States to "wildcat" state banks occurred after President Jackson vetoed the bill extending the charter of the bank. This enabled the wildcats to make credit available on easy terms. It also led to soaring land sales in the West (up from $2.6 million in 1832 to $24.9 million in 1836) and an accompanying boom in canal and road construction, the latter largely financed by British investors. But in July 1836 Jackson issued the "Specie Circular," which required purchasers of government land to pay for it with gold or silver. This caused people to withdraw specie from the banks and to buy less land. The loss of their gold and silver reserves in turn led to the restriction of bank credit and to many bank failures. The panic occurred when every bank in the country had to suspend the conversion of paper currency into specie on demand. Conditions improved thereafter, and the banks resumed specie payments in 1838. But the revival was short-lived; the economy remained depressed until 1843.

973 Panic of 1857. This downturn was the result of falling grain prices caused by a big increase in Russian exports of wheat after the Crimean War. As a result, western farmers could buy less, and their declining consumption hurt the business of both eastern manufacturers and the railroads. The bankruptcy of the Ohio Life Insurance and Trust Company in August 1857 was followed by the collapse of many hundreds of rural banks. The southern states escaped the bad times because the European demand for cotton remained high. This strengthened the Southerners' confidence in the viability of their slave economy, and contributed to the popularity of the slogan "Cotton is King." (see number 60).

974 Panic of 1873. The failure of the banking house of Jay Cooke and Company precipitated this panic, which was by far the most severe one up to that date. The New York Stock Exchange had to be shut down for ten days to check the steep decline of prices. But like all others, the causes of the following economic downturn, which lasted for several years, were complex. Dislocations caused by the Civil War played a part, but more important was the reckless overbuilding of American railroads and the opening of the Suez Canal, which caused major readjustments of world trade patterns. The year 1873 also marked the beginning of a period of severe worldwide price deflation (the above-mentioned Great Depression) that extended far beyond the bad times of the mid-1870s.

Cleaning up on Wall Street, *The Daily Graphic*, September 27, 1873. CULVER PICTURES, INC.

975 Panic of 1893. This panic, triggered by the failure of the National Cordage Company in May and marked by many bank failures and business bankruptcies later in the year, exacerbated an already serious economic decline. The causes were worldwide, but in the United States the conflict over the coinage of silver, which was advocated by groups hurt by the long deflationary cycle, was a major factor. The Treasury's declining gold reserves, which fell below $100 million (considered a danger point), further eroded public confidence in the economy. The next few years were among the darkest in American history, being marked by the Pullman strike, in which federal troops were used to keep the trains running (see number 982) widespread protest marches by unemployed people, and the spectacle of the government having to turn to a private banker, J. P. Morgan, to obtain enough gold to avoid bankruptcy. The question of the free coinage of silver seems less important today than it did in the 1890s, but it split the Democratic Party, gave force to the Populist movement, and made a national figure of William Jennings Bryan (see number 412).

976 Panic of 1907.

This was known as a "rich man's panic." In October, the failure of F. Augustus Heinze, a big specu-

Cartoon from the *Philadelphia Enquirer,* September 1907.
CULVER PICTURES, INC.

lator, led to runs on a number of banks. When depositors suddenly began to withdraw money in huge amounts from the Knickerbocker Trust Company, whose president had been associated with Heinze, the bank had to close its doors. This precipitated a full-fledged panic. The hero of the resulting crisis was the same J. P. Morgan, who had been pictured as a villain during the depression of the 1890s. Morgan rallied other bankers to raise cash to help hard-pressed but sound institutions withstand the pressure of frightened depositors and to bolster sagging prices on the stock exchange. President Theodore Roosevelt helped by authorizing the deposit of federal funds in New York banks to bolster their reserves. The president also agreed to allow U.S. Steel to swallow the Tennessee Coal and Iron Company in order to save the brokerage house that owned it, a decision he was later to regret (see number 561). The long-

range effect of the panic on the economy was not great, but it led to important reforms, most notably the creation of the Federal Reserve system in 1913.

977 Panic of 1929.

This was the famous "Black Thursday," the stock market collapse of October 29, 1929. Actually, there had been an earlier crisis on October 24, and the trend of securities prices had been down for several weeks. Although it certainly had a psychologically depressing effect of millions of people, the "crash," as it was called, did not cause the Depression that followed. By the end of the year, stock prices had regained a good part of what had been lost in October, and it was only in the spring of 1930 that the serious economic downturn began. What was most remarkable about the Great Depression was its length and the persistent high un-

"Sold Out," cartoon by Rollin Kirby, October 25, 1929.
CULVER PICTURES, INC.

employment that was its most tragic aspect.

STRIKES

978 **The Railroad Strike of 1877** broke out when firemen and other workers of the Baltimore and Ohio Railroad walked out to protest a wage cut. The strike spread throughout the East and Midwest until roughly two thirds of the nation's tracks were tied up. Rioting, arson, and looting convulsed Pittsburgh, Baltimore, and other cities. Federal troops were called in, and a number of people were killed before order was restored. This was the first industrial strike to approach national proportions.

Looking up the track opposite 25th Street, rail strike in Pittsburgh, July 21–22, 1877.
CULVER PICTURES, INC.

979 **The Missouri Pacific Railroad Strike,** 1885, began after two wage cuts had been im-posed. In March, when the entire southwestern rail network controlled by Jay Gould had been paralyzed, the management agreed to restore the cuts. A few months later, the Knights of Labor struck the Wabash Railroad, another Gould line, and again won a victory. But in March 1886 a general strike against the Gould system— involving sixty thousand workers—was broken. This was a heavy blow to the Knights of Labor.

980 **The McCormick Harvester Machine Company Strike,** in Chicago, 1886, was part of a campaign for the eight-hour day that involved about eighty thousand workers. The strike's chief historical importance rises from the fact that local anarchists staged a protest meeting in Chicago's Haymarket Square after a striker was killed by the police. When 180 policemen arrived to break up this meeting, someone threw a bomb. Seven policemen were killed, some apparently as a result of bullets fired into the crowd by their fellows. Eight anarchists were convicted of the crime on very flimsy evidence and four of them were hanged. Although the strikers were uninvolved in the bombing, the incident caused a reaction against them and against organized labor in general. The eight-hour movement suffered a serious setback.

Lithograph celebrating the eight-hour day won by government employees in 1868.
LIBRARY OF CONGRESS.

981 **The Homestead Strike,** 1892, involved the Carnegie Steel Company's plant in Homestead, Pennsylvania, a town on the Monongahela River near Pittsburgh. When the Amalgamated Association of Iron and Steel Workers struck Homestead, Henry Clay Frick, Andrew Carnegie's man in charge, determined with Carnegie's full approval to prove that "we had a right to employ whom we pleased and discharge whom we pleased." He engaged three hundred Pinkerton guards to "protect" the plant. But when the guards arrived by barge from Pittsburgh on July 4, they were met by a hail of bullets from picketers. After a day-long battle, in which seven Pinkertons and two strikers were killed, the Pinkertons surrendered and were allowed to march off. Troops were then brought in, and by late July the plant was again operating, using nonunion workers. The attempt of anarchist Alexander Berkman to assassinate Frick in his Pittsburgh office was a further blow to the union, though Berkman had no connection with it. In any case, the strike was crushed and Homestead remained nonunion for nearly half a century. A number of strikers were tried for murder but acquitted.

Strikers assailing the Pinkerton men, *Harper's Weekly,* **1892.**
CULVER PICTURES, INC.

982 **The Pullman Strike,** 1894, began as a walkout in the Pullman Palace Car factory outside Chicago. Since some Pullman workers belonged to the newly formed American Railway Union, the union refused to move trains with Pullman cars, and this closed down most of the railroads leading in and out of Chicago. Trains were stopped and a certain amount of railroad property was damaged in resulting clashes. The fact that the mails were tied up by the strike led to the issuance of a federal court injunction against the union on the ground that it was a combination in restraint of trade. (The union was willing to move mail trains if no Pullmans were attached, but the railroad operators would not agree to this.) When the union ignored the injunction, President Cleveland sent troops to Chicago to preserve order and move the mails. The strike then collapsed. Eugene V. Debs, president of the union, was sentenced to six months in jail for ignoring the court order.

983 **The Anthracite Coal Strike,** 1902, was called by John Mitchell, head of the United Mine Workers, in an effort to obtain recognition of the union by the mine companies, most of which were owned by railroads. A strike two years earlier had resulted in a 10 percent wage increase, but not in recognition of the union. This walkout began in June and dragged on throughout the summer and early fall. The strikers won much public support by avoiding violence and by offering to submit the dispute to arbitration, a proposal the operators rejected (see number 323). With coal in short supply and winter approaching, President Theodore Roosevelt summoned both sides to Washington and sought to force a settlement. When the operators refused even to discuss the issue with the union, Roosevelt announced that he would send in troops to mine the coal. The operators then agreed to abide by the determination of a presidential commission, and the strike ended. The commission granted the miners a wage increase, but did not compel the operators to recognize the United Mine Workers.

984 **The Steel Strike of 1919.** The union movement, and labor in general, made important gains during World War I, and when the war ended there were many strikes as workers sought to preserve these gains during a period of inflation. In the steel industry, largely unorganized since the time of the Homestead Strike, the AFL created a special committee in an effort to unionize the work force. When the steel companies, led by Elbert H. Gary of U.S. Steel, refused to recognize the union, engage in collective bargaining, and put an end to the twelve-hour day, the committee called a strike. About 350,000 workers walked out. The strike was a failure, however. State and federal troops were called in and the companies hired strike-breakers. The Red Scare hysteria was at its height, and public opinion was much influenced by the fact that the most important strike leader, William Z. Foster, was an avowed revolutionary, head of the Syndicalist League of North America. Early in January 1920, the committee called off the strike without obtaining any concessions from management.

Representatives of the Steel and Metal Workers Union of A.F. of L., 1919. CULVER PICTURES, INC.

985 **The Boston Police Strike,** 1919. This was another of the many strikes of the postwar period. When the Boston police commissioner, Edwin Curtis, discharged nineteen officers who were active in the local policemen's union, more than two thirds of the 1,500-man force walked out. The result was widespread looting and other unlawful activity in the city. Curtis refused to arbitrate the dispute, fired the strikers, and began recruiting a new force. Though he had done nothing to try to prevent the strike or to negotiate a settlement, Governor Calvin Coolidge then called out the state militia and announced, "There is no right to strike against the public safety by anybody, anywhere, any time." The largely undeserved praise that Coolidge received for having broken the strike led to his choice as Harding's running mate at the 1920 Republican National Convention.

Sit-Down Strikes, 1936–37. The wave of sit-down strikes that swept through the automotive industry began in February 1936, in the Akron, Ohio, plant of the Goodyear Tire and Rubber Company. The most important sit-downs, however, occurred the following winter, when seven thousand workers in General Motors' Fisher Body plant in Cleveland sat down. Within days the movement spread to Fisher factories in Flint, Michigan, and then to other GM plants. The strikers succeeded in winning union recognition —in part because the tactic discouraged employers from seeking to hire strikebreakers, and in part because neither Governor Frank Murphy of Michigan nor President Franklin Roosevelt would call up troops to dislodge the workers. The movement spread to other fields; by the end of 1937, some four hundred thousand workers had taken part in sit-down strikes. The tactic was eventually declared illegal by the Supreme Court, but the occupations certainly sped the organization of American heavy industry.

"Hello, Momma. We're Makin' History," cartoon depicting sit-down strikers. CULVER PICTURES, INC.

987 **The Steel Strike of 1952.** The steel industry had finally been organized during the New Deal, and the United Steelworkers of America had become one of the most powerful unions in the country by the end of World War II. When its contract expired in January 1952, the union sought a wage hike and other benefits, but the manufacturers balked, arguing that government price controls (this was during the Korean War) made it impossible for them to grant increases. The union agreed to continue working without a contract, and when the Wage Stabilization Board proposed a small wage increase in late March, the union went along. The companies, however, refused, and six hundred thousand steelworkers then walked off the job. President Truman blamed the companies for the impasse. He therefore issued an executive order authorizing the seizure of the mills on the ground that a national emergency existed, and the union called off the strike. The companies, however, turned to the courts for relief, and in June the Supreme Court upheld a lower court ruling that the seizure was an unconstitutional usurpation of legislative power by the executive. The strike was then resumed and was not settled until August, when the companies agreed to wage increases roughly similar to those proposed by the Stabilization Board.

988 **The PATCO (Air Traffic Controllers') Strike,** 1981.
Though it was forbidden by law to strike, PATCO, the union of the workers who directed the movement of planes in and out of the nation's crowded airports, went on strike in August 1981. President Reagan immediately ordered the controllers to return to work,

and when the vast majority of them, more than eleven thousand men and women, refused to do so, he discharged them and began a crash program to train replacements. Even after the strike collapsed, Reagan refused to give the PATCO controllers back their jobs, and the union was destroyed. His tough stance had a generally chastening effect on all labor organizations.

FIASCOS

At what point does a political indiscretion or a diplomatic tempest in a teapot become a serious embarrassment? When does a military defeat become a disaster? Here are some American fiascos, "in-between" incidents where things went wrong but, where the long-range effects were relatively minor.

989 **Battle of New York,** August–
October 1776. This was George Washington's first experience as a commander in a major battle, and his lack of experience was almost fatal to the Patriot cause. He had taken up defensive positions on Long Island when a powerful British fleet reached New York waters. A Redcoat army commanded by General Sir Wil-

liam Howe landed on Long Island and easily outflanked and drove back the Americans, but Washington managed to get his men across the East River to Manhattan. After some delay, Howe followed and in a direct attack routed the Americans. Had he used his fleet to move troops to the northern end of Manhattan, he could have trapped Washington's entire army; fortunately he failed to do so. Yet for weeks Washington failed to grasp the danger of remaining on an island while the enemy controlled the surrounding waters. He finally did cross to the mainland and eventually went on to the brilliant victory at Trenton (see number 944).

990 **Treason Trial of Aaron Burr,** 1807.
In 1806 former Vice President Aaron Burr, already under indictment for having killed Alexander Hamilton in a duel, concocted an elaborate scheme for a filibustering expedition in the West. Whether his objective was Spanish territory in the Southwest or New Orleans and part of the Mississippi valley recently purchased from France (see number 213) is still unclear. Before he undertook his expedition, however, one of his associates informed President Thomas Jefferson of the

scheme. Jefferson, who detested Burr, ordered him arrested and put on trial for treason. Fortunately for Burr, the judge in the case was another political foe of Jefferson's, Chief Justice John Marshall (see number 197). In his charge to the jury, Marshall applied the narrow definition described in Article III, section 3, of the Constitution—that treason consisted "only of waging war" against the United States or in "adhering" to the nation's enemies, and must consist of "an overt act" testified to by two witnesses. This gave the jury no choice but to find Burr not guilty, much to Jefferson's chagrin.

Aaron Burr. LIBRARY OF CONGRESS.

991 **Attack on USS Chesapeake,** 1807. This was the most notorious of the examples of high-handed impressment (see number 15) by British naval officers during the Na-

poleonic Wars. The forty-six-gun American frigate *Chesapeake,* out of Norfolk, Virginia, on a routine patrol, was hailed by HMS *Leopard.* The American captain, James Barron, expecting some ordinary communication, hove to and permitted a British party to come on board. The officer in charge, however, demanded that Barron turn over to him four sailors who he claimed were deserters from another British warship. Barron refused, but since the United States was not at war, and he was barely out of sight of land, his vessel was unprepared to fight. But the guns of the *Leopard* were loaded and primed. As soon as the boarding party was back on deck, the Britisher opened fire and Barron was forced to surrender and turn over the sailors. Impressing anyone from a warship was in plain violation of international law, but President Jefferson contented himself with urging Congress to pass the Embargo Act (see number 54).

992 **General William Hull's Invasion of Canada,** 1812. When the War of 1812 broke out, American military leaders expected to overrun Canada easily because the colony had only half a million people. It did not work out that

way. In July, General William Hull, governor of Michigan Territory, crossed from Detroit into Canada with two thousand militiamen. But his communications were soon attacked by Indians. Hull hastily retreated to Detroit and then surrendered the fort to pursuing Canadians without firing a shot.

Surrender of General William Hull, August 1812. LIBRARY OF CONGRESS.

993 **General Henry Dearborn's "Attack" on Montreal,** 1812. Henry Dearborn had fought with distinction during the Revolution and had served as Secretary of War throughout the Jefferson Administration, but as his biographer put it, his military skills "appeared to have evaporated with age and long disuse." He had grown so obese that he needed a special cart to get from place to place. He was supposed to coordinate his attack on

Montreal with Hull's invasion of Upper Canada from Detroit, but when his army reached the Canadian border the men refused to cross and Dearborn had to march them back ignominiously to his base at Plattsburg, New York.

994 **Hartford Convention,** 1814–15. Opposition to the War of 1812 was concentrated in the New England states because the powerful Royal Navy had bottled up their ports, thus gravely injuring their mercantile economies. This had given the moribund Federalist Party a new lease on life in the region, and in 1814 some of its more conservative leaders organized a convention at Hartford to discuss strategy. There was some talk of seceding from the Union and forming a New England Confederacy, but the Convention contented itself with claiming that a state had a right "to interpose its authority" to correct "infractions" of the Constitution by the federal government, and calling for a new convention if a number of changes in national policy were not forthcoming. The negotiation of the Treaty of Ghent and the American victory in the Battle of New Orleans (see numbers 214, 947) changed the political climate in New England, however, and put an end to the Federalist Party and all talk of secession.

995 **John Quincy Adams's Annual Message to Congress,** 1825. Although he was one of the most intelligent men ever to serve as President and there have been few more dedicated public officials in any land, John Quincy Adams was a spectacularly inept politician. He became President at a time when sectional rivalries were on the rise and the Jeffersonian slogan "that government is best which governs least" had wide public support. Yet in his first annual message he called for a large program of road and canal construction, "multiplying and facilitating the communications and intercourse between distant regions"; the support of "public institutions and seminaries of learning," including "a national university"; and an astronomical observatory staffed by "an astronomer, to be in constant attendance of observation upon the phenomena of the heavens." He went on to compare American activities in such areas unfavorably with those of France, Great Britain, and Russia, and to urge the Congress not to be "palsied by the will of our constituents" in cases where public backing for these projects was lacking. Needless to say, his schemes were rejected, and he was not reelected to a second term.

996 **President William Howard Taft on the Payne-Aldrich Tariff,** 1909. The 1908 Republican Party platform had called for revision of the high tariff then in effect, and when he took office as the new President, William Howard Taft had summoned Congress into special session to carry out that pledge. A modest downward revision was passed in the House of Representatives, but the cuts were restored in the protectionist Senate. Although Taft insisted both privately and in public, "I am a low-tariff man," he signed the resulting (Payne-Aldrich) bill into law. Then, in a politically unfortunate speech in Winona, Minnesota, an area where opposition to tariffs was strong, he described the

"Taft embraces the Tariff," 1912. CULVER PICTURES, INC.

measure as "the best tariff bill that the Republican Party ever passed." He went on to say that if people wanted free trade they "ought to put the Democratic Party in power," a suggestion the voters adopted in 1912, though not only because of Taft's advice.

997 **President Franklin Roosevelt's attempt to "pack" the Supreme Court,** 1937. Frustrated by the overturning of important New Deal legislation by the conservative majority on the Court and emboldened by his overwhelming victory in the 1936 presidential election, Roosevelt sought congressional approval for a bill adding new justices in cases where sitting members of the Court failed to retire after reaching the age of seventy. Although couched in terms of a general reform of the federal judiciary, the bill was taken as an attempt to destroy the independence of the Supreme Court. It was unable to muster congressional support, despite the large Democratic majorities in both houses. However, criticism of the Court had its effect; several justices retired, and the Court ceased to invalidate New Deal legislation. It is commonly said that "Roosevelt lost the battle but won the war."

998 **Bay of Pigs Invasion,** 1961. During the latter stages of the Eisenhower Administration, the CIA had secretly trained a small army of anti-Communist Cuban emigrés for a planned invasion of Cuba, the hope being that masses of Cubans would flock to the invaders' banner and overthrow the Cuban regime of Fidel Castro. When he became President, John F. Kennedy learned of the scheme, and after some hesitation, permitted it to go ahead. It was a disastrous failure. The landing at the Bay of Pigs in western Cuba was successful, but the local people showed no interest in joining the invaders. Castro's troops quickly pinned them down and forced them to surrender. Kennedy quickly admitted his mistake, but the incident was a most unfortunate beginning to his presidency, for it made him appear both weak-willed and impulsive.

999 **George Romney's "Brainwashing,"** 1968. During his campaign for the 1968 Republican presidential nomination, Romney, who was opposing the Vietnam War, tried to explain his earlier support of the war by saying that on an inspection trip to Vietnam in 1965 he had been subjected to "the greatest brainwashing that anybody can get," administered by American military and diplomatic personnel there. As a result, he was attacked both by supporters of the war and by people who felt that he must be indecisive and naive, and his presidential campaign soon collapsed.

1000 **Jimmy Carter's "Montezuma's Revenge" Remark.** While on a state visit to Mexico, President Carter, replying to a toast by Mexican President José Lopez Portillo, mentioned that he had in common with Portillo the habit of jogging, and that he had first acquired the habit in Mexico City. All would have been well if he had stopped with that almost certainly inaccurate remark, but he went on to say that while in the city "I was affected with Montezuma's revenge." Carter thought he was making a small joke, but the Mexicans, quite reasonably, took the remark as "a typical Yankee slur."

1001 **The Commando Raid on Iran,** 1980. In the fall of 1979, angered by President Carter's decision to permit their hated ex-Shah, Mohammed Riza Pahlevi, to enter the United States for medical treatment, Iranian militants occupied the American embassy in Teheran and held its occupants hostage. For months, while resentment in the United States mounted, Carter searched unsuccessfully for a peaceful way of obtaining the hostages' freedom. Finally, in April 1980, he authorized a helicopter raid on the embassy by Marine Corps commandos. The raid was a classic fiasco. Several helicopters broke down and there was an accident at the nighttime rendezvous point in the desert south of Teheran in which eight marines died. Carter then felt compelled to call off the attack. When they discovered what had happened, the Iranians made much of the incident. The hostages remained captive and Carter's reputation was further damaged.

INDEX

(Whittier), 147
Barlow, Joel, 146
Barnburners, 9, 10
Barron, James, 189
Barton, Bruce, 112
Baruch, Bernard, as the Lone Eagle, 20
Bataan, Battle of, 173–74
"Battle Hymn of the Republic, The," 148
Bay of Pigs invasion (1961), 191
Beard, Charles A., 92
Beast, B. F. Butler as, 12
Beauregard, Pierre G. T., 13, 158–59
Beecher, Henry Ward, 11
"Beecher's Rifles," 11
"Being thus arrived in a good harbor . . ." (Bradford), 47
Bell, John, 42
Benedict, Ruth, 107
Benét, Stephen Vincent, 147
Benton, Thomas Hart, 9, 54; on Jefferson, 124; on J. Q. Adams, 125; as Old Bullion, 112
Berkeley, Sir William, 154
Berkman, Alexander, 186
Berlin, Irving, 149
Bethune, Mary McLeod, 106; and the "Black Cabinet," 106
Bet-You-a-Million Gates, 20
Beveridge, Albert, "March of the Flag" speech by, 71–72
Biddle, Nicholas, as Czar Nicholas, 7
Big Bill (Haywood), 19
Big Bill (Taft), 19
Big Ditch (Erie Canal), 7
Billings, William, "Chester" by, 148
"Billion here and a billion there . . . , A" (Dirksen), 60
Birdseye, Clarence, 182
Birney, James, 41
Black Dan, Daniel Webster as, 8
Black Hawk (Sauk chief), 93–94
Black Hawk War, 94
Black Jack, Pershing as, 20
Blackwell, Elizabeth, 68, 105
Blaine, Harriet Stanwood, 131
Blaine, James G., 14–15, 17, 55, 98; and "Burchard Break," 98;

and Mulligan Letters, 98; on Van Buren, 125
Bland, Richard P., as Silver Dick, 15
Bleeding Kansas, 11
Bloomer, Amelia, 67
Bodmer, Karl, 3
Boll Weevils, 25
Bonhomme Richard, 166
Booth, John Wilkes, 87–88; on Lincoln, 129; as Lincoln's assassin, 87–88
Border Ruffians, 11
Boston Police Strike (1919), 187
Bourbons, 17
Bowie, Jim, 172–73
Boxer Rebellion, 14
Boy Orator of the Platte, 15
Braddock (Edward), Ambush of, 172
Bradford, William, 47, 92–93; *Of Plymouth Plantation* by, 47, 141
Bradwell, Myra, 105
Bragg, Braxton, 159, 162
Briand, Aristide, 38
Bridegroom on the Wedding Cake, Thomas Dewey as, 24
British Empire . . . , The (Gipson), 4, 116
Brook Farm, 75
Brooks, Preston S., as Bully, 9
"Brother, Can You Spare a Dime?" (Great Depression song hit), 149
Brown, Antoinette, 105
Brown, John, 11, 54, 87, 148, 161, 162; his statement before being hanged for Harpers Ferry raid, 54
Brown v. Board of Education of Topeka (1954), 34
"Bryan, Bryan . . ." (Lindsay), 147
Bryan, William J., 15, 37, 42, 184; as the Boy Orator of the Platte, 15; "Cross of Gold" speech by, 71; as the Great Commoner, 15; as the Peerless Leader, 15
Bryant, William Cullen, 146
Bryce, James, 56

Buchanan, James, 128; Polk on, 128; Strong on, 128; Van Buren on, 128
Buckner, Simon H., 172
Bucktails, 9
Buell, Don Carlos, 162
Bull Moosers, 21–22, 43
Bull Run (First Manassas), Battle of, 12, 156, 173
Bull Run (Second Manassas), Battle of, 12, 156, 173
Bully, Preston S. Brooks as, 9
Burchard, Samuel D., 98
"Burchard Break," The, 98
Burger, Warren E., 60
Burgoyne, John, 5, 171, 174; as Gentleman John, 5
Burnside, Ambrose E., 162–63, 164, 173
Burr, Aaron, 101; and Hamilton duel, 188–89; on Madison, 124–25; treason trial (1807), 188–89
"Businessmen have a different set of delusions . . ." (Keynes), 59
Butler, Andrew P., 9
Butler, Benjamin Franklin, 12, 13–14, 118, 159
Butler, Nicholas Murray, on Coolidge, 133–34

Cabet, Étienne, 76
Cactus Jack, Garner as, 21
"Caesar had his Brutus . . ." (Patrick Henry), 61
Calhoun, John C., 6, 27; on Harrison, 126; on Monroe, 125; on Van Buren, 126
Canada, Hull's invasion of, 189
Cannon, Joseph G., 19–20; as Foul-mouthed Joe, 20; as Hayseed, 20; on McKinley, 132; as Uncle Joe, 19–20
Captain Shrimp, 4
Carnegie, Andrew, 56, 119, 185
Caroline, destruction of (1837), 38–39
Carpetbaggers, 16
Carr, Joseph, 34
Carrothers, Wallace H., 181
Carter, James Earl (Jimmy), 25,

38, 136–37; Goldwater on, 137; his "Montezuma's revenge" remark, 191; and raid to free hostages in Iran, 191–92; Sadat on, 136; Schmidt on, 137
Carter, Rosalynn, as the Steel Magnolia, 25
Cass, Lewis, 41, 97–98
Cato, Marcus Porcius (the Elder), 8
Cato of the Senate, Silas Wright as, 8
Catt, Carrie Chapman, 68
Cattell, James McKeen, 64
Cellophane, invention of, 181
Cermak, Anton J., 88
Champagne Charlie, Charles Townshend as, 5
Chancellorsville (Civil War battle, 1863), 157
Charles I, King, 116
Charles II, King, and Old Dominion, 113
Charles River Bridge v. Warren Bridge (1837), 33
Chattanooga (Civil War battle, 1863), 158
Chesapeake, USS, attack on, 189
"Chester" (Billings), 148
Chickamauga (Civil War battle, 1863), 158
Chicken in Every Pot . . . (election slogan), 22
Chilean Crisis (1891), 40
Choice, Not an Echo, A (slogan), 26
Churchill, Winston, 24; on Hopkins, 24; on Truman, 134; on Wilson, 133
Civil War, 29, 98, 114–15, 153; battles, 156–58, 173, 175–76; generals, 158–66; nicknames, 12–13; slogans, 13. *See also* Slavery; specific aspects, battles, developments, individuals
Clark, Frank, 64
Clay, Henry, 5, 7–8, 10–11, 27, 28, 36, 50, 53; and Alabama Letters, 97; as the Great Compromiser, 8; as the Great

Pacificator, 8; and Hammet Letter, 97; as Harry of the West, 7; on Madison, 124; as the Mill Boy of the Slashes, 7–8; as Prince Hal, 7; and Raleigh Letter, 97
Clermont (steamboat), 169
Cleveland, Grover, 15, 17, 40, 118, 131; Lodge on, 131; Lowell on, 131; and Pullman strike, 186; Tillman on, 131
Clinton, DeWitt, 7, 9; as Magnus Apollo, 7
Clintonians, 9
Cold Harbor, Battle of (1864), 157, 173
Cold War, 23, 119
Collazo, Oscar, 89
"Colonies and plantations in America . . ." (Declaratory Act, 1766), 95
Columbia (battle, 1865), 158
Columbian Exchange, 3
Common Sense (Paine), 144
Communes, utopias and, 74
"Compelling the colonies to pay money without their consent . . ." (Franklin), 47
Compromise of 1850, 28, 70, 97
Compromise of 1877, 28
Compromise Tariff (1833), 27–28
Conkling, Roscoe, 88; on Chester Arthur, 130
Conscience Whigs, 10
Constitution (frigate), 166
Constitutional Union Party, 42
"Constitution regulates . . . , The" (Seward), 53
Contras, aid to, 101
Cook, Tennessee Claflin, 105
Coolidge, Calvin, 22, 133; and Boston Police strike, 187; Butler on, 132–33; on Hoover, 134; Keep Cool with (slogan), 22; Lippmann on, 133; and "Prosperity" and New Era, 111; as Silent Cal, 21
Copperheads, 13
Corinth (Civil War battle, 1862), 157
Cornwallis, Lord, 175

Corregidor, Fort, 172
Corrupt Bargain (campaign slogan), 10–11
Cotton Is King (slogan), 11–12
Coughlin, Father Charles E., 20–21; as the Radio Priest, 20–21
"Count me out . . . I will not accept . . ." (Sherman), 56
Cox, Archibald, 100, 101
Crawford, William H., 10
Crazy Horse, and Big Horn battle, 173
Creole (slave ship), 169
Crèvecoeur, Michel Guillaume de, 49
Crisis Papers (Paine), 141
Crittenden, John J., 28
Crittenden Compromise, 28
Crockett, Davy, 172
Croker, Richard, 102
Crosby, Alfred W., Jr., 3
"Cross of Gold" speech, Bryan's, 71
Crump, Edward H., 103
Cuban Missile Crisis (1962), 23
Cuffe, Paul, 90
cummings, e. e., 147
Curley, James Michael, 103
Curtis, Edwin, 187
Custer, George Armstrong, 173
Czar, Thomas B. Reed as, 15
Czar Nicholas, Nicholas Biddle as, 7
Czolgosz, Leon F., 88

Daley, Richard J., 104
"Damn the torpedoes! . . ." (Farragut), 62
Dana, Richard Henry, 41–42
Dartmouth College Case (1819), 32
Davis, Jefferson, 159, 160, 161; on Johnson, 129
Davis, Katharine Bement, 106
Davis, Matthew L., 101
Davis, Pauline Wright, 104; as founder of *Una*, 104
Dawes, Charles G., 21, 115
Dawes Plan, 115
Dearborn, Henry, 189–90
Debs, Eugene V., 42–43, 186; on

Ford, Henry, 58; his "Peace Ship," 170
"For the first time . . . women's labor . . ." (Robinson), 65
"For the Union Dead" (Lowell), 147
Fort William Massacre (1756), 4
Forty Thieves, 9
Foster, William Z., 187
"Fourteen Points" speech, Wilson's, 72
Franklin, Benjamin, 37, 47; and Albany Plan, 114; on John Adams, 123; and Paxton Boys Uprising, 155
"Franklin Roosevelt is no crusader . . ." (Lippmann), 59
Fredericksburg, Battle of (1863), 153, 157, 173
Freeman, Douglas Southall, 159, 160
Freeport Doctrine (1858), 98
Free Soil, Free Speech, 11
Free Soil Party, 11, 41
Frémont, Jessie, 9
Frémont, John C., 9, 11
French and Indian War, 4, 35, 116, 178. *See also* Seven Years' War
Frequency Modulation (FM), 181
Frey, Captain, execution of, 39
Frick, Henry Clay, 185–86
Friedan, Betty, 146
Fugitive Slave Act (1850), 97
Fulton, Robert, and "Fulton's Folly," 169

Gallatin, Albert, 36
Garfield, James A., 30, 113, 130; Adams on, 130; assassination of, 88; Grant on, 130; on Grant, 129; on Hayes, 130; McKinley on, 130
Garner, John Nance, 21
Garrison, William Lloyd, 51; on Hayes, 130; on woman suffrage and Negro rights, 64
Garvey, Marcus M., 90
Gary, Elbert H., 186
Gaspée, 169
Gates, John Warne, 20
Gaulle, Charles de, on Nixon, 136

"General prosperity of the country . . . , The" (Henry Ford), 58
Genet, Edmond Charles, 96
Gentleman Johnny, 5
George, David Lloyd. *See* Lloyd George, David
George, Henry, 56, 142
George II, King, 153
George III, King, 48
Geronimo, 94–95
Gerry, Elbridge, 5
Gerrymander, 5
Gettysburg (Civil War battles), 157, 175
Gettysburg Address, 71
Ghent, Treaty of (1810), 36
Gibbons, Thomas, 33
Gibbons v. Ogden (1824–25), 33
Gilman, Charlotte Perkins, 68
Gilmore, Patrick S., 148
Gipson, Lawrence Henry, 4, 116
Gladstone, William E., 55
Glynn, Martin Henry, 22
Godlike Daniel, 8
Goldman, Emma, 69
Goldwater, Barry, 26; on Carter, 137
Gompers, Samuel, 119
Gordon, Kate M., 69
Gould, Jay, 14, 185
Government employees, Rotation in Office and, 6
Grady, Henry, and New South, 111
Grant, Ulysses S., 12, 62, 129, 163, 164; as Civil War general, 62, 163, 164, 165, 166, 173, 176; Garfield on, 129; Henry Adams on, 129; Lincoln on his drinking, 62; on McKinley, 130; and Old Guard, 113; *Personal Memoirs*, 142; Sherman on, 129; and Vicksburg siege, 176
Gray, L. Patrick, 60
Great Awakening, 6, 69, 116; First, 6; Second, 6, 116
Great Commoner, the, 15
Great Compromise, 27, 114
Great Compromiser, Clay as, 8
Great Depression (late nineteenth

century), 182, 183
Great Depression (1930s), 23, 117, 182, 184
Great Eastern (steamship), 116–17
Great Gatsby, The, 117
Great Migration, 116
Great Northern Railway, 117
Great Pacificator, Clay as, 8
Great Society, LBJ's, 117
Great War for the Empire, 4, 116. *See also* Seven Years' War
Great Western (steamship), 116
Greenback Labor Party, 42
Greer (U.S. destroyer), 168
Grenville, George, 95
Grimké, Sarah, 66, 67
Guadalupe Hidalgo, Treaty of (1848), 37
Guiteau, Charles J., 88

Had Enough? (election slogan), 26
Hague, Frank, 103; his "I am the law," 103
Hale, Nathan, 48
Hale, Sarah Josepha, 65
Half-Breeds and Stalwarts, 17
Halleck, Henry W., as Old Brains, 112
Halve Maen (Half-Moon), 168–69
Hamilton, Alexander, 49, 61; and Burr duel, 188–89; on John Adams, 123; on "the people are a Great Beast," 61
Hamilton, Alice, 105–6
Hammet Letter, 97
Hammond, James H., 54
Happy Warrior, the, Smith as, 21
Harding, Florence K., 20
Harding, Warren G., 20, 133, 187; Alice Longworth on, 133; cummings on death of, 147; Debs on, 133; on his friends and enemies, 133; McAdoo on, 133
Harlan, John Marshall, 34
Harmony community, 74
Harper, Robert Goodloe, 61
Harpers Ferry. *See* Brown, John
Harrington, Michael, 145
Harrison, Benjamin (1726–91), 80

Roosevelt, Elliot, 82
Roosevelt, Franklin Delano, 21, 22, 34, 36, 43, 59, 81, 102, 106, 134; attempted assassination of, 88; and attempt to "pack" the Supreme Court, 191; First Inaugural Address (1933), 72; and *Greer* incident, 168; Jung on, 134; Laski on, 134; Lippmann on, 134; and Nine Old Men, 113–14; on "only thing we have to fear," 72; and Pearl Harbor, 173; "Quarantine" speech, 72–73; and strikes, 187
Roosevelt, Franklin Delano, Jr., 82
Roosevelt, James, 82
Roosevelt, Theodore ("T.R."; "Teddy"), 16, 18, 22, 43, 57, 81, 132, 145, 184; attempted assassination of, 88; and coal strike, 186; Corollary, 18; Holmes on, 132; James on, 132; McKinley on, 132; on McKinley, 132; and New Nationalism, 72, 111; on Pierce, 128; Platt and, 102; and Rough Riders, 16, 153–54; on Taft, 132; and U.S. Steel antitrust suit, 99
Roosevelt, Theodore, Jr., 81
Roosevelt Corollary, 18
Roosevelt family, 81, 82. *See also* individual members
Rose v. Wade (1972), 34–35
"Rosie the Riveter," 149
Rotation in Office, 6
Rough Riders, 16, 153–54
"Royalists of the economic order . . . , The" (FDR), 59
Ruef, Abraham, 103
"Rum, Romanism, and Rebellion," 98
Rush, Benjamin, 36
Rush-Bagot Agreement (1818), 36

Sacagawea, 93
Sadat, Anwar, on Carter, 136
Sage of Nininger, 15

SALT II. *See* Strategic Arms Limitation Treaty
Salutary Neglect policy, 3–4
Sanger, Margaret H., 68, 106
Saratoga, Battle of, 5, 35, 174–75
Savannah (Civil War battle, 1864), 158
Scalawags, 16
Schmidt, Helmut, on Carter, 137
Scholar in politics, Lodge as, 20
School and Society, The (Dewey), 145
Schrank, John F., 82
Schurz, Carl, 16
Scott, Dred, 33
Scott, Harriet, 33
Scott, Winfield, 39, 113, 163, 164; and Anaconda Plan, 114–15; and Mexico City campaign, 175; as Old Fuss and Feathers, 113; on Taylor, 127
"Secession, like any other revolutionary act . . ." (Jackson), 52
Second Bank of the U.S., 7; as the Monster, 7
Second Great Awakening. *See* Great Awakening
Selden's (George B.) "road engine," 182
"Sell (our) country! Why not sell the air . . . ?" (Tecumseh), 50
Sequoyah (Cherokee craftsman), 93
Servants: headright and, 3; indentured, 3
Seven Years' War, 4, 35, 116. *See also* French and Indian War
Seward, William H., 53, 101; and Alaska purchase, 17
Seward's Folly, 17
Sexual Behavior of the Human Male (Kinsey), 145–46
Shaker communities, 74
Share Our Wealth movement, 23
Sharp Knife, Andrew Jackson as, 8
Shaw, Anna Howard, 69
Shays, Daniel, 155
Shays's Rebellion, 49, 155

Sheppard-Towner Act (1921), 31
Sheridan, Philip H., 63, 165; as Little Phil, 12; quoted on Indians, 63
Sherman, John, 15; as the Ohio Icicle, 15
Sherman, William T., 56, 165–66; on Civil War, 153; as Civil War general, 153, 165–66; on Grant, 129; on Johnson, 129
Sherman Antitrust Act (1890), 30–31, 119
"Shiloh, A Requiem" (Melville), 147
Shiloh (Civil War battle, 1862), 157; Melville's "Requiem," 147
Silent Cal (Coolidge), 21
Silent Majority, 23
Silent Spring (Carson), 145
Silver Dick, Bland as, 15
Silver Grays, 10
Simpson, Jeremiah, 15
Sinclair, Upton, *The Jungle* by, 145
"Sinners in the Hands of an Angry God" sermon (Edwards), 69–70
Sirhan, Sirhan B., 89
Sit-down strikes, 187
Sitting Bull, 94, 95
Sixteenth Amendment, 31
Slavery, ix, 3, 6, 9, 10, 11–12, 13, 27, 28, 29, 32, 54, 65; compromises, 27–28; Nullification and, 6, 27; as the Peculiar Institution, 6; Young America and, 7. *See also* Civil War; specific aspects, developments, events, individuals
Slow Trot, 13
Smith, Alfred E., 87, 102, 106; as the Happy Warrior, 21
Smith, Bessie, 87
Smith, David, 87
Smith, Gerald L. K., 87
Smith, Gerrit, 87
Smith, Horton, 89
Smith, James ("Boss"), 87
Smith, John, 63, 86; Pocahontas

and, 92
Smith, Joseph, ix, 76, 87
Smith, Preserved, 87
Smith, Sophia, 86
Smith, Walter B., 87
Smiths, the, 86–87. *See also* individual members
"(Smoking tobacco is) lothsome . . ." (James I), 47
Socialist Labor Party, 42
Socialist Party, 42–43
Social Security Act (1935), 31–32
Sockless Jerry, 15
Souls of Black Folk, The (Du Bois), 143
"Southern women are . . . abolitionists . . ." (Ella Thomas), 65
Spanish-American War, 16, 17–18, 37, 99, 119. *See also* specific aspects, developments, events, individuals
Spoils System, 6
Spotsylvania Courthouse (Civil War battle, 1864), 157
Squanto (Indian leader), 92–93
Stalin, Joseph, 24; on Eisenhower, 135; on FDR, 134; as Uncle Joe, 24
Stalwarts and Half-Breeds, 17
Stamp Act (1765), 95
Standard Oil Company, antitrust movement and, 118–19
Standish, Myles, 4, 61; as Captain Shrimp, 4
Stanton, Charles E., 63
Stanton, Elizabeth Cady, 66
Stanwix, Fort, 171
"Star-Spangled Banner, The" (Key), 146, 171
"Statesman is a politician who is dead, A" (Reed), 15
States' Rights "Dixiecrat" Party, 43
Steel Magnolia, Rosalynn Carter as, 25
Steel Strike of 1919, 186–87
Steel Strike of 1952, 187–88
Steffe, William, 148
Steffens, Lincoln, 18, 58
Steinem, Gloria, 69, 146

Stevens, Thaddeus, 55; his epitaph written by himself, 55; on Johnson, 129
Stevenson, Adlai E., 26
Still, Charity, 67
Stimson, Henry L., 19; on Hoover, 134
Stimson Doctrine, 18–19
"Stonewall" Jackson, 12. *See also* Jackson, Thomas J. ("Stonewall")
Stowe, Harriet Beecher, *Uncle Tom's Cabin* by, 144
Strasser, Adolph, 55–56
Strategic Arms Limitation Treaty (SALT, 1972), 38; SALT II (1979), 38
Strong, George T., on Buchanan, 128
Stuart, Gilbert: portrait of George Washington by, 123; on Washington, 123
Stuart, James E. B. ("Jeb"), 162
Sturgis, Maria A., 67
Sullivan, Timothy D. ("Big Tim"), 102
Sumner, Charles, 9; on Fillmore, 127–28
Sumter, Fort, 171
Supreme Court, U.S., 57; FDR's attempt to "pack," 191; as Nine Old Men, 113–14. *See also* specific decisions, individuals
Susan Constant (caravel), 168
Sutter's Fort, 171
Swope, Gerard, 115
Swope Plan, 115

Taft, William H., 18, 19, 43, 132; as Big Bill, 19; and Dollar Diplomacy, 18; Dolliver on, 132; on McKinley, 132; on Payne-Aldrich Tariff, 190–91; T. Roosevelt on, 132; and U.S. Steel antitrust suit, 99; Will Rogers on, 132
Tail Gunner Joe, 24
Talleyrand, Charles-Maurice de, 62
Taney, Roger B., 33
Tarbell, Ida M., 18

Tariff Act of 1832, 6
Taylor, Zachary, 113, 127; Mann on, 127; as Old Rough and Ready, 112; Scott on, 127
Tea Act (1773), 96
Tecumseh, Chief, 11, 50, 93, 94
Teflon President, 25
Tenskwatawa ("the Prophet"), 11, 93
Tet (Vietnam War), 174
Theory of the Leisure Class, The (Veblen), 143
"There is a vulgar persuasion . . ." (Wright), 65
"There is in all the past . . ." (Henry George), 56
"There is many a boy here today . . ." (Sherman), 153
"There is no foundation in reason . . ." (Mott), 67
"There is on the globe one single spot . . . New Orleans . . ." (Jefferson), 50
"There is something noble . . ." (Hamilton), 49
"They won't let me alone about slavery . . ." (Dickens), 53
"This Government is menaced with great danger . . ." (Catt), 68
Thomas, Ella, 65
Thomas, George H., 13, 166; as the Rock of Chickamauga, 13; as Slow Trot, 13
Thoreau, Henry David, 54; *Walden* by, 142
Three-Fifths Compromise, 27
"Th' Supreme Coort . . ." ("Mr. Dooley"), 57
Thurmond, J. Strom, 25, 43
Ticonderoga, Fort, 171
Tillman, Benjamin, 15; on Cleveland, 131; as Pitchfork Ben, 15
"Times that tried men's souls . . . , The" (Paine), 48–49
Tippecanoe, Battle of, 11
Tippecanoe and Tyler Too, 11
Tocqueville, Alexis de, 52; on Jackson, 125
Tolstoy, Leo, on Lincoln, 128

Washington Treaties (1922), 37–38
Watergate Affair (1973), 100–1
Waving the Bloody Shirt, 13–14
Wealth Against Commonwealth (Lloyd George), 145
Weaver, James B., 42
Webster, Daniel, 8, 32, 37; as Black Dan, 8; as Godlike Dan, 8; "Second Reply to Hayne" by, 70; "Seventh of March" speech, 70
Webster, Noah, 49
Webster-Ashburton Treaty (1842), 36–37, 39
We Do Our Part (NRA slogan), 22–23
Weed, Thurlow, 101
"We have met the enemy . . ." (Perry), 153
"We in America . . ." (Hoover), 58
Weiss, Dr. Carl A., 88–89
Wellman, Walter, on Benjamin Harrison, 131
"We ought to let him hang there . . ." (Ehrlichman), 60
"We provide for each slave . . ." (Fitzhugh), 54
"We shall tax and tax . . ." (Hopkins), 63
West Coast Hotel Co. v. Parrish (1937), 34
"We the people of the Confederate States . . . ," 54
"What's good for General Motors . . ." (Wilson), 63
"What then is the American . . ." (Crèvecoeur), 49
"What this country needs . . . is a really good five-cent cigar" (Marshall), 57
"What you say, do . . ." (Ervin), 60–61
Wheeler, Wayne, 119
"When Johnny Comes Marching Home Again" (Gilmore), 148
"When men who are willing to work . . ." (Willard), 59
"When spinsters can support themselves . . ." (Cattell), 64
Whig Party, 10, 11

Whiskey Rebellion, 155
White, Sue Sheldon, 69
White, Theodore, 136; on LBJ, 136
White, William Allen, on Benjamin Harrison, 131
"Whites want slaves . . . , The" (Walker), 51
Whitman, Walt, 147
Whittier, John Greenleaf, 147
Who but Hoover? (election slogan), 22
"Why don't you speak for yourself, John?," 61
Wilderness, The (Civil War battles, 1864), 157
Willard, Daniel, 59
Willard, Emma, 104
Williams, Kenneth P., 164
Williams, Roger, 47
Williams, T. Harry, 89
"Will it play in Peoria?" (Ehrlichman), 60
Wilson, Charles E., 24, 63
Wilson, Woodrow, 18, 20, 37, 43, 87, 99, 132–33, 170; "Address to Newly Naturalized Citizens" (1915), 58; "Appeal" for a Democratic Congress (1918), 99; and call for war against Germany speech, 72; Churchill on, 132; "Fourteen Point" speech, 72; Hearst on, 132; Lloyd George on, 133; and Missionary Diplomacy, 18; and New Freedom, 111; as Peck's Bad Boy, 20
Winthrop, John, 47
Wirt, William, 41
Wise, John S., on Pierce, 128
Withholding Tax Act (1943), 32
"With women as half . . ." (Steinem), 69
Wizard of Ooze, Dirksen as, 24–25
Wobblies (Industrial Workers of the World), 19
"Woman's body belongs to herself . . . , A" (Sanger), 68
Woman's Rights Convention (1848), "Declaration of Sentiments" presented at, 66

"Women have the same invaluable right . . ." (Woodhull), 66
"Women may, if they exert their talents . . ." (Hale), 65
"Women of America . . . , The" (Norton), 69
Woodhull, Victoria Claflin, 66, 105
Workingman's Party, 41
World War I, 23, 37–38, 72, 99, 115, 117, 176; Dawes Plan, 115; Versailles Treaty, 37; Young Plan, 115. *See also* specific aspects, battles, developments, events, individuals
World War II, 23, 26, 28, 72, 115, 173. *See also* specific aspects, battles, developments, events, individuals
Wright, Frances, 65, 75; called the "Priestess of Beelzebub," 75; and Nashoba, 75
Wright, Jim, on Reagan, 137
Wright, Richard, *Native Son* by, 143–44
Wright, Silas, as Cato of the Senate, 8

Yalu, Battle of the, 174, 177
Yamamoto, Isoroku, 176
"Yankee Doodle," 148
Yorktown (battle, 1781), 174–75
Yorktown, USS, 176
"You may fire when you are ready, Gridley" (Dewey), 153
Young, Brigham, 76
Young, Owen D., 115
Young America, 6–7
Young Fox, John Van Buren as, 9
Young Napoleon, McClellan as, 13
Young Plan, 115
"You white folks . . . ," 67

Zangara, Joseph, 88